Bob Chenowith

June 1995

BLACK WALNUT

*The History, Use, and Unrealized Potential
of a Unique American Renewable
Natural Resource*

à

Bob Chenoweth

SAGAMORE PUBLISHING
Champaign, IL

Production Supervision: Susan M. McKinney
Cover and photo insert design: Michelle R. Dressen
Editor: Susan M. McKinney
Proofreader: Phyllis L. Bannon

*Front cover photo of Bicentennial Tree courtesy of Al Huff of the Atlantic
Veneer Company, for further information, see pages 30-33.
Back cover photo taken by author in Shenandoah Valley.*

All other photographs provided by author unless otherwise specified.

Library of Congress Catalog Card Number: 95-67286
ISBN: 1-57167-008-4

Printed in the United States
Printed on 100% recycled paper.

To Tom and Vera Chenoweth,
who gave me the land, a love for books,
and a yearning for knowledge

and to Iris,
who accompanied me on my quest
and who sustains me

The Prayer of the Tree

Man! I am the warmth of your home in the cold winter night
and the protective shade when summer's sun is strong.
I am the framework of the roof to your house and the top
to your table, the bed in which you sleep and the timber
with which you fashion your boats.
I am the handle to your hoe and the door to your hut.
I am the wood of your cradle and the boards of your coffin.
I am the bread of kindness and the flower of beauty.
            Hear my prayer: Destroy me not!

—Unser Wald[1]

[1] *In the German language, "unser wald" means "our forest."
While the author and origin of this prayer are unknown, the message
and the truth of the message are universal.*

CONTENTS

ACKNOWLEDGMENTS

The generosity and help of many people are reflected in this book. It is not possible to mention by name all who have helped to make this book a reality. However, some who have been most generous and helpful are:

Ken Asmus, Michigan Nut Growers Association, Kalamazoo, Michigan; Bill Baitinger, Director, Office of Technology Transfer, Purdue University; Walt Beineke, Department of Forestry and Natural Resources, Purdue University; Leo C. Bird, Walnut Grower, Dibble Creek Tree Farm, Stockton, Kansas; Francis A. Bishop, Owner, O'Neill & Bishop, Haverford, Pennsylvania; Robert J. Blair, District Forester, Illinois Dept. of Conservation; Manfred Bohlke, President, M. Bohlke Veneer Corporation, Fairfield, Ohio; Jay R. Book, Walnut Grower, Elizabethtown, Pennsylvania; John Bowers, Walnut Buyer, Hoosier Veneer Company, Trafalger, Indiana; James Brown, Buyer, Henredon Furniture Company, Spruce Pine, North Carolina; Harold Bruner, Consulting Forester, Walton, Indiana; D.C. Burton, Timber Manager, David R. Webb Company, Edinburgh, Indiana; John C. Callahan, Writer, Bradenton, Florida; Philip G. Carew, Manager, Timberlands, Pike Lumber Company, Carbon, Indiana; Lloyd R. Casey, Forester, USDA Forest Service, Radnor, Pennsylvania; John Cole, District Wildlife Biologist, Gibson City, Illinois; Andy Cook, Reader, Eden, Utah; Marie Cook, Reader, Eden, Utah; Ralph L. Davis, Retired, Clearwater, Florida; Kenneth Dooley, Walnut Grower, Merion, Indiana; Eddie Ferguson, President, Waterford Furniture Makers, Lynchburg, Virginia; Walt Fields, Forest Custodian, Fulton, Illinois; Gaston G. Fornes, Inventor, Professor of Machine Design, Charlottesville, Virginia; Larry Frye, Executive Director, Walnut Council, Zionsville, Indiana; Gene Garett, Dept. of Forestry, University of Missouri, Columbia, Missouri; Calvin Gatch, Nurseryman, Cascade Forestry Nursery, Cascade, Indiana; Richard D. Goldner, Walnut Nurseryman, Birch Run, Michigan; Robert A. Green, Walnut Farmer, Nashville, Tennessee; Fritz

Greenman, Landowner, West Lafayette, Indiana; Robert A. Gross, President, Gross Veneer Sales, High Point, North Carolina; John A. Grunwald, President, David R. Webb Co, Edinburgh, Indiana; Nancy Gunning, Secretary, Walnut Council, Zionsville, Indiana; Brian Hammons, Vice President, Hammons Products Company, Stockton, Missouri; Donna Hammons, President, Missouri Dandy Pantry, Stockton, Missouri; R. Dwain Hammons, President, Hammons Products Company, Stockton, Missouri; Larry Harper, *Missouri Ruralist Magazine*, Columbia, Missouri; Randall B. Heiligmann, Forestry Specialist, Ohio State University; A. W. Heiman, Landowner/Walnut Grower, Anderson, Indiana; Tucker Hill, Editor, *The Nutshell*, Northern Nut Growers Association, Etters, Pennsylvania; Robert T. Hollowell, President, Pierson-Hollowell Company, Lawrenceburg, Indiana; William L. Hoover, Professor of Forest Economics, Purdue University; Bob Horey, Reader, Lake Worth, Florida; Al Huff, Vice President, Atlantic Veneer Company, Beaufort, North Carolina; Norman E. Hughes, Owner, Good Hope Hardwoods, Landenberg, Pennsylvania; Lawrence Hunt, Inventor, Hartford, Iowa; Jim Jones, Forester, Hammons Products Company, Stockton, Missouri; Larry Junker, Reader/Walnut Enthusiast, Merritt Island, Florida; William Kidd, Professor of Forestry, University of West Virginia, Morgantown, West Virginia; Ken Konsis, President, Illinois Chapter, Walnut Council, Danville, Illinois; Jack Koss, President, Capital Machines International, Indianapolis; Victor L. Lechtenberg, Dean of Agriculture, Purdue University; Bill McKinley, Nurseryman, Potsdam, New York; Dave Mercker, Professional Forester, Forest Management Services, Terre Haute, Indiana; Boynton Merrill, Walnut Grower, Henderson, Kentucky; Bill Miller, President, Curry-Miller Veneer Company, Indianapolis; Thomas B. Mills, Lafayette Marketing Inc., West Lafayette, Indiana; Carolyn Moye, Receptionist, Henkel-Harris, Winchester, Virginia; Ivan Odle, Landowner, Largo, Florida; Larry Owen, Professional Forester, Forest Management Services, Terre Haute, Indiana; Hugh B. Pence, Landowner/Walnut Grower, Lafayette, Indiana; Judith Pence, Landowner/Walnut Grower, Lafayette, Indiana; Steve Pennington, Iowa Dept. of Natural Resources, Des Moines,

Iowa; John E. Phelps, Forestry Science Lab, SIU, Carbondale, Illinois; Bob Plater, Bowman/Hunter, Danville, Illinois; R. Felix Ponder, Forester, North Central Experimental Station, Columbia, Missouri; John E. Preece, Professor, SIU, Carbondale, Illinois; Charles A. Richcrick, Walnut Grower/Nurseryman, York, Pennsylvania; William Reid, Dept of Horticulture, Chetopa, Kansas; George Rink, Research Geneticist/*Bulletin* Editor, Carbondale, Illinois; Gary L. Rolfe, Head, Dept. of Forestry, University of Illinois, Urbana, Illinois; Tom Rutledge, Walnut Nut Buyer, Hammons Products Company, Stockton, Missouri; Robert Schaub, Reader/Editor, *Boone News Republican*, Boone, Iowa; Richard C. Schlesinger, Research Forester, University of Missouri, Columbia; Larry Severeid, Walnut Farmer, LaCrosse, Wisconsin; Dr. Robert W. Shultice, Walnut Grower, Amana, Iowa; Sally Smith, Reader, Pittsburgh; Bill Schneeberger, Landowner/Walnut Grower, Waukon, Iowa; Archie Sparks, Walnut Breeder and Grower, Beaver, Iowa; Brian Sparks, Walnut Grower/Nurseryman, Beaver, Iowa; James P. Stafford, Ohio Dept. of Natural Resources, Zanesvile, Ohio; Jeff W. Stringer, Professor of Forestry, University of Kentucky, Lexington; Charles Thatcher, Nutgrower, Clairton, Pennsylvania; Bob Trimble, Landowner/Walnut Grower, Monticello, Illinois; Jerry Van Sambeek, Project Leader, Forestry Science Laboratory, Carbondale, Illinois; Bruce Wakeland, Wakeland Forestry Consultants, Culver, Indiana; Ann Walsh, Reader, Wayne, Pennsylvania; Ed Workman, Physical Science Technician, SIU, Carbondale, Illinois; Richard L. Wertz, President, Amos-Hill Associates, Edinburgh, Indiana; William E. Ziegler, Forester, F.S.G. Nurseries, West Lafayette, Indiana.

The search for a publisher was discouraging. Several private and land grant college presses rejected this book, believing that it lacked commercial value (i.e., they did not believe they could make money from it.) I persisted despite this, because I believe there is a need for this book. You can help me prove them wrong by reading and recommending this work.

Fortunately I found the wonderful and helpful people at Sagamore Publishing who have been most cooperative and encouraging. I am particularly grateful to Susan M. McKinney, my editor and production manager, who has guided me but allowed me to express myself. It has been a great pleasure to work with her and all those at Sagamore.

While many have contributed thoughts and ideas through their published work, interviews, or letters, the words selected herein are mine, and I accept full responsibility for any errors of fact or judgment.

Not everyone will agree with what is written here. Growing black walnuts is a particularly challenging and frustrating task. One thing I have learned for certain—no one knows all the answers.

INTRODUCTION

"I cannot live without my books." —Thomas Jefferson

"The things I want to know are in books; my best friend is the man who'll give me a book I ain't read." —Abraham Lincoln

"The real world is nothing but a vast jumble of noises, shapes, colors, smells, and textures—essentially meaningless until human mind imposes some order upon them." —Robert B. Reich *The Work of Nations*

The Eastern black walnut, *Juglans nigra,* is a native hardwood tree that European immigrants found in some quantity and excellent quality in the northeastern one-third of the United States and the lower regions of Canada. For thousands of years, native Americans valued the rich nutmeats of this tree and traded it over a wide range. When causes unknown and diseases introduced by the Europeans killed large numbers of the agrarian native Americans we call Mississippians, the abandoned fields and burned-over brushlands they left behind were excellent forest sites, providing sunlight for oak and walnut forests to emerge and thrive.

When the Europeans moved inland and occupied the vast forests of North America, they found trees of immense size and numbers that they rapidly exploited and cleared to farm the land. In the last century, second-growth trees have emerged, but the quality and quantity are much below that first cutting. Over the last 30 years, black walnut wood and veneer have become increasingly popular in Europe and Asia. Exports of black walnut logs and veneer have consumed as much as 80 percent of annual production during this period. Both the quality and quantity of black walnut logs have declined, and prices for quality logs have risen sharply, reflecting this shortage.

What can and is being done to grow more and better black walnuts? This book gives some of the history of the use of the Eastern black walnut and explains what is being done by some people to produce more and better trees for future generations. It tries to explain *why* they do it as well.

Growing black walnut trees of quality is not easy and takes many years. Various government organizations have encouraged and supported this effort, but recent economic constraints have reduced this support, and more reductions seem likely. Black walnut research has been productive, but more people need to study it and act upon it. For the most part, landowners are unaware and are not acting; their forests are neglected and unmanaged.

Black walnut trees were common and taken for granted in central Indiana and Illinois, where I grew up. We sometimes harvested the nuts and occasionally heard stories that black walnut trees were valuable for veneer, but we did not know much about the tree. We were a farm family for five generations, and knew more about corn, soybeans, chickens, hogs, and cattle than about black walnuts.

There were black walnut trees on the Vermilion County, Illinois land where my ancestors had been pioneer settlers in 1828. We paid little attention to these trees other than making an occasional visit to "tramp around the woods" and absorb the timber atmosphere. A walk in the woods was a pleasing and calming experience, but we never managed it, and never pruned or planted trees except for one occasion.

In the fall of 1928, my father returned from studying at the University of Illinois and planted two buckets full of black walnut nuts in two rows on two very different sites. That was five years before I was born. I have watched these trees grow since I was a child, and I am now 61 years old.

In 1987, I employed a professional forester to evaluate the timber on this Illinois land. This led to a timber sale in 1988 and a decision to reforest 22 acres to hardwoods. This 22 acres had been cleared of timber over 100 years earlier, but was subject to erosion and consisted of two small fields that did not lend themselves to farming in constant row crops with modern machinery. Our efforts to turn these long tilled fields into a forest have been interesting, challenging, and tough, and have led me into new and unexpected adventures.

From my foresters, I learned about the Walnut Council, which was founded with 400 members in 1969, and has since grown to about 1,000 members. I joined this organization to learn more about black walnut. In August 1991, 1992, 1993, and 1994, I attended the Walnut Council annual meetings in Leavenworth, Kansas; Amana Colonies, Iowa; Stockton, Virginia; and Nebraska City, Nebraska. At these four meetings, I found myself in a group of dedicated walnut lovers and exposed for the first time to a religion I had not known existed. I observed that Walnut Council members were of all ages, but most were eligible for senior discounts. Why do older people plant trees?

As a member of the Walnut Council, I began receiving the Walnut Council *Bulletin,* which is a quarterly publication of about 20 pages filled with facts, details, and general information about black walnut. I bought a copy of the Walnut Council publication *The Continuing Quest for Quality, Proceedings of the Fourth Black Walnut Symposium,* which had been held at Southern Illinois University at Carbondale, Illinois, July 30 to August 2, 1989. This added further to my knowledge of black walnut and the many state, federal, and private organizations and individuals who were devoting time and money to cultivating black walnuts. I still had many unanswered questions.

I began searching for other reading material on the subject of black walnut, talking to woodworkers about the use of the wood, and corresponding with individuals knowledgeable about various aspects of the black walnut. There was little published or available to the layperson. Most information was in technical publications that were readily available only to those within the black walnut community. Some consider these dry reading.

I found that most laypeople had not heard of the Walnut Council and knew little about black walnut history, wood, nuts, veneer, plantation plantings, pruning, or species improvement. Many people have a vague idea that black walnut trees are valuable, and recall black walnuts as part of their youth, but they lack specific facts. Most land-owners do not manage their woodland, care for those trees that come naturally, or plant trees. I began to realize what tremendous opportunity was being lost.

There is much to learn in life. Some learning comes early, quickly, and easily, such as the fact that stoves are hot and ice is cold. However, we often never learn, or learn too late, what should have been learned much earlier. This is true of individuals, families, and nations. Landowners need to know more about their woodlands and trees. Proximity to a subject does not guarantee learning. In fact, we often take for granted that which is close and familiar. Often, we assume we know all about something when we actually know very little. In this way, we often close our minds to what we should notice and overlook something that, on closer examination, deserves our study. We are surrounded by things we do not understand. Opportunity knocks, but we do not listen.

Few individuals have the extraordinary curiosity of a Charles Darwin, Luther Burbank, or John Audubon. Few have the opportunity or the dedication to pursue one line of study for a lifetime. As the world grows more complex and society becomes more integrated, specialty professions pro-liferate and many individuals devote their efforts toward greater and deeper understanding of a single subject. By sharing their learning with other professionals through publication of technical papers, the cumulative understand-ing of a specific subject grows.

While society as a whole may benefit from the efforts of a dedicated few, the vast majority of people never know or perhaps do not care what these few have accomplished. When accumulated knowledge can benefit many, and many are needed to act upon it, education has specific meaning. Someone wishing to know more about a subject can usually satisfy his curiosity at a good library.

Libraries have always been a pleasure to me, and I have found them a prime source of knowledge on many subjects I wanted to understand more fully. When I went to the library in search of information about the Eastern black walnut, *Juglans nigra L*, I found no single source devoted to the subject.

While I did not find a book exclusively on black walnut, I did find a wealth of material and learned much as I talked with walnut growers and users of walnut products. I traveled from Pennsylvania to Missouri, South Carolina, North Carolina, Illinois, Kansas, Iowa, Kentucky, Indiana, Tennessee, Wisconsin, Virginia, West Virginia, Ohio, Nebraska, Michigan and Ontario looking for more information about black walnut. I found many people who were interested but were not currently involved in any way with black walnut. Many recalled black walnut trees in their youth and remembered cracking black walnut nuts long ago.

The full story of this interesting and unique natural resource and the people associated with it reflects the full range of the American character. The story reflects great greed and uncommon generosity; pitiful neglect and extraordinary care; heedless waste and passionate conservation; common stupidity and uncommon wisdom; mass ignorance and rare intelligence. And it reflects some of the divisions in our national personality. Animal lovers face off against plant lovers, and advocates of more rapid economic growth are obstructed by preservationists and conservationists.

Our national history is one of forest exploitation to achieve record standards of living and home ownership unequalled elsewhere in the world. The speed with which we deforested much of the Eastern United States was unparalleled in human history. Natural reforestation has often been by inferior species and individuals. Efforts to assist natural reforestation by planting hardwoods are comparatively new in the United States, and have met with only limited success. There is much yet to learn about planting hardwood trees and improving all species of hardwoods. Because black walnut is such a fine, rare, and valuable hardwood, it deserves greater attention and effort from more landowners.

There are many poorly managed stands of natural black walnut throughout its growing region. Black walnuts grow readily in regions that are among the least prosperous in our nation. These regions would benefit directly from the added value provided by more and better black walnut trees. The black walnut tree represents an opportunity for individuals, regions, and the nation as a whole to accumulate wealth.

Walnut trees do not require a large capital investment or skilled labor to plant and nurture. They do not require much space and could be planted on land that is well drained and fertile but neglected and not used for anything else. A small investment and some effort can reap great psychic, physical, and monetary rewards.

Failure to recognize this simple fact has limited the economic prosperity of the black walnut growing range. Had former generations planted more black walnuts, current generations would have more wealth, more jobs, and more income. Walnut veneer exports would help reduce our balance of payments deficit. Should we not learn from the past? Should we not act now to improve the future?

The world supply of hardwood timber is being depleted at a rate that cannot be sustained. Many hardwood forests are showing stress, decay, and death from various forms of pollution. Almost certainly, we will see hardwoods become more rare and valuable in the future. Most foresters agree that it takes 40 to 80 years to grow a quality black walnut veneer log. Growing black walnuts is truly a long-term investment.

We Americans have a reputation for impatience and short attention spans. However, a few individuals and corporations have planted small plantations of black walnut trees. Most of the individuals involved will never live to see the trees they planted grow to harvest size. Most will never have the pleasure of sitting in a walnut chair at a walnut table built from wood they machined from wood they grew. Some plant trees in a search for immortality, some for their grandchildren, some for wealth, and some for the pleasure of watching them grow. For whatever reason, more people should plant trees.

It is to inspire action that this book is written. I hope it will lead more landowners to manage their woodlands and walnut trees in a better manner, plant more walnut trees, and join the Walnut Council and further Council objectives. If you enjoy and learn from this book, share it with another. If you know someone who can gain from it and act upon it, give it. Despite the lure of television and mania for computers, books remain the most economical and efficient way to transfer knowledge. As Emily Dickinson wrote:

> *There is no Frigate like a Book*
> *To take us lands away*
> *Nor any Coursers like a Page*
> *Of Prancing Poetry—*
> *This Travel may the poorest take*
> *Without offence of Toll—*
> *How Frugal is the Chariot*
> *That Bears the Human Soul.*

Readers who wish to know more of the author's background and motivation for writing on this subject may wish to begin with Chapter 8, "Some Illinois History." Chapter 8 is presented as an example of land use and is a case study that reviews material presented in the first seven chapters. Those who begin with Chapter 1, "Sylvania," will find much earlier American history.

Come share with me some of what I've learned about black walnut.

1

SYLVANIA

O Lord, how manifold are thy works!
In wisdom has thou made them all.
The earth is full of thy riches.

—Psalm 104, verse 21, *Holy Bible*

On June 1, 1680, William Penn formally asked King Charles of England for a grant of American land. He proposed that his province should be called "Sylvania," because so much of it was forested. However, the King ordered that the prefix "Penn" be added, and thus was born Pennsylvania. This prefix was added not to honor William, but his father, Admiral Sir William Penn, who had served the King honorably by accepting the blame for a naval blunder committed by the King's brother, the Duke of York.

Sylvan is derived from the Latin, *silva*, which means "composed of or abounding in, woods, groves, or trees." Penn's surname was a Welsh prefix meaning "head" or "high." Thus, Pennsylvania would mean high or head woodland. While Penn had not yet been to North America, he had heard reports describing the new land as heavily wooded and covered with forest, which it generally was.

In his classic book, *The Great Forest*, (1947) Richard G. Lillard describes it thus:

When explorers landed, America was trees. Explorers looked down from the mountaintops to an ocean of trees that stretched in every direction as far as the eye could reach. (p.3)

Rutherford Platt writing in *The Great American Forest* (1965) describes it also:

The American hardwood forest of history—the domain of the woodland Indians, the forest which was so dangerous and unlivable in the eyes of the first English settlers and which we call primeval today—was in truth a luminous, youthful, supple forest, new-born out of the Ice Age. In the nobility and quality of trees, in the number of species of trees, bushes, vines and flowers; in the purity of lakes and streams, in the abundance and color of its birds and fish and in the personalities of its animals, no other forest that ever grew on earth could be compared with it. (p. 43)

In the spring of 1773, the naturalist William Bartram came upon some of this forest near present Washington, Georgia, and thought it "the most magnificent forest" he had ever seen. For seven miles the way lay through it. He wrote:

We . . . entered this sublime forest; the ground is perfectly a level green plain, thinly planted by nature, with the most stately forest trees . . . whose mighty trunks, seemingly of an equal height, appeared like superb columns. To keep within the bounds of truth and reality in describing the magnitude of those trees, would, I fear fail of credibility; yet, I think I can assert, that many of the black oaks measured 8,9,10 and 11 feet diameter five feet above the ground, as we measured several that were above thirty feet girt (sic), and from hence they ascend perfectly strait (sic), with a gradual taper, forty or fifty feet to the limbs . . . (p. 78)

In addition to the black oaks, he listed tulip trees, black walnut, sycamore, hickory, beech, elm, and sweet gum in this cathedral forest.

In 1788, near the junction of the Ohio and Muskingum Rivers, where present day Marietta, Ohio lies, early settlers measured a black walnut tree 22 feet in circumference. The rings on a nearby tulip tree, counted with a magnifying glass, came to 441, dating the tulip tree back to 1346. In the Cumberland Basin in the 1780s, walnuts 11 feet in diameter, as tall as English elms were reported.

Trees were so thick and heavy upon the land that there was not enough clear space to grow grain for livestock or man, and not enough space for gardens. The first priority of the pioneer was to clear land for agricultural use. Clearing these "nuisance" trees was an immense task that took years and often lives as well.

Many trees were burned. Two byproducts of burning trees were potash and pearl ash. Both were important sources of income to pioneer farmers. Some farmers asserted that they derived enough income from these products to pay the cost of clearing new ground. Potash was a combination of various crude salts of potassium—mostly potassium carbonate—resulting from burning wood. It was used in making soap, scouring wool, bleaching and dyeing cloth, making glass, and other purposes. Potash from wood was important until about 1856, when great potassium deposits at Strasbourg, Germany were discovered.

Equipment needed for making potash was within every farmer's reach. Lye, made by leaching wood ashes, was boiled down in great iron kettles and evaporated to dryness. The resulting crude "black potash" could be sold or it could be refined into pearl ash. In 1805, pearl ash sold for $200 to $300 per ton. Being highly concentrated, pearl ash could be economically transported to market from distant farms.

Charcoal was another important forest-farm product until coal and coke supplanted it around 1840. Much charcoal was made by farmers who could produce 30 bushels of charcoal, valued at five to nine dollars, from a cord of wood. The average iron furnace used 800 bushels of charcoal every 24 hours, and over a year's time, a furnace consumed 240 or more acres of woodland. Tanbark was another byproduct of clearing land. Tanning was a rural community enterprise until about 1830, when it gradually became concentrated in a few large plants.

When timber was not burned on the site, much of the wood produced from clearing land could be used for fuel or to build cabins, tools, containers, or fences. Early pioneer life revolved around wood. Wood was the essential raw material of the frontier, and to be successful on the frontier required woodlore and woodworking skills.

The Dutch, coming from The Netherlands, lacked these skills since their homeland had few trees, so they learned from the English, Germans, French, and Scandinavians. It was important to identify tree species and to know which species was good for what purpose. In every settlement, craftsmen who knew woodlore or had woodworking skills were valuable members of the community.

Lillard wrote:

> Pioneers learned that smooth rockers of black walnut did not make the chairs creep forward when the sitter rocked, as it did when the rockers were of maple or hickory slick with wear. In a thousand ways, Old World tools, used to work timbers from the ever-present forest, gave early American history a period characterized not by stone or bronze or iron, but by wood. They devised ways to substitute wood for stone, iron, or leather. With their ingenious exploitation of the forest, they made wood play a greater part in the development of the United States than in the rise of any other nation in history. (p. 138)

Eric Sloan's excellent book on the early uses of wood, *A Reverence for Wood* (1965), describes the period this way:

> That century of magnificent awareness preceding the Civil War was the age of wood. Wood was not accepted simply as the material for building a new nation— it was an inspiration. Gentle to the touch, exquisite to contemplate, tractable in creative hands, stronger by weight than iron, wood was, as William Penn had said, "a substance with a soul." It spanned rivers for man; it built his home and heated it in the winter; man walked on wood, slept in it, sat on wooden chairs at wooden tables, drank and ate the fruits of trees from wooden cups and

dishes. From cradle of wood to coffin of wood, the life of man was encircled by it. (p. 72)

In 1765, everything a man owned was made more valuable by the fact that he had made it himself or knew exactly from where it had come. This is not so remarkable as it sounds; it is less strange that the eighteenth-century man should have a richer and keener enjoyment of life through knowledge than that the twentieth-century man should lead an arid and empty existence in the midst of wealth and extraordinary material benefits.

Those days, when the nation was struggling to be born, were perhaps our most poignant times, for it was an era when each man was forced to live with piercing awareness and perception. Two centuries later, when an American turns on the water and lights in his apartment, he has little awareness of where these things come from; the greatest pity, however, is that he says, "Who cares where it comes from, as long as it keeps on coming?" (p. 72)

Today, the best place to see the value and importance of wood to early pioneers is the Museum of Appalachia: "The most authentic and complete replica of pioneer life in the world." Located in Norris, Tennessee near I-75 north of Knoxville, this 65-acre museum, farm, and village reflects over 25 years of intelligent thought, effort, and love for the people of Appalachia by John Rice Irwin, founder-director. Irwin collected over 30 authentic log structures now filled with thousands of frontier and pioneer relics. Woodworking tools and items made from wood are a major factor in the large display barn. Oak baskets made by Cherokee Native Americans are also displayed, in which dark patterns were made by dye produced from black walnut roots. (See Directory.)

ଈ

It was a struggle to clear the timber for agriculture. Lillard described the size of the "problem" in this way:

In less than three centuries backwoodsmen cut off most of the virgin stands of the Great Forest. But though the eastern third of North America was the largest area in history to be so greatly changed so quickly by human labor, the process viewed in detail, called for a tedious, painstaking labor. Trees were more of an obstacle than hostile Indians. In some parts of early New England it took one axman as many as thirty days merely to cut the timber on an acre of land, and as many days more to remove wood and rocks and make the land at all farmable. (p. 32)

Early settlers knew the best land was where the best and biggest trees grew. In his book about immigration from the U.S. and Europe into Upper Canada and what is now Ontario, *The Trail of the Black Walnut* (1957), G. Elmore Reaman observed:

It has been said that the Germans in selecting their land in Upper Canada followed the trail of the black walnut. Because this type of tree grows best on limestone soil and because this was the kind of soil the Germans preferred, the black walnut tree made the selection easy. But the method of selection had also to do with all trees: the land that grew the tallest trees must be the best land. Of course, choosing land covered with heavy timber meant that the settler was selecting a location which would require much physical labor. (p. 65)

The first thing the settler had to do after acquiring his land was to clear four or five acres to produce a garden and forage for his livestock. The quickest way was Indian fashion, which was to deaden the trees by girdling them with an axe. This let sun penetrate to growing crops planted between the still-standing tree trunks that had no leaves. As time permitted, the settler would then drop the dead trunks and clear the land of stumps, roots, and rocks. It was hard, dangerous, time-consuming work, and the trees were a constant hindrance.

Even today, descendents of these early settlers often look upon trees as a hindrance, give trees little respect or care, and consider trees of little value. Trees are now often taken for granted. Many do not realize the importance of trees; they have learned little about trees and show no inclination to learn. Few shared the view of John Burroughs, log cabin poet-naturalist, who felt the spiritual wealth of trees and wrote: "The most precious things of life are close at hand, without money and without price."

Lillard describes the early settlers' attitude this way:

> Any tree on his horizon irritated his eye and made him reach for his axe. He wanted to see bare ground. Maybe certain swamp oaks or elms were so "venerable" that "in view of their antiquity it seemed almost wrong to cut them," and if they were huge, demanding hours of labor, the settler left them for a few years until he had a spare day; but the day came for sure when he chopped them down and burned them up, just to get rid of them. Oblivious of the pleasures and uses of shade, the settler left no hedge trees, no trees by the cabin or water trough. He had no eye for graceful branches or contrasts in shades of green. His interest in a tree was how many blows would it take to fell its trunk. (p. 74)

To protect crops from freely roaming livestock, fences were constructed of the most readily available excess material: trees. The most common fence was called a snake fence, worm fence, or Virginia rail fence. These fences were made of wooden rails, and consumed tremendous amounts of labor and a huge amount of timber to create and construct.

Lillard explains:

> Experienced woodsmen split fifty to a hundred ten-foot rails a day. A visitor to Illinois met a settler who took a day to convert a tall tree into upwards of two hundred heavy rails. After the crosscut saw came into general use, a pair of men could turn out five hundred rails per day.
>
> Historically, the rail fence was a free fence for the poor man. But by present-day standards rail fences were extravagant users of time, energy, and timber. By 1875, American fences had cost more than the land was worth and were the most valuable class of property except railroads and city real estate. Illinois had ten times as much fencing as all of Germany. Fences in New York were worth one hundred and fourteen million dollars with an annual repair bill one tenth of this. (p. 78)

During the Civil War, rail fences often provided fuel for the evening campfire. On the march south, soldiers of the Army of the Potomac warmed themselves and heated coffee with the flames from Virginia rail fences. Lillard continues:

> The abundance of cheap fuel and timber, which so obviously aided the settler, contributed as greatly to the growth of cities and the rise of commerce and industry. Lumbering itself rose to great prominence. It played a major role in the settlement of the treeless West and the boom times of the Gilded Age all over the country. Always it supplied cheap housing and cheap furniture, making America a nation of home owners. (p.139)
>
> As inventors and scientists began to make sweeping transformations in the lives of people, they made heavy demands on cordwood and lumber. The railroad itself, key enterprise in the period, consumed whole forests. Wood went into the construction of early locomotives, of passenger cars, sleeping cars, freight cars, trestles, and stations. Wood blazed in the firebox. Each year railroads required millions and millions of new crossties. Hand-hewn ties of walnut, white oak, and chestnut oak were expected to last only seven years. In 1869 rolling stock on United States railroads used the lumber from a third of a million acres, tracks required thirty million ties (cut from one million and a half acres), and locomotives burned a total of nineteen thousand cords of wood a day. (p. 146)

ða

In 1850, lumber production was the No. 1 manufacturing industry in the United States. As Eastern timber was depleted, the center of the timber industry moved west with the growth of the country. It moved from Maine and New York to Pennsylvania, to Ohio, to Indiana, to the states on Lake Michigan and Lake Superior, and then west and northwest to Oregon and Washington. Some virgin forests yet remain and are now being cut in Oregon, Washington, and Alaska. But most virgin forests fell to the saw and the lumbermen moved on to new forests. When the land was not farmed, the forest regenerated but was not the same.

After 1860, Pennsylvania became the leading lumber producing state. For 30 years, the lumber capital of the world was Williamsport, Pennsylvania, which once had 25 sawmills. The Pennsylvania Lumber Museum in the north edge of the Susquehannock State Forest on Route 6, Potter County, illustrates the life of the early logging camps and describes the activites of the Civilian Conservation Corps (CCC). A slide show at the museum shows old photographs of logging camp life and bare hills clear cut of all timber.

The hills of northeastern Pennsylvania are no longer bare. Trees have returned, but the magnificent forest is gone forever. The trees that grow now are harvested earlier, and smaller, and many have foliage reduced by gypsy moths and deer browse. Regeneration of these forests is seriously threatened.

ら

Further west, early geological survey reports documenting trees from five to 12 feet or more in diameter at three feet above ground were not uncommon. Forty-two species of hardwoods in the Wabash Valley were reported to have reached a height of 150 feet or more. Initially, this magnificent forest covered 87.5 percent of Indiana, which became a state of the Union in 1816.

In 1966, the Indiana Academy of Science reviewed Indiana history in the book *Natural Features of Indiana.* They said:

In the year 1899, Indiana led the nation with a lumber production of 1,036,999,000 board feet. The period 1880 to 1900 saw 2,604,000 acres cleared and timber acreage was estimated to have dropped from 4,355,000 acres to 1,500,000 acres. Second growth timber was often thought of as brush and, unfortunately, this same idea prevails yet in certain areas. Mass clearing had visibly affected stream flow. Wildlife was disappearing to an alarming degree. The white-tail deer was gone. The passenger pigeon was gone from Indiana. In the period of slightly over 50 years the great forests had been reduced to sad remnants and some of the finest hardwoods in the world were gone. By 1919, Indiana had dropped to 13th place nationally in hardwood lumber production. (p. 550)

By 1930, only 15 percent of Indiana was forest covered. Over 70 percent of Indiana had been cleared of forest in under 80 years. By 1992, 19.3 percent of Indiana was forested, and 15,119 acres of new forests had been planted in the previous five years.

The Great Smokies and the Blue Ridge (1943), contains a chapter titled "Men, Mountains, and Trees" by Donald Culross Peattie. His comments on lumbering practices of the 1940s follow:

At first, about 60 years ago (1883), only the most precious cabinet woods were culled — walnut, cherry, magnolia . . . The mills did not bother with logs less than twenty inches thick at the small end! In a decade, they were glad to get logs 24 inches at the stump end. Today (1943), the average grade of lumber has been lowered as much as 40% of what was acceptable in 1905. The result has been that all the finest trees, and most valuable species, have been pulled out of the forest as if they were objectionable weeds, while the species of little commercial value, like dogwood, have been left to multiply. The only trees that were certain to be spared were superannuated specimens, usually full of disease and decay and taking up far more than their share of the light and moisture. This is selective logging with a vengeance! By comparison, clean-cutting of the hardwood forest is wiser practice. For it gives all the seedlings, of all kinds of trees, an equal chance to come up in a swift, uniform, healthy growth. Indeed, such second growth is worth more to the owner and the miller than many a virgin forest with its too large proportion of superannuated and seedling trees. (p. 170)

In the 1900 *Yearbook of Agriculture*, William L. Hall, Assistant Superintendent of Tree Planting, Division of Forestry, wrote:

The diminution of natural timber in the Mississippi Valley has been general. On the eastern side the destruction of forests has been greatest because there the supply was greatest. The valley of the Wabash River is now cleared in most places to the banks of the stream. A prominent farmer of Vigo County, Ind., told the writer recently that he had but a half dozen remaining white oaks to use for posts, and that he would soon have to grow his own posts or buy them.

On the west side of the Mississippi a condition of great scarcity prevails. Little timber is left in western Iowa and Missouri. The valleys of eastern Kansas, which produced large quantities of Black Walnut and Bur Oak, have largely been cleared. Arkansas holds the greatest supply of valuable timber in the Middle West, but it is filled with sawmills, many of them of immense capacity, running day and night. The most valuable post and tie timbers of Arkansas are White Oak and Bur Oak, the supply of which is rapidly diminishing. (p. 78)

Early forestry legislation was faulty and unworkable, but gradually more concern developed for the quickly vanishing forest. In 1903, Indiana legislation provided for the first State Forest Reservation. Two thousand acres in Clark County were purchased and became the early scene of field investigations in the reforestation of hardwood species. Beginning in 1905, courses in forestry were first offered at Purdue University, and by 1913, ten forestry courses were offered. Taxes were lowered on forest land held by private owners, and incentives were offered for reforestation. By 1932, state forestry lands had expanded to 25,000 acres and by 1966 to 126,288 acres.

ია

In 1944, through the efforts of private citizens who worked toward and contributed half the funds, 88 acres near Paoli, Indiana called Cox's Woods were acquired and designated as the *Indiana Pioneer Mothers' Memorial Forest*. Thus was preserved one of the last vestiges of the virgin Indiana forest. Here lies a strange tale.

"Whadaya wanna go out thar fer? Ain't nuthin out thar but trees."

Thus spoke the young service station attendant in Paoli, Indiana on October 14, 1945, when my father asked him for directions to Cox's Woods. Service station attendants then would pump gas, check under the hood, clean the windshield and give directions.

My father, an avid reader, had read and saved the January 31, 1942 issue of *The Saturday Evening Post*, which told of the history of a tract of magnificent old stand timber and the successful effort to save it from being cut. Father had brought me and my mother to see the trees, and we did. They were majestic and all that the article said they would be. But that was in 1945. (See Appendix I, "Joe Cox's Trees Live On" by Andrew H. Hepburn.)

The opinion expressed by the service station attendant is not uncommon in much of the country. Many Americans show a basic disregard and lack of respect for trees. This may reflect the relative abundance of trees on our land or the historic "war" against trees to clear the land to grow grain and forage. Or the attitude may be simply thoughtlessness based on ignorance. John Muir, the famous naturalist and first president of the Sierra Club said, "The wrongs done to trees, wrongs of every sort, are done in the darkness of ignorance and unbelief."

Lack of respect for trees is reflected in many ways: mutilated trees; trees with nails driven into them holding wire fence; trees with yard lights attached to them; and various items hung from the branches such as swings and tires. In recent time, a deer hunter building a hunting seat drove 20 large steel spikes into a 36-inch diameter black walnut tree planted by my father in 1928.

Very seldom are trees properly pruned. Few trees are planted or properly cared for. Bulldozers clear "junk" trees from stream banks and fence rows. Many woodlands are grazed by cattle and slowly destroyed. Dead trees are often left standing in pastures and woodlots. Woodlands are often ignored by landowners, and anyone wanting to just "see trees" was suspect.

❧

In March 1992, I visited my father in Florida and he gave me the January 31, 1942 issue of the *Saturday Evening Post* that he had kept for 50 years. Later the same month, I drove north on Indiana Route 37 through the Hoosier National Forest and into Paoli, Indiana, to visit again Joe Cox's Woods. (Appendix I)

Homes along Route 37 south of Paoli display a bewildering array of abandoned vehicles, machinery, various appliances, assorted trash and junk. Much fruit from the consumer society has been left to rust and rot beside the road. We are a truly rich society to discard so easily and so carelessly so much of our material wealth. At the same time, many ignore the restoration of our forests. While we discard and waste our material wealth, we neglect to care for and improve our natural wealth. It is a combination of traits leading to poverty.

How different the scene was from Bavaria in Germany, for example, where such displays of trash do not exist. An executive of a veneer company who had lived in Germany but was now living in America gave his view on why Germany was so clean while America was not. He said, "You have so much land and so many things, that it is unappreciated. You have so much freedom. You take it all for granted. In Germany, there are rules and you cannot cut some trees which are over seven inches without permission. I love it here. I love the sense of freedom." Being able to simply throw things away is a very powerful measure of freedom.

ᶻ⋅

Approaching Paoli, Indiana from the south, I thought I recognized the entrance to Cox's Woods from my visit 47 years before. But a single sign on the opposite side of the road from the woods confused me. I parked, but found no trail markers or identifying signs. There were two modern signs with red pistols and a red diagonal stripe across them which I assumed meant no hunting but may have meant no guns.

In Paoli, the service station of 47 years before had "modernized." It was now a self-service station with only a cashier who had never heard of Cox's Woods or the Indiana Pioneer Mothers' Memorial Forest.

The office of the Paoli Ranger District, USDA Forest Service was moving and merging with the local Chamber of Commerce office. There I found Helen Collier, senior volunteer, who had put together a loose leaf binder of material about the Indiana Pioneer Mothers' Memorial Forest. The local district forest ranger had decamped in October to Tell City, which was 40 miles south, and Helen was left holding the fort. Helen was most helpful and explained that she worked only three days a week under a senior citizen program. She thought the forest rangers did not want to serve in the Paoli office because it was a low-rated position.

Helen gave me a photocopy of a very dim photocopy of a map of the Memorial Forest and directions. She explained that I would find a sign on Route 150 and the Memorial Forest went through to Route 37 and one could walk east or west from highway to highway. She said the forest rangers were not encouraging visits because of vandalism and reported rumors of "satanic rites" about 20 years ago. For those reasons, the parking area had been closed.

I then drove southeast on Route 150 looking for the entrance to the forest and drove past it. There was no sign. I returned and found the roadway back to the forest blocked by a heavy chain leaving room to park only four cars and three were parked there already. One was owned by a young man fishing in a small stream nearby and another by an old man just embarking on a walk. He acknowledged that this was indeed the entrance to the famous Indiana Pioneer Mothers' Memorial Forest.

There were no trail markers or road signs. I followed the old road about 1/4 mile to a surfaced parking area with room to park 20 cars. There were no cars because of the chain across the the old road back at the entrance on Indiana Route 150.

A dim trace of an unmarked trail headed up the hill from the parking area. A short distance up that trace, I came to a large stone memorial that read, "INDIANA PIONEER

MOTHERS' MEMORIAL." Behind the stone memorial, the sad remains of what had been a magnificent white oak were rotting into the forest floor. Around the white oak carcass, an old wood rail fence was falling into decay.

It was a lovely, warm, quiet, very early spring day in March, and the flowers of the forest floor were just beginning to appear. There were yet some of the magnificent black walnuts Joe Cox loved so much. The trees reached 80-100 feet without a limb and were several feet in diameter at the base. They only tapered gradually as they rose higher and higher searching for sunlight.

But these trees, too, were dying and the tops showed decay and death. Several of these huge walnuts had died and fallen, and several appeared to be dead but not yet fallen. There were not only oak and black walnut, but big beech and hard maple as well. It was evident that this virgin forest had changed in fifty years and was changing still.

Some who had visited this forest left their initials in the bark of the big beech trees as evidence of their visit and their lack of respect for trees. At least there was no recent

Indiana Pioneer Mothers' Memorial in Cox Woods, Paoli, Indiana.

fresh carving. The most recent "vandalism" was a metal "no guns" sign attached at eye level to a big beech tree by steel bolts. Two huge black walnuts showed evidence of having been painted with some orange paint and this covered with darker paint in an attempt to match the color of the bark. I heard two stories about how this had occurred.

One story was that a new log buyer happened into the woods, and finding no signs, assumed the land was private. He marked several trees for harvest and went looking for the owner. He must have believed he had stumbled into heaven because trees of this size cannot be found or bought anymore. Only in state parks and nature preserves does one find trees of this stupendous size.

The second story was that someone wanted to make a TV commercial and marked the trees to film the commercial. I don't know if either is true, but I did see two huge magnificent black walnuts on Forest Service land that had been marked with orange paint.

It was evident to even the untrained eye that 50 years after the effort to preserve Joe Cox's Woods as the Indiana Pioneer Mothers' Memorial Forest, things were not going as planned. The trees Joe Cox so loved were dying just as Joe and the Pioneer Mothers had. Many pioneers would have considered trees a strange memorial. In the early days, there was little love for trees.

In *The Awakening Land* (1966), a descriptive novel of pioneer life in Ohio, Conrad Richter gives a superb description of the fear and loathing Sayward Luckett Wheeler felt for the towering forest. She longed to see the sun and sky but they were blocked from her view all summer by the massive trees and leaves thick overhead. Her younger sister was lost in the forest and taken by Indians. Her mother had not wanted to leave Pennsylvania for the Northwest Territories and feared the forest wilderness.

When her mother died, Wheeler's thoughts about the "bury hole" are described by Richter.

> It was dug more with the axe than with the shovel.
> The black ground was all roots. As far as their hands went
> down, the roots lay atop each other, this way and that,

thick and thin, like a great den of snakes froze up for the winter and not knowing it was long spring. Sayward hated having to put her mother in a place like this. Those greedy, flesh-minded roots would slink around that box trying to get in. (p. 34)

After a long life cutting the massive trees and grubbing stumps to clear land for farming, Wheeler faced death. At the last, she wanted her bed moved so she could see the few remaining trees. Her son, Chancey, thought this strange. Richter wrote of Chancey's thoughts:

> Could it be even faintly possible that the children of pioneers like himself, born under more benign conditions than their parents, hated them because they themselves were weaker, resented it when their parents expected them to be strong, and so invented all kinds of intricate reasoning to prove that their parents were tyrannical and cruel, their beliefs false and obsolete, and their accomplishments trifling? (p.628)
>
> He remembered a dozen stories of her abhorrence and bitter enmity for what she called 'the big butts.' And yet now all she lived for was the sight and sound of those green leaves moving outside her window. Was there something deeper and more mysterious in his mother's philosophy than he and his generation who knew so much had suspected; something not simple but complex; something which held not only that hardship built happiness but which somehow implied that hate built love; and evil, goodness? (p. 629)

Perhaps Cox's Woods was a suitable memorial for the Pioneer Mothers even though many hated the forest and feared the wilderness. Some of the current generation show the same lack of respect for the big woods as their pioneer ancestors. Was that the lesson? Are we just like them? Have we not learned to love the forest as Joe Cox did? What will it take for more of us to learn to appreciate and respect trees? If people were discouraged from visiting this forest and could not be trusted to visit it without vandalizing it, what kind of a memorial was this? What had been preserved and what had been accomplished here by this effort?

Well, the trees have been preserved for 50 years longer than they would have been if harvested in 1942. Many have died, but some yet remain for you to see. Many people have seen these trees over this 50 years, and some of these people may have been moved or inspired to do other than vandalize or wonder what the fuss was all about. Some people admire big trees.

Black walnuts in Cox Woods. March, 1992, author in foreground.

ॐ

Apparently, reverence for trees, even big, majestic trees such as these, is quite rare in the human species. A few people are moved and touched by exposure to trees such as this, but most seem not to be so touched. A few are inspired to write poetry such as Joyce Kilmer's famous poem *Trees*. Others feel compelled to carve their initials. I've heard that tourists visiting the Grand Canyon spend an average of six minutes admiring the canyon and 40 minutes in the gift shop and snack bar. My own observations confirm this to be the case.

Some who have visited the forest may have been reminded and impressed with what the Pioneer Mothers encountered when they arrived. For those who will look, this forest still serves to demonstrate how much we have lost of our heritage. Although some of the trees have been preserved for fifty years, many have died and decayed. It is of course a natural process, but sad, nevertheless.

But for photographs and memories, the dead trees, like our Pioneer Mothers, are lost forever. The beautiful wood they were has been lost. It was not preserved as tables, chairs, desks, or paneling. It cannot be passed from generation to generation and admired by those yet to come.

George Nakashima, the famous woodworker of Bucks County, Pennsylvania, described the beauty of trees and his philosophy in his book, *The Soul of A Tree* (1988). He wrote:

> We are left in awe by the nobility of a tree, its eternal patience, its suffering caused by man and sometimes nature, its witness to thousands of years of earth's history, its creations of fabulous beauty. It does nothing but good, with its prodigious ability to serve, it gives off its bounty of oxygen while absorbing gases harmful to other living things. The tree and its pith live on. Its fruits feed us. Its branches shade and protect us. And, finally, when time and weather bring it down, its body offers timber for our houses and boards for our furniture. The tree lives on. (p. 27)

Preservation of living things is an ideal not based on reality.The *Holy Bible*, Ecclesiastes, Chapter 3, Verses 1 and 2 reads: "To every thing there is a season, and a time to every purpose under the heaven: A time to be born, and a time to die; a time to plant, and a time to pluck up that which is planted." William Shakespeare wrote: "Everything that grows, holds in perfection but a little moment." You cannot preserve living things.

The essence of the forest that Joe Cox so admired, a majestic forest of black walnut and oak has not been preserved because it was only a temporary condition whose permanence was against the laws of Mother Nature. Mother Nature has her own laws, which are complex and unbending. Her laws dictate that living trees die and are replaced by others. Her laws dictate that while black walnuts and white oaks may sprout and live a short time in the shade of the deep woods, these species soon die in deep woods from lack of sunlight.

The trees Joe Cox loved had sprouted and grown in an environment of open sunlight many years before he knew them. His woods were only one scene in nature's play. Although it was a beautiful scene, it was only temporary. The next scene has begun to form. The next generation of trees, now growing on the forest floor, is not black walnut or oak, but hard maple and beech. These latter species can tolerate dense shade and will become the dominant species in only a few more years. If you want to see Joe Cox's walnut trees and his forest, you must hurry. The scene is changing. The next act has begun. The walnut and oak scene is coming to a close, and the maple and beech scene will soon dominate.

ಎ

This attempt at preservation teaches many lessons if only we can learn them. To learn these lessons, the U.S. Forest Service is studying this forest as a Research Natural Area. In 1978, permanent sample plots were established by the Forest Service and Southern Illinois University. After 10 years, the plots were reassessed. In this 10 years (from 1978 to 1989) the total number of trees decreased by 16 percent. An average of 71 trees per acre died, and about 30 smaller trees grew large enough to be counted. Although a quarter of the dead trees were hard or sugar maples, more than half of the new trees were also sugar maples. This species was the most numerous of all, increasing from 48 percent of the trees in 1978, to 55 percent in 1989.

Thus, one lesson learned is that natural change in a forest is inevitable. Another is that if there is little sun, the shade-tolerant species will increase, and the species that require more sun will decrease. Since black walnut and white oak require more sun, they can only be increased by the provision of more sun. This means larger openings in the forest canopy must be created. In an established forest, larger openings may be created by disease, fire, tornado or harvesting of mature trees. Without one of these events, the forest will be dominated by shade-tolerant species such as maple or beech. Nature's law prevails.

This was not a new lesson. Zane Grey, dentist, world class fisherman, hunter, and author, wrote *The Young Forester* (1910). It contains this insightful passage:

> This is an old hardwood forest. Much of the white oak, hickory, ash, maple, is virgin timber. These trees have reached maturity; many are dead at the top; all of them should have been cut long ago. They make too dense a shade for the seedlings to survive. Look at that bunch of sapling maples. See how they reach up, trying to get to the light. They haven't a branch low down and the tops are thin. Yet maple is one of the hardiest trees. Growth has been suppressed. Do you notice there are no small oaks or hickories just here? They can't live in deep shade. (p. 8)

Nature's law was no secret in 1910. But, unless we recall past lessons, we often must relearn lessons forgotten. In 1992, Dick Burton, timber manager for David R. Webb, (a large and successful veneer company in Edinburgh, Indiana) spoke to his daughter's fifth grade class. "How many believe it is wrong to cut a tree?" he asked. Every hand went up. Preservationists all!

Burton states and asks:

> I'm a conservationist but not a preservationist. You can't preserve living things! All living things eventually die. Is it better to have plastic desks and chairs made from petroleum, which is an imported nonrenewable resource, or these items made from hardwoods, which are renewable resources and locally grown?

Is it better to conserve or preserve? Burton is strongly for conservation of soil, the environment and conditions that promote the growth of trees. He believes that preserving living things is not practical. He believes we should plant more trees and manage our forests so that future generations will have more trees and more wealth. A small investment now will be worth a great deal in 50, 80, or 100 years.

Burton said:

> We've been harvesting trees for over a hundred years throughout the Midwest and there are yet trees and will be trees but the quality is declining and the more desirable species are being replaced by less desirable species. We should manage our forest land to encourage more desirable species such as black walnut and white oak.

&a.

The Eastern black walnut is native to an area bounded by eastern Kansas, Oklahoma, and Texas on the west, Minnesota, Michigan, Ontario and New York on the north, and Alabama to Georgia on the south. It is seldom found in solid natural stands. Since it grows best in deep, fertile, well-drained soil, the best trees are often found in close proximity to streams. In any natural forest, the black walnut seldom constitutes as much as five percent of the total stand.

The black walnut has always been comparatively rare even in the period of pioneer and commercial exploitation of the virgin forest. Because it was and is comparatively rare, and because the wood has so many desirable characteristics and uses, the black walnut has always been the premium tree of the land. While it has been proposed as the National Tree, it has not been so designated and surprisingly has never been adopted as the state tree of any state. The nut is the state fruit of Missouri.

&a.

Attentive readers, at this point, may have some questions. If the terminal forest is hard maple and beech, how was it that the first settlers into Pennsylvania and the Ohio, Mississippi and other river valleys found forests with so many walnut and oak? If these species grow only in open sunshine, where did the open spaces necessary for their establishment come from? Good questions!

These questions puzzle some people, but there is an explanation. When La Salle led his expedition down the Illinois and Mississippi rivers in 1682, he found evidence of large numbers of native Americans, but relatively few living persons. University of Indiana students, conducting an archaeological dig just outside Cox Woods, have found a farming village of native Americans and carbon dated charcoal from firepits to the late 1300s — but no later. What had been a large agrarian native American culture throughout the Midwest was largely gone. Where had the people gone? Did their presence and then sudden disappearance provide the conditions for the growth of the magnificent forests found by Europeans?

Indiana University students conducting an archaeological dig at the edge of Cox Woods discovered native American carbon materials dated to the late 1300s, but none later.

America in 1492: The World of the Indian Peoples Before the Arrival of Columbus, edited by Alvin M. Josephy, Jr. (1992), describes the many varied civilizations and their ways which existed in America before Columbus. It says:

If Columbus had ascended the Mississippi River and gone ashore in Illinois across the great river from present-day St. Louis, he would have seen the already crumbling ruins of the greatest Indian metropolis north of Mexico. This was Cahokia, onetime capital of a highly sophisticated society which archaeologists have called Mississippian. Its refined artistic production, hierarchical social and political organization, and effective economic structure flourished in a riverine habitat. (p. 136)

About three hundred years before Columbus's voyage, the central city of Cahokia reached the peak of its architectural development and political prestige. Rising above the five square miles that constituted "downtown" Cahokia was a gigantic pyramid now called Monks Mound. An artificial heap of shaped earth, its base was 1,040 feet long and 790 feet wide; it rose 100 feet high to support a wattle-and-daub-walled temple on its truncated summit. More than a half million cubic meters of mound fill had been piled in stages over the decades by a local population that probably numbered more than 10,000 at its height. Whatever precipitated the abrupt decline of this civilization a few hundred years before Columbus remains a matter of scholarly debate. (p. 138)

Some scholars believe Cahokia declined because the population grew beyond the means of the local area to support it. Evidence of three great wooden stockades surrounding Monks Mound have been found by archaeologists. These stockades were made of tree trunks buried four feet deep and standing upright for 20 feet above the soil level. The three stockades were built in succession, with a new one built outside the older as it decayed. Built at about 40-year intervals, each successive stockade was built of smaller and smaller trees indicating the local forests were being depleted.

Firewood would have been harder and harder to get and would have come from longer and longer distances. Pollution of local water, accumulation of garbage, and the resultant diseases could also have contributed to the decline of Cahokia.

Regardless of the cause, a city with a greater population than London in 1250, and which is believed to have had the largest population of any city in North America until surpassed by Philadelphia in 1800, declined and died and the forest returned.

ે

The centuries between A.D. 800 and 1100 saw a dramatic development in American farming and mound building. The Mississipian culture was widespread throughout the range of the Eastern black walnut. Monks Mound was larger in volume than the largest pyramid at Giza, Egypt. Thousands of smaller mounds were found throughout the Midwest. These people grew marsh elder, goosefoot, maize, squash, pumpkins and other crops in small plots of land in the fertile river valleys. These small fields were tilled by hand and by hoe. They had no beasts of burden. When the native American population ceased to exist, these abandoned fields were excellent sites for young oaks and walnuts to grow.

After 1500, a period of great dying hit native Americans that was the worst in the history of man. The Europeans who followed Columbus introduced diseases that caused millions of deaths. In America, twice the proportion of the population was lost as was lost to the Black Death in Europe.

In 1738, smallpox was brought to the Carolinas on slave ships. It traveled up the trading paths and burst upon the Indians with fearful effect. One half the entire population is said to have been devastated. Some scholars believe the population of native Americans in North America dropped from 18 million in 1492 to as low as 350,000 by 1900. Where the people had been, trees grew.

For centuries before Columbus came, native Americans had cleared land for farming and hunting by burning or girdling trees. Wherever plant cover would burn, it was burned repeatedly as part of the cultural way of life. Each year, the aboriginal intentionally fired thousands of square miles in the historic range of white-tail deer. Deer were driven by fire into the arms of hunting parties. In so doing, native Americans "harvested deer," but helped sustain deer populations as well. How could this be?

Deer require browse, which is low-growing shrubs and trees. Deer find little of this in deep forest; they may live in deep forest, but they feed in glades and open areas. Fire provided open browse for deer and openings for oak and walnut seedlings to find sun.

White-Tailed Deer: Ecology and Management, compiled and edited by Lowell K. Halls (1984), further supports the link of deer with the forest. It says of native American hunting methods:

> One of the most widespread and successful hunting methods was the fire drive, and for this procedure the dormancy of the vegetation was of critical importance in both spring and autumn. In both seasons, fires could be set before departure to alternative-season camps and, in addition to the venison harvested, burning served to prepare the areas for the group or tribe to return later. Turner wrote of fire-surround hunting of white-tails by the Iroquois Indians of New York in the late 1700s. He described a site near current Groveland where about 500 Indians ignited a nearly 49 square mile area, driving deer and other animals toward the center where hunters were stationed. Another such burning area existed near Masonville, New York. (p. 39)

White-tailed deer were as essential to the life of Eastern native Americans as the bison or buffalo were to the life of native Americans living on the western plains. Most people are familiar with the role of the bison or buffalo in the American west. Stories of white hunters slaughtering vast herds of buffalo for sport, or only their tongues or hides, are common knowledge. Less understood is the role of the white-tail deer and the slaughter of it, which occurred in two phases.

In the first phase (1500-1800), the white-tail deer population was reduced from an estimated 30 million to 12 million by native American hunters who traded deerskins for items of "civilization" such as tin and iron implements, guns, knives, traps, powder, rouge for war paint, cotton and woolen stuffs, mirrors, cheap jewelry and trading beads proffered by European fur traders. The "simple savage" still saw little but good in the white man's "civilization" with its goodies and gadgets. But there was a price to pay for this "civilization."

Halls' book states:

> For countless centuries a venerated kin, the white-tailed deer now was reduced to a commodity, with the North American Indian acting as the white merchant's functionary in a three-century spate of exploitation that left the land nearly barren of certain wildlife and the Indians themselves destitute of subsistence and cultural options. It was the Indian who killed by far the greater number of animals involved in the fur trade . . . the slaughter was inveigled by the white tradesman and underwritten by the European buying public.

> In 1833 came John James Audubon's epitaph to the aeon-old Indian/white-tail relationship . . . and epilogue to American influence on the continent: "For as the deer, the caribou, and all other game is killed for the dollar which its skin brings in, the Indian must search in vain over the deserted country for that on which he is accustomed to feed, until, worn out by sorrow, despair, and want, he either goes far from his early haunts to others, which in time will be similarly invaded, or he lies on the rocky shore and dies." (p. 59)

Thus, greed drove the destruction of wildlife, the burning of more land, and contributed to the self-destruction of native Americans. The destruction of the native American contributed in two ways to the growth of the magnificent forests. Abandoned fields and burned forests provided open space and light for oak and walnut.

ॐ

The Father of American Forestry was French. Francois Andre' Michaux traveled widely across North America in the early 1800s, and wrote extensively of his travels. In 1817, his works were published in Philadelphia as *The North American Sylva*. In his travels and writings, he carefully observed the quality and uses of every tree species he found being utilized by the inhabitants. He noted that the species of trees indigenous to an area was a reliable index of the quality and value of the soil. He observed the contrast between the nature of a forest surrounding an abandoned clearing and the one beginning to grow up in the clearing, and in this he anticipated what is now a well-known tenet of forest management, *the sequence of species domination.*

Related observations led him to the conclusion that the prairie regions of Kentucky and Tennessee owed both origin and continued existence to repeated wildfires. He noted the rapidly mounting timber shortage in the east, and recommended elimination of the less desirable species and encouragement of the better sorts to offset the timber drain. Many have not yet learned this lesson.

Thinking and writing scientifically about the future of the American forests was something new. Americans had grown accustomed to regarding their forests as impediments to be surmounted, as nuisances in the way of cultivation of land or building a road. Americans continued to cut, burn and use the timber without regard for the future. It would be a century before they would awaken to a sufficient realization of what they were losing and begin to study the science and wisdom of Francois Andre' Michaux.

Michaux left in his will a substantial legacy to the American Philosophical Society of Philadelphia, Pennsylvania, for the encouragement of forest studies. This money enabled the Society to support studies that played no small part in the creation of the Pennsylvania Department of Forestry. This department was the stimulus, as well as the seed bed and nursery, of the forestry services of several states during the early 1900s.

By 1899, when Indiana became the center of logging in the United States, many forests, because farmland had been abandoned and forests burned by native Americans, could have been *only* 250 to 500 years old and in scene two, which was the oak and walnut scene. Now, about a hundred years later, Cox's Woods is passing into scene three, and the oaks and walnut are to be more rare. It could be that the Europeans arrived at just the right time to find the forest in its most productive and valuable period, thanks to the native Americans who had farmed and used fire to "harvest" deer.

ﻉﺍ

Recently, Professor William L. Hoover, at Purdue University's Department of Forestry and Natural Resources, has researched and recorded black walnut tree harvest statistics. His records show a nearly steady decline in production of black walnut logs from 1966 to 1980. And, an even steeper decline in the top-quality veneer log production as a percent of total production. He found that over 90 million board feet of black walnut logs were harvested in 1966. By 1978, the harvest had declined to less than half or below 45 million. Veneer log production had been over 45 percent of the total in 1968, but declined to less than 30 percent of the smaller total by 1979. It was evident to all that the quantity and quality of black walnut timber was declining drastically.

As black walnut became rare and valuable, stories of tree rustling began to surface. Bob Lark, who has been associated with Valley Forge National Historic Park for 21 years, related an event that occurred in 1972, when he was employed with the law enforcement agency of then-Valley Forge State Park. Bob said:

> We had 8-10 huge black walnut trees stolen from the park near Maxwell's Quarters at the base of Mount Misery. The trees had huge trunks and several had no limbs for 50 feet. They were valued at about $10,000 and although they were illegally harvested, we never caught the rustlers.

Walnut trees were not safe even in Valley Forge State Park.

ﻉﺍ

As quality walnut trees became more rare and valuable, the cutting of these aged giants became newsworthy. On December 30, 1976, *The New York Times* carried an article

by Reginald Stuart titled: "Perfect" Walnut Tree is Among
18 Sold for $80,000. The *Times* reported:

> PIONEER, OH—Roger Herrett, a state forest service
> officer in the northwestern part of Ohio for some 17 years,
> is not one who gets easily excited over a new tree story.
> But recently, Mr. Herrett and many of the so-called tree
> veterans in this region witnessed a tree story that they will
> be talking about for years. It was the sale, for $80,000.01 of
> 18 black walnut trees, including one that the hardwood
> industry considered the most perfect and valuable black
> walnut tree in the nation. When the bidding was over,
> Herman Meyer, the head of the Atlantic Veneer Company
> of Beaufort, N.C. the new owner of "the perfect tree," put
> its value at $30,000.
>
> The tree, now called the "Bicentennial Tree" by its
> new owners, was between 180 and 200 years old. It mea-
> sured 57 feet to its first limb and was more than 130 feet
> high. Its diameter was 38.4 inches at 4 1/2 feet above
> ground and its circumference at that height was 10 1/2
> feet. "It was majestic," said Mr. Herrett, who was among
> those who gathered for the cutting of the tree with cam-
> eras in hand."I've seen perfect logs 20 feet long, but to
> have this perfectness spread over 57 feet, well, as old
> George Geobel said, 'They don't make them kind any-
> more.'"
>
> "I've known about this tree for 15 years," said Mr.
> Meyer, president of Atlantic Veneer. "We get a lot of calls
> and letters on other trees, but it is very unlikely that there
> would be another one like this. Very unlikely. We're
> cutting hundreds of trees a day, but this one is special."
> The second highest bidder, the David R. Webb Company
> of Indiana, offered $78,750 for the lot.
>
> The sale of "the tree" has generated a new wave of
> enthusiasm in this region and in other parts of the Corn
> Belt known for its fine quality black walnut trees. And
> although Pioneer, a village of 1,000, has seen the best of its
> days as a walnut tree town, there are still some good ones
> around.
>
> "Selling trees in this region is primarily a sideline,
> for growing crops such as corn and wheat are the main-
> stay here in addition to a sprinkling in recent years of
> industry. Having salable trees was simply a combination
> of the workings of nature and the claiming of certain
> parcels of land decades ago when settlers, most of them

of German ancestry, moved to this area from the East. Even when there was a much greater abundance of black walnut trees in the area," Mr. Herrett said, "selling those trees was only of secondary importance to the farmers' perceived need to clear them and burn them in order to make way for more farming." He said, "many trees, possibly of equal value to 'the tree' had probably been cut and burned years ago or used on the farm without second thought."

Speculation that there may be more highly valuable trees around this region, if not on the farm from which "the tree" was cut, has prompted the three brothers who sold it to shy away from publicity. They fear, as do some state officials, that there may be renewed tree rustling should speculation grow that this may be one of several highly valuable trees left in the region but not yet found. Tree rustling was once commonplace in this region, but it is somewhat rare today. One farmer was said to have had nearly 20 trees stolen from his property in a single day.

There is little likelihood that "the tree" will be stolen, however, primarily because of its size. And until it is cut next month, it is on display at the Atlantic Veneer mill in North Carolina. Once cut, officials say, it will yield nearly 2,000 board feet of walnut veneer, nearly enough to cover three acres of land. (p. 1) *Copyright © 1976 by The New York Times Company. Reprinted by permission.*

The Bicentennial Tree, cut November 28, 1976, in Williams County, Ohio. Length: 30 meters, Diameter: one meter, Volume: 15 cubic meters. Estimated to be 200 years old and valued at $30,000. Photo courtesy of Al Huff, Atlantic Veneer Company.

Actually it would cover desks, walls, pianos, furniture or caskets. It also stimulated great excitement and interest in black walnut, which lasted for several years. Some believe the interest in black walnut has now waned and another great black walnut tree story is needed to rekindle interest. But trees like this are extremely rare.

Did this experience and publicity make a lasting impression on the residents of Pioneer, Ohio, where the tree was cut in 1976? In 1994, I visited Pioneer and talked with several current residents. They recalled the tree and the publicity but all agreed it had not changed the community. The money, they said, was spent for more land. They knew of no one who was planting black walnuts or pruning natural stands of black walnut. The local nursery was growing and selling silver maples, which grow fast and make shade but are brittle and of no commercial value. "The tree" is almost forgotten.

While this magnificent tree was cut and turned into veneer, it yet lives. How could this be? Before it was cut, live cuttings were taken from the tree and grafted onto roots of young black walnut seedlings by the foresters of the Ohio Department of Natural Resources. As part of a tree improvement program, clones of this tree, and many other superior trees, are growing in a plantation outside Zanesville, Ohio. The objective of this program is to improve the black walnut seedlings grown by the Ohio state nursery.

In June 1993, James P. Stafford, Coordinator of the Ohio Tree Improvement Program, showed me a clone of "the tree" which was about 20 feet tall. The clone was not an impressive individual. Stafford observed, "Quite possibly, that magnificent old tree just happened to be growing in an Indian garbage dump. Clones of 'the tree' may never equal the original." Jim and many others believe superior black walnut trees are determined more surely by their *environment* than by their genes.

Despite this belief, Stafford and others are striving to preserve the genes of superior individual black walnut trees and much effort has been devoted to selecting superior black walnuts for continued propagation. It is a long and difficult process, and money to finance the effort is not always forthcoming. In 1994, Jim told me he will be leaving the tree improvement program and a replacement is not guaranteed. A sign of waning interest? (More about this in Chapter 6.)

Jim Stafford stands beside a clone (cultivar) of the Bicentennial Tree, which was harvested in 1976. This tree grows in the Ohio Tree Improvement Plantation near Zanesville, Ohio. Photo taken June 1993. Note that this tree is branching at a low height.

❧

Other black walnut stories have appeared in the press. In 1984, Lori Epps of the Covington Bureau of the *Commercial News* of Danville, Illinois, reported another outstanding walnut sale in Cayuga, Indiana.

> No one can make Bud Myers believe that money doesn't grow on trees. Myers and his wife, Sue, of Cayuga Route 1 have sold an assortment of prime lumber for more than $300,000.
>
> The 352 trees, purchased by Atlantic Veneer Corporation of Beaufort, N.C., sold for an average price of $903 apiece, with the highest price paid for a single tree being an astounding $20,000, a record for the state of Indiana. The sale is believed to be one of the largest hardwood timber sales ever conducted, dollar-value wise, in the United States.
>
> Mr. Myers contacted a private forester and together they surveyed Myers' 140 acres of timber. They surveyed the land and selected 146 oak and 206 black

walnut for sale. Of the trees chosen, 70 of the black walnut and 104 of the white oak were classified as prime timber with each containing an average of between 201 and 224 board-feet of lumber. The sale was by invitation only with 60 major companies across the United States asked to participate. Eighteen companies sent representatives to inspect the timber and of these, eight submitted quotes on the lot. The high bidder, Atlantic Veneer Corporation, outbid all competitors by more than $50,000.

Bill King, agent for the company, explained that Atlantic, one of the largest veneer mills worldwide, makes "every effort possible" to buy quality trees. "We tried to make our bid high enough to assure the purchase." King said the highest-priced tree of the group, a black walnut, is among the finest he has bought in his 15 years with Atlantic. The 150-year-old tree measured approximately 128 feet from base to top and was estimated to contain slightly more than 1,000 board feet of lumber. King said the tree and others harvested will be trucked to a railroad siding in Spiceland, Ind., where they will be shipped by train to Beaufort, the company's base. Upon arrival in Beaufort, the logs will be sliced into thin veneer and then shipped to worldwide markets. According to King, Atlantic is one of the largest veneer mills in the world.

As Myers and about 25 curious neighbors watched the harvest of the prize tree, Myers reflected on what he had learned during the past several months. "For one, I learned the value of my timber. I'd say 90 percent of most farmers don't know what their forest is worth. I can look at a tree now and tell if it's got prime veneer." Not sure whether his family will replace the trees, he noted one thing for certain — they will continue to practice good management and protection of their forest land. (p. 4)

❧

On April 25, 1989, the *Wall Street Journal* carried a front-page article by Robert Johnson, staff reporter for the paper, entitled "Walnut Trees Now Are Often Grown for Different Nuts." He reported in the article the adventures

of Allan Ware, a professional "spotter" of trees for Frank
Purcell Walnut Lumber Company, in Kansas City, Kansas.

His (Mr. Ware's) quarry, the elusive black walnut,
occurs naturally only about once per wooded acre in the
U.S., compared with 100 oaks per acre. Walnut trees have
long been a scant three percent of the nation's tree population. Desperation is rising in sawmills because walnut,
with its golden swirls and purplish feathering, has become trendy. "Oak is boring," says Holli Pearson, wife of
a Kansas City lumber-store chain owner. "Walnut is so
iridescent, it almost beckons you into another dimension,
like a story by Lewis Carroll."

The price of walnut lumber is up almost 20 percent
since 1984. Walnut inventories are badly depleted amid
rising demand. New plantings aren't harvestable for at
least 50 years, despite recent U.S. Forest Service experi-
ments with speeding growth. Thus, baby boomers, who
aren't known for waiting patiently, won't soon enjoy a
plentiful supply of walnut.

To satisfy the conspicuously intelligent, Allan Ware,
the professional "spotter" must trek further and further
into the woods on slimmer leads, looking for what his
boss, Tom McMillan calls "the Hope Diamond of logs:
about 20 feet long, 20 inches in diameter, free of big knots
and unbattered by woodpeckers." "Many walnut trees
are too wormy or small and sappy to be worth cutting,"
says the 14-year veteran spotter. When he does find a
good tree, he is authorized to write a check of up to
$10,000 on the spot.

A spectacled alumnus of the University of Missouri's
forestry school, Mr. Ware bemoans the scarcity. "Sometimes I wonder when this will end, when there won't be
any walnut left," he says. Others bemoan Mr. Ware and
those like him. Says Carl Zichella, spokesman for the
Sierra Club, an environmental group: "Cruising the timber to satisfy market pressure when trees are scarce is
outrageous. They could put themselves out of business,
and I say good riddance," he adds.

His first day at work, he mistakenly paid $500 to a
man posing as a landowner who apparently took the
money and ran. The real owner later refused to sell.

Spotters are sometimes accused of cheating landowners out of fair prices, destroying crops to haul trees

away and even "rustling" trees in the dead of night. "I don't want nothing to do with you. I never got paid for the last trees I sold somebody." says a farmer, peering at Mr. Ware from a slight opening in his screen door. The spotter stands his ground and extols the virtues of his employer. The farmer slams the door in his face. But Mr. Ware's visit the next day is successful: He purchases 40 trees.

Yet those trees are barely a morning's work for Frank Purcell Lumber's computerized saws. That company's five percent share of the nation's fragmented $85 million wholesale walnut lumber market is probably the largest. To maintain that volume, Mr. Ware advertises for leads in about 30 small-town newspapers; drives more than 50,000 miles a year, mostly in Kansas, Missouri and Illinois; and hikes inestimable distances.

Lately, Mr. Ware's turf has been infested by foreign competition. Farmers tell of a snuff-sniffing German in his 70s who proffers cheap cologne in return for leads on walnut. Benefitting from exchange rates on deutsche marks, he is paying top dollar with only a cursory inspection of the wood, a casual approach that Mr. Ware can't afford. Mr. Ware's trail is also being dogged by a mysterious Japanese gentleman who frequents remote Midwest diners and is known only as "Mr. Moto." He is said to pretend ignorance of English while negotiating for lumber but celebrates with articulate orders for steak dinners when the deals are done.

Such competition, accompanied by rumors of soaring prices, are prompting unrealistic expectations among landowners. High-grade 20-foot logs typically fetch $100 to $1,000 from spotters. A few trees, fit to produce many feet of the best veneer, have brought $20,000; but they are extremely rare. Nevertheless, "talk of top prices travels fast and everyone thinks their tree is Fort Knox," says Mr. Ware.

Others look to the future. Speculating on a sweeter sellers' market to come, Douglas Dawson, a Unisys Corp. marketing representative, recently planted 36 black walnut trees on his five-acre lot in Waukee, Iowa. He got the idea from a relative who turned down surprise offers of $500 apiece for three front-yard walnuts. Mr Dawson's Arbor Day vision: that his land "will be worth thousands more to my children." (p. 1) *Reprinted by permission of Wall Street Journal, ©1989 Dow Jones & Company, Inc. All Rights Reserved Worldwide.*

୨ୟ

The *Walnut Council Bulletin* (Winter 1990) carried an article from Bob Burke about an estate sale of walnut trees that yielded $528,000.

Bob Burke, Industry Representative to the Walnut Council Executive Board, reported on the sale of approximately 550 large black walnut trees from the estate of Mrs. Margaret Burns of Elkhart, Illinois. At the time of the sale, the trees were between 110 and 140 years old and probably overmature by 50 to 60 years. The standing trees were sold to the International Veneer Company with a bid of $528,000.

The trees were apparently established as part of a large planting, because tree rows were still obvious even after the harvest. The overmature condition of the stand was manifested by narrow growth rings and extensive top dieback on some of the trees. Although over 100 years old, few trees exhibited heartrot in the butt log.

Little if anything is known about the early management of the plantation. The total land area involved was approximately 28 acres. The interior of the area was occupied by a horse exercise tract; thus most of the trees were confined to 18 acres surrounding the horse track. Examination of the annual rings on the stumps told a story of relatively rapid diameter growth during the first 30 to 35 years with ring widths of approximately 1/4 inch.

Subsequent growth was very slow with individual rings often running together making it impossible to obtain a precise age determination. (p. 6)

୨ୟ

While the wood of the black walnut is almost universally admired, some people find the growing tree undesirable. Black walnut is one of the latest species to leaf in the spring, and one of the first to defoliate in the fall. It typically has a growth period of only 90 to 135 days. In poor soil, the tree may often be misshapen, the trunk may not be straight, the tree may have poor condition and lack good form. However, when a tree stands alone in pasture or open field and grows in good soil, it develops a form which most admire. The foliage has a lovely green color and the leaves give the tree the appearance of a huge fern.

The compound leaves are one to two feet long in overall dimensions with 15 to 23 leaflets. These leaves are palmlike and glossy in attractive shades of green, but are often pitted or spotted with foliage diseases. Walnut leaves, placed under a dog's bed or in his house, are reported to ward off fleas. Leaves turn yellow in the fall and their attraction cannot rival the lovely reds and yellows of maples, or the subtle browns and maroons of the oaks.

Black walnut leaves in bloom.
Photo courtesy of Jerry Van Sambeek.

In suburban lawns, walnuts present some problems. Walnut nuts stain driveways, sidewalks, and hands. Falling nuts can dent cars and heads. Tomatoes and many other common garden plants do not grow well in the vicinity of walnut trees.

In 1951, the West Virginia University Experiment Station published *Effect of Black Walnut Trees and Their Products on Other Vegetation* by Professor Maurice Brooks. Results of an extensive field study at the University of Missouri of 300 black walnut trees in relationship with their surrounding vegetation revealed the unusual nature of the black walnut.

Brooks concluded that black walnut trees often prove to be detrimental to certain other plants growing within the walnut's root spread. Brooks found evidence of antagonism between black walnut and red pine, apple, tomatoes, potatoes, alfalfa, blackberries, rhododendrons, mountain laurel, and azaleas. The latter three members of the heath family may be negatively effected by the tendency of the black walnut to raise the pH of the soil in its root zone. These plants prefer more acid soils.

However, Brooks reported that black walnut trees stimulate the growth of black raspberry and bluegrass. In 1940, a study by Richard Meriweather Smith at Ohio State University comparing weight gains of cattle grazed on bluegrass under black walnuts showed an average yearly gain of 46 pounds per acre over cattle on a check plot, and 71 pounds per acre over cattle on a locust plot. He concluded that many pastures would benefit from well-spaced black walnut plantings.

Perhaps black walnuts are of more value to soils and pastures than just for wood or nuts. In Kentucky, black walnut trees are often planted along the fences of thoroughbred horse paddocks to provide shade for the valuable horses, to encourage blue grass growth, and to provide eventual income. These trees are called blue grass walnuts by the veneer buyers.

&.

Selective logging during the past 100 plus years, in which the constant search to find and harvest the best and the most beautiful black walnuts has left poorer and poorer residual stock. This selective harvest may have resulted in the inverse of Darwin's survival of the fittest. When allowed to regrow, the forest must spring from seed of stunted and malformed trees that the loggers did not want. A forest of the highest quality may not result. Our natural forests may have been genetically degraded for many years.

Unfortunately, many state nurseries obtain their seeds from trees that also may be genetically inferior. Nuts are often collected by individuals without regard to the form or vigor of the parent tree and from barnlots, pastures, roadsides and other easy-to-reach places where the best forest trees do not grow. The expressions, "the nut does not fall far from the tree," and "like father like son," seem applicable to black walnuts also.

In good soil, the eastern black walnut is a top-quality tree. If it stands alone, its limbs spread widely, the head becomes a great green dome, and the whole tree seems to luxuriate in space, deep soil and abundance of sunshine and rain. At all times its appearance suggests massive strength, the trunk solid and heavily furrowed.

❧

A few of these old, massive, solitary trees remain in the eastern area called Penn's Woods. A book listing 300 of the oldest trees in Pennsylvania, New Jersey, Delaware and Maryland was published in 1982. *Penn's Woods 1682-1982,* reports the work of The Penn Tree Committee, which traveled the roads and highways to locate the historic Penn trees listed in an earlier book by Edward Wildman titled *Penn's Woods 1682-1932,* published 50 years before.

Most of the 300 trees that were estimated to have been living from the time of William Penn are oak or other species, but the book lists five huge old black walnuts. For each, it gives the 1982 circumference at breast height (CBH) and Wildman's measurements from 50 years before. The location of each tree is given along with a short description of the tree. The five are:

Black Walnut, Shiloh Road off Route 926, near Westtown, Westtown Township. PA CBH:14'6" (Wildman: 12'5") Estimated age: 250-300 years. Since colonial times, black walnut lumber has been the most desirable wood for making furniture. Consequently, black walnut trees of this age are extremely rare, especially in Pennsylvania where the manufacture of furniture was a booming industry in the early 1700s. The only reason this specimen was rejected by loggers over the years was its lack of a straight bole to make knot-free lumber. The ravages of time are clearly visible in this tree. The site is not exactly ideal. Contributing to this gloomy picture is the loss of two large limbs many years ago. The ministrations of a tree surgeon are sorely needed. Yet without care this patriarch of walnut trees lives on, apparently well fed by fertile soil. Access to it is excellent, since it stands within inches of the roadside. (p. 68)

Black Walnut - Grange Black Walnut, Grange Estate, Myrtle Avenue at Warwick Road, off City Line Avenue, Haverford Township, PA. CBH: 14'6", Estimated age: 250-300 years. The "bell tree" no longer signals workers to meals as it did more than 200 years ago. It has added only 6 inches to the 14-foot girth measured in 1912, but it continues to survive even though its center is largely hollowed. It bears still the green leathery fruits which contain the black walnuts that squirrels and people find so tasty. (p. 87)

Black Walnut - Lower Cross Road at the intersection of Sheridan Avenue, Saddle River, Bergen County, New Jersey. CBH: 16'5", Estimated age: 300 or more years. There are three of four record-sized black walnut trees in New Jersey in the central corridor from Burlington to Bergen counties; all measure the same within inches in circumference. This tree, with its large and spreading branch crown, is the present State Champion. (p. 146)

Black Walnut - Along Riverton Road, 1/2 mile north of the center of Morrestown, Burlington County, New Jersey. CBH: 15'4" (Wildman 13'4") Estimated Age: 250-300 years. This was the largest black walnut in New Jersey until it was recently "defeated" when a larger tree was found in Bergen County. This tree has many large limbs that extend almost horizontally from its short trunk and present a rounded, massive crown. An extensive wooded area on the north and west sides protects the tree from winter winds. (p. 150)

Black Walnut - Washington Walnut, 425 Ridgewood Road, Maplewood, Maplewood Township, Essex County, New Jersey, CBH: 14'3", Estimated age: 250-300 years. Standing within a few feet of the old Timothy Ball house built in 1743, this fine old tree is linked with Revolutionary days as well as more peaceable times. This walnut is at least as old as the Ball house. It is said that Washington, a Ball relative, visited his cousins before and after the Battle of Springfield. According to tradition, he hitched his horse to an iron ring that was attached to the trunk. The tree has since grown over the ring, which is no longer visible. Some among the older residents in the vicinity remember when it could be plainly seen. Within the Timothy Ball house there is a huge fireplace. The tale is told that Washington stabled his horse in the fireplace when staying there overnight. (p. 153)

❧

Many people have an interest in record big trees. The American Forest Foundation (AFF) has maintained the national registry of big trees since 1940. Organized in 1875, the AFF is the nation's oldest citizens conservation organization and publishes the magazine *Tree Farmer* six times a year. Every two years the National Register of Big Trees is updated and included in the magazine. AFF also sponsors Global ReLeaf, which is a national and international tree-planting and education campaign.

The current American champion Eastern black walnut, *Juglans nigra L.* is located in Sauvie Island, Oregon, and measures 278 inches in circumference at breast height, stands 130 feet tall and has a branch spread of 140 feet. Adding the circumference in inches to the height in feet, plus one fourth the branch spread in feet is the system used to compare trees of different shape. Using this system, this record champion black walnut scores 443 points. It just replaced the former champion which was in Humbolt County, California, with 427 points. In 1984, the record holder, with 280 points, was in Ohio. New champions replace former ones because they score more points or the former champion died or was cut down.

Forty-eight states have American Forestry Foundation Big Tree State Coordinators who keep track of champion trees in their individual states. Anyone can nominate a tree for consideration by contacting his own state coordinator or the Washington office. (See Directory.)

The current Pennsylvania champion Eastern black walnut stands in Valley Forge National Historical Park not far from where black walnut trees were rustled in 1972. The tree circumference at breast height is 203 inches, height 98 feet, spread 111 feet and thus it scores 328 points. It stands alone in a bluegrass pasture where horses graze, just off Yellow Springs Road and beside the covered bridge over Valley Creek. It appears to be quite healthy, is protected from strong winds by Mount Misery, and never wants for moisture, since Valley Creek flows constantly nearby on its way north past Washington's Headquarters. The nearest competing tree is 60 feet away.

Pennsylvania champion Eastern black walnut in Valley Forge National Historical Park in the summer of 1992.

The black walnut was native to a wide range of North America when the European pioneers arrived and available in both good quality and considerable quantity. This great natural resource, like many others, was useful in the building of a great nation and was consumed quickly without consideration for the future. Barns were framed in walnut and roads built from the wood. Walnut was burned.

Now, over 100 years after the great hardwood forests of the Midwest were first harvested, by clear cutting in most cases, loggers are harvesting the second or third growth timber. Clear cutting was practiced then, but now clear cutting is unpopular and great objections to it exist. However, clear cutting provided good opportunity for white oak, red oak and black walnut to regenerate.

Loggers and landowners have benefited from regeneration in the heavy cutting of these species over the past 30 years. The next generation of timber users and landowners may not be so fortunate. There are yet many black walnut trees throughout its range, but the quantity and quality of timber and veneer-size trees have greatly diminished. Black walnut trees are hunted like fugitives and many are harvested before they have reached full maturity. Who owns these fugitive walnut trees? Who ultimately acquires the logs?

2

WHO OWNS
THE TREES?
WHO GETS THE LOGS?

ð.

For of all sad words of tongue or pen,
the saddest are these:
It might have been!

—John Greenleaf Whittier

The vast majority of standing black walnut trees and hardwood forests are owned by farmers and miscellaneous private individuals. A diverse group of about 7.8 million individuals, corporations, groups, and associations control these private forest lands; in sharp contrast to the conifer forests of the United States, which are largely owned by the United States Government or commercial forest products companies.

The Renewable Forest and Rangeland Resources Planning Act of 1974 provided for forest surveys every ten years. Forest surveys are conducted by the U.S. Forest Service, Department of Agriculture, on a state-by-state basis. The objective of the surveys is to periodically inventory the nation's forest land to determine the extent, condition, volume, growth, and depletions of timber.

The 1986 forest survey of Indiana revealed that non-industrial private owners held 87 percent of the state's timberland and 85 percent of the growing-stock volume. The 1985 survey of Illinois found that private individuals owned 84 percent of the timberland, and the 1981 Kansas inventory found nonindustrial private parties owned 96 percent of that state's commercial forest. The 1989 Missouri survey found that farmers and miscellaneous private owners held 83 percent of that state's timberland. In Pennsylvania, there are 490,000 private forest landowners who own an average of 25 acres each. Over the full range of the Eastern black walnut, over 85 percent of woodlands are privately owned.

Throughout the Midwest, the pattern of hardwood forest ownership can be seen when driving the highways. While most of the land is pasture or tilled row crops, such as corn or soybeans, timber is seldom out of view. In small groves, generally away from the highway, one sees hardwood trees. Close examination of these groves would show that many were never cleared for farming because they were in a wet spot unsuited for tillage, or because the land had a severe slope and was subject to erosion. Most have had logs removed several times in the years since the land was first occupied by the new arrivals from Europe.

Many timber groves are owned by farmers who consider them a sideline, if they consider them at all. The trend toward larger and larger farms and bigger and bigger machinery has corresponded with a declining farm population. These wooded groves once provided fuel, fence material, and construction material for the farm unit, but they seldom provide these functions now. Most are not managed, and few receive any timber stand improvement (TSI).

The forest surveys reveal a picture that is not totally bleak, however. The total acreage and volume of timber have been increasing, but the quality and percentage of desirable species are declining. Thus, there is more timber and hope for timber, but both the quality and desirability have declined. These trends reflect widespread neglect of land and forest.

&

Throughout the Eastern United States, an abandoned pasture or cultivated field will eventually revert to trees, but the species often will not be the most desirable. Birds fly long distances and carry seeds of wild cherry, mulberry, hackberry, cedar, locust, and other species that they leave behind in their droppings.

The seeds of other species, such as maple and cotton-wood, are carried by the wind. These wind- and bird-carried seeds will fill an abandoned pasture or cultivated field with their species. Blue jays will carry and bury acorns farther than a squirrel will carry a walnut, but blue jays do not carry walnuts. Squirrels are the primary transporters and propagators of black walnuts. It is not known exactly how far a squirrel will carry a walnut, but most estimates place the distance at under 200 yards.

Let us assume the Arnold Schwarzenegger of squirrels carries a walnut 400 yards in one direction, plants it, and the nut becomes a tree and produces another nut in 10 years. If this process is then repeated by Arnold Schwarzenegger II, and repeated every ten years thereafter, it would still take over 40 years for walnut trees to advance only one mile from the first mother tree. It would take over 400 years for walnuts to advance 10 miles. Thus, unless an abandoned pasture or field is already close to walnut trees bearing nuts, no walnuts are likely to occur naturally in that field. Without the help of man, walnuts do not move far.

General observation supports this scenario. Walnut trees grow in groves and are rarely found remote from other walnuts. Without the help of man, abandoned pastures and fields remote from nut-bearing walnut trees do not produce walnut trees. Native Americans who valued the nuts of this tree and were students of nature may have understood this walnut immobility. They carried walnuts great distances and may have left some close to their camps and hunting grounds. This transportation surely expanded the range and increased the number of black walnut trees found by Europeans.

Selecting and harvesting desirable species, such as the oak and black walnut, and leaving the undesirable species only increases the percentage of undesirable species. And those remaining species provide the shade that discourages regen-eration of oak or black walnut, which both require sun. With-out intervention by man to plant desirable species in aban-doned fields and pastures, and TSI to improve the ratio of

desirable species in established timberlands, both the quality and desirability of timber have declined. Unless land and
forest management practices change, both will continue to decline.

ৈ

Indiana's Timber Resource, 1986: An Analysis, published by
the U.S. Forest Service in 1990, serves as an example of what is
happening to American hardwood forests. It included these
observations:

Timberland area increased from 3.9 million acres in
1967 to 4.3 million in 1986. Primary reason for the increase
is the reversion of wooded pasture and improved pasture to
timberland. The 1986 maple-beech forest type (includes
cherry-ash-yellow poplar type to be comparable with 1967
maple-beech type) covers the largest area of the State (1.6
million acres), displacing oak-hickory, which led in 1967 with
2.4 million acres, but slipped to second in 1986 with 1.4
million. Sawtimber stands accounted for 64 percent of the
timberland area in 1986, compared to 52 percent in 1967.
Thirty-seven percent of the timberland supports more than
5,000 board feet of timber per acre. Fifty-two percent of the
stands are less than 50 years old. Two-thirds of the privately
owned timberland has been held by the same owner for at
least 10 years, and one-third has been held for 20 years or
more. Seventy-six percent of the timberland grows trees
taller than 70 feet at age 50, considered good sites in the
Midwest. Growing stock volume increased from 3.7 to 5.2
billion cubic feet between 1967 and 1986, a 43-percent rise.
Sawtimber volume rose from 12.5 to 19.2 billion board feet
between inventories, a 54-percent gain. Oaks account for 30
percent of the growing stock volume in 1986, largest of any
species group. However, in 1967, oak volume represented 40
percent of the volume. Eighty-three percent of the sawtimber volume is in log grades three and four, poorest of the four
grades.

More than 87 percent of the State's timberland is held
by nonindustrial private owners. Historically these owners
have not engaged in forest management of their lands for a
number of reasons. In Indiana, improving the resource will
require that private owners practice active forest manage-

ment. To accomplish this will require an increased education, information and assistance program for landowners. An added inducement to forest management, however, may be the prospect of a declining supply of timber. As supplies dwindle, prices of acceptable and available timber should rise. As owners contemplate an expected rise in stumpage prices, they may become more aware of the value of their timberland. As this happens they are also likely to become interested in ways to increase its value beyond what nature alone can do.

If this has happened, the results are hardly noticeable. Supplies of black walnut have been dwindling for 20 years and stumpage prices have risen, but few owners show little tendency or interest in helping nature do better. Apathy or ignorance reign.

ᢞ

Where are the black walnuts in these surveys? They are there, but scarce. In Indiana, in the 1986 survey, black walnut accounted for 2.29 percent of the total net volume of sawtimber of all classes of hardwood. By measure of the number of growing-stock trees on timberland, black walnuts were 1.3 percent of the total hardwoods. By the measure of the number of all live trees on timberland, black walnut were again 1.3 percent of the total. Of all trees over 17 inches diameter at breast height, black walnuts were just over one percent of the total. Indiana is acknowledged by everyone as a prime source of black walnut veneer and the center of the veneer industry in America, but big, veneer-quality walnuts are very rare.

Black walnut is so rare in the forests of Pennsylvania it is not even mentioned in *The Atlas of Pennsylvania, 1989*. As a percent of total hardwoods and live trees, black walnut is less abundant in American forests than when the Europeans first arrived. Of course, the total forest area is much, much smaller. Big walnuts are more rare in America than ever before.

Undoubtedly there are more black walnut trees than the surveys reflect. Since black walnut, which requires sunlight, almost never regenerates in established woodlands and the survey looked only at timberland, it would have missed black walnuts in barn lots, fence rows, roadsides, lawns, ditches, streambanks, and pastures. Although these areas are often partially tree covered, they are not classed as commercial forest land because of their small size. Therefore, standing timber from these sources is not included in the black walnut timber-volume estimates reported. Studies in Kansas and Kentucky, for example, indicate that volumes on non-commercial land equal roughly one-fourth the walnut inventory volumes on commercial forest lands. There are more black walnuts than the surveys indicate, but the quality of these unsurveyed trees is usually very poor.

Driving north from Hot Springs, Arkansas, the terrain suddenly changes about 50 miles from the Missouri state line. Black walnut trees appear in locations such as those mentioned above. There are many walnut trees, but they are a lonely, forlorn, and badly shaped sample. You see black walnut trees in increasing numbers as you drive into southern Missouri.

These "non forest" black walnut trees are part of the hardwood resource and are found in various parts of some 24 states from Arkansas to Pennsylvania. Those in Pennsylvania look much like those in Arkansas and Missouri, and most are acceptable for black walnut lumber. However, most of these walnuts do not attract great interest from the veneer companies. They want the best, and pay the most only for forest-grown high-quality walnut logs.

ᵗᵃ

Black walnut trees grow today in Valley Forge National Historical Park where General George Washington and his Army survived the terrible winter of 1777-78. In the 1930s, several were planted near the stone farmhouse Washington used as his headquarters during the encampment. Walnuts grow in the park along roadsides, through the center of the park where fence rows once sheltered them, and where squirrels or farmers planted them. Over the rolling hills where Washington's soldiers built their huts, park personnel now mow the fields and, in mowing, destroy any sprouting walnuts. This urge to have neat fields of grass is the greatest hazard to walnuts in the park and elsewhere. Mowing prevents reforestation in Valley Forge Park and in farm pastures too.

Washington's headquarters during 1777-1778 encampment at Valley Forge with black walnuts planted in the 1930s.

At Gettysburg, Manassas, Antietam, New Market, and in the valleys of the Shenandoah, Rappahannock, Tennessee, and Rapidan, where so many walnut gunstocks were stained with the blood of Blue and Gray, black walnut trees grow like poppies on Flanders Field. They grow singly and in groups. Where mature walnut trees grow near unmowed, ungrazed and untilled land, younger walnut trees grow as well.

Black walnut trees growing alone or outside the close competition of other young trees usually branch low to the ground, have crooked trunks, show damage to the trunks, and grade below the standard required by veneer companies. They are satisfactory for gunstocks, lumber, novelty items, flooring, etc., but usually do not meet veneer company standards, and therefore do not bring top dollar.

Thus, the black walnut is in a *Catch 22* situation. It produces the best veneer timber only where it cannot regenerate. It does best in the forest environment where excessive shade prevents young walnut trees from growing. On rare occasions, an abandoned pasture is not mowed and is close to producing black walnut trees. Then, squirrels will bury nuts and produce a grove of young black walnut trees that will grow with others to produce a new forest and the desired veneer-quality black walnut. However, these natural stands are rare.

è▲

Indiana's Timber Resource, 1986: An Analysis, outlined the importance of forest products to the state's economy.

Nearly 44,000 Hoosiers employed by more than 1,000 businesses owed their livelihood to the forest resources of Indiana in 1982. As a collective group, the Indiana forest products industries (lumber and wood products, furniture and fixtures, and paper and allied products) ranked as the State's sixth-largest employer in terms of employment and payroll within manufacturing industries. The three forest products industries combined generated $2.4 billion in value added by manufacture to the State's economy in 1982.

Nationally, Indiana ranks ninth in total lumber production and third in hardwood lumber production with only North Carolina and Pennsylvania producing more. Neither North Carolina nor Pennsylvania grow high-quality black walnut trees, which are highly regarded by veneer companies. Veneer companies will take quality trees from these states and will cut veneer from them, but they prefer Indiana, Ohio, or Iowa black walnut logs for veneer.

Many landowners who hold title to land upon which the supporting natural resource timber grows, say they are not interested in managing their forest property for income. Many look upon the woodland as their private park. They value it for recreation, wildlife, hunting, a place to relax and observe nature and as a means of passing their heritage on to future generations. Many have little knowledge of proper forest management or the desire to practice it. The forest manages itself and occasionally, for one reason or another, some trees will be cut.

A 1977 Pennsylvania landowner survey indicated that forest land is owned for the following reasons (in descending order of preference): (1) recreation, (2) investment, (3) part of farm, (4) farm and domestic use, (5) other, (6) aesthetics, (7) part of residence, and (8) timber production. With such a low regard for timber production, it may seem surprising that 73 percent of Pennsylvania's forest products are harvested from the property of private landowners.

When motivation for harvesting or not harvesting timber is examined, it is apparent that economics plays a major role in the decision to harvest. Landowners who hold forest land for recreational reasons, or simply because it is part of their farm, are *likely* to harvest if they need money or are offered a "good price."

For the owner of a small forest, selling timber may be a once-in-a-lifetime occurrence. Often sales are generated by a timber buyer who approaches the owner seeking logs. When a landowner sells timber in this way, it is a haphazard business with little or no consideration for management of the timberland. Probably, the buyer will want only the best-quality trees of select species. The removal of these few selected trees can do much overall damage to the timberland and leave less desirable species as the dominant species. In this way the future value of the timberland will be reduced. Often little or no consideration is given to the long-term management of the timberland.

The West Virginia University Extension Service offers four videotapes that provide clear and simple guidance to timberland owners. *Woodlot Management: How it Grows, Woodlot Management: Helping It Grow, Harvesting and Renewing It,* and *Selling Timber* are great sources of information about timberland management. Any owner of timberland who wants to learn how to better manage his timber could benefit from these tapes. (See Directory).

In Illinois, it is estimated that a professional forester or state forester is used in less than 10 percent of all private timber sales. The Indiana figure is higher, but still low. Without the assistance of a professional forester, the owner dealing with one buyer can hardly expect to receive full value for his standing timber. The buyer has knowledge and experience on his side, along with a strong incentive to pay as little as possible.

Timber companies may use computers to give buyers even more incentive to buy low. One of the largest Indiana veneer companies now tags each veneer log when cut and assigns it a number that identifies it. With this assigned number, the log proceeds to the mill where it is sliced, and the resulting veneer sold and the realized value recorded. At the end of any period, the veneer company can, by computer, compare the end result of all purchases by each buyer and post the record for all to see.

Working just like the batting average of a baseball player, the buyer's comparative performance can be a powerful tool of management that puts pressure on the buyer to buy low. A timber buyer armed with knowledge, experience, and such incentive can be a powerful force, and the typical timber owner is no match for such a buyer.

The timber owner should not feel rushed. One big advantage of timber is that it can be inventoried *live* for long periods. While inventoried, the trees grow and usually increase in value. There are risks of tornado, fire, aging, or disease to standing timber, but these are rare or slow occurrences. The landowner should not be pressured into a hurried decision and should seek the advice of a professional forester before he agrees to sell.

There are no state requirements for consulting foresters. However, some states publish lists of foresters and their qualifications. The Indiana Forestry and Woodland Owners Association, Inc. publishes an annual directory of private professional foresters. The 1991-1992 *Directory* listed 24 consulting foresters and seven industrial foresters. Some listings represent more than one forester, some work for a fee, and some provide a service in conjunction with a timber survey. All have completed a four-year college-level curriculum accredited by the Society of American Foresters and have received a bachelor's degree in forestry.

In Indiana, there is one listed professional forester for each 3,225 owners of timber. Foresters would seem to be spread very thin, but each landowner seldom requires the service of a consulting forester and, when he does, service will not be required for a long period.

Most consulting foresters have eight to 20 years of experience and devote nearly all of their time to providing professional assistance to landowners. Some of the services they provide include: timber management plans, timber marking and sales, timber stand improvement, tree planting, timber inventory, timber taxation assistance, timber appraisals, sale of forest land, plantation maintenance, Christmas tree management, logging supervision, forest damage appraisals, multiple land use planning, and wildlife management plans.

A landowner who contemplates selling timber should contact a consulting professional or a state forester who will walk the land with the owner and advise him on how to proceed with a sale. The landowner should inform the forester of his personal goals, and the landowner should always retain the final word on what trees are sold. Reflecting the scarcity of good logs, the trend of late has been to cut smaller and smaller trees. Resisting pressure to sell before trees are mature may be difficult, but selling too soon will most certainly reduce total income.

Most consulting foresters are paid a *percent* of the *gross* sale. Therefore, they have some incentive to recommend harvesting the more desirable species and immature trees better left for another time. More timber owners, foresters, and timber buyers should resist the trend to prematurely harvest young, healthy, productive trees.

Some consulting foresters work for a fixed fee. Most foresters will willingly cooperate with a conservative owner who prefers to take no log before its time. While big trees grow slowly, trees of good quality will gain value more rapidly as they get larger.

A 16-foot log, which is 12 inches in diameter at breast height (DBH), will contain 30 board feet of lumber using a Doyle scale. Doubling the diameter to 24 inches DBH increases the content of the log to 220 board feet. Another increase in DBH to 30 inches raises the volume of wood to 380 board feet, and a log 36 inches DBH will contain 580 board feet of lumber. Not only does the total volume of wood increase with the size of the tree, but the value of each board foot increases as well.

Veneer companies are eager for good quality black walnuts of large size. However, some timber buyers may hesitate to buy large, higher-quality logs because of the high value of such logs. Some prefer smaller logs with less cost and less risk per log.

Occasionally, there are valid silviculture reasons for cutting small trees. If a stand is too dense and thinning will release better quality trees for further rapid growth, smaller trees may be cut to make room for others. Economic considerations, such as the urgent need or desire for cash or concern for market prices in the future, may lead to the early harvest of trees. Thoughtful and careful consideration should be given before a tree is cut. Once it is cut, it is gone, and it may take 80 years to grow another.

Working with the owner, the forester should mark the woodland for harvest in a manner that enhances the owner's goals and the woodland's productivity. The forester may cruise the timber, prepare a complete inventory of what is to be sold, note the diameter, merchantable height, species, and condition or vigor of the trees and prepare a prospectus for sale. He may advertise the sale, conduct the sale, negotiate the contract, and supervise the harvest. For these services, he may receive a percent of the gross amount realized or he may be paid a fixed fee. In either case, he usually will justify his commission or fee, and the landowner will have a more satisfactory sale.

In this age of litigation, a prudent seller should have a legally enforceable contract with the purchaser. This contract should specify what is sold, when it is to be cut, road maintenance, erosion control, reseeding of exposed soil, ownership of treetops, fence damage, etc. Lack of an enforceable contract is a common deficiency in many private sales. The experience of the professional forester in this area can save the landowner many problems.

The owner should be paid in full before the first tree is cut. Indiana licenses all tree buyers, but obtaining a license is easy and does not guarantee the owner will get full *value*. It only guarantees he will receive what he agreed to sell his trees for.

A landowner who jumps at the first offer from a timber buyer who comes knocking at his door may be filled with doubts and ill feelings that have plagued many woodland owners and turned them off future sales. The logs should go to the bidder willing to pay the most, as it should be in a free market economy.

Regardless of who buys the standing timber, veneer-quality walnut logs almost always end up at a veneer mill. Sawmills receiving superior black walnut logs set them aside for veneer log buyers. The veneer companies want the best and pay the most for quality logs of substantial size. Until the 1960s, these veneer companies were domestic. A timber seller could expect his trees to be processed into lumber or veneer in this country by a locally owned company.

ða

American native hardwoods, and the black walnuts in particular, are unique natural resources that provide employment for thousands of Americans. The black walnut's botanical range extends into parts of 33 states, but its prime commercial range is limited principally to the six midwestern states of Indiana, Iowa, Ohio, Illinois, Kentucky, and Missouri. The veneer industry, which uses only the best quality logs, was developed close to this resource base. In the late 1800s, most logs, which were huge at that time, were delivered to the veneer mills by animal power.

In 1910, Indianapolis, Indiana claimed to be the largest veneer-producing city in the United States and had at least nine mills. Only two have survived in Indianapolis. The center of veneer mills gradually shifted 30 miles south of Indianapolis to Edinburg, Indiana, which now claims to be the "Veneer Capital of the United States." Proximity to the resource is not as important as it was in 1910. In the early 1990s, Indiana veneer mills imported 65 percent of the logs they needed from 19 other states. Logs are now transported great distances at great expense, but closer proximity is still better and cheaper.

In 1989, 15 hardwood face veneer mills were operating in Indiana. This was the largest number of mills in any state. The industry has survived tremendous changes, economic cycles, fires, changing fashions, and vicious competition. In the 1960s, a new threat arose. The black walnut timber, a resource unique to the United States and upon which much of this industry was based, was being claimed by others. A battle for control of the American black walnut resource ensued.

This battle is expertly documented in detail by John C. Callahan in his book, *The Fine Hardwood Veneer Industry in the United States: 1838-1990*. Basically, this battle was waged between those favoring free trade and those favoring protectionism. Was it jobs for Americans or free markets? Was it logs for our American veneer companies or logs for foreign veneer companies? Who was to get the logs?

Log exports do generate foreign exchange, but loss of logs impacts on domestic employment and the loss of value added through manufacture may result in a net loss of foreign exchange. In other words, if you want American black walnut veneer, don't buy our logs and make it there, but let us make it, and then you buy our veneer.

Callahan notes:

> The first request for control of black walnut log exports was made to the U.S. Department of Commerce on December 1, 1959, by a walnut veneer manufacturer in Indiana. This was undoubtedly a reaction to the numerous foreign buyers in the state who were out-competing his and other local companies for the best walnut veneer timber and cut logs. At the time of the request to control the export of black walnut logs, 17 of the 23 manufacturers of walnut veneer were located in Indiana. Between 1958 and 1959, the total export of walnut logs from U.S. ports increased nearly 65 percent, and the average value of the logs exported increased from $454 to $584 per thousand board feet. (p. 254)

The volume of black walnut log exports had been increasing since 1954, when it was under a million board feet. By 1959 it had risen to 3.73 million board feet, and by 1960 to 10.18 million board feet. Callahan continued:

> As walnut log exports increased exponentially, primary manufacturers of black walnut products became acutely aware of a potential imbalance between growth and harvest volumes. This was particularly true of old growth black walnut trees suitable for veneer. Although the request in 1959 had been rebuffed, manufacturers continued to petition the Department of Commerce, requesting that the federal government control the export of walnut logs. (p. 254)

The American Walnut Manufacturers Association (AWMA) led the fight in 1960, and again in 1961, to secure export controls on black walnut logs. They provided data on overcutting and inflationary prices of timber and logs and sought an embargo or quota on exports of walnut veneer logs based on provisions of the Export Control Act of 1949. All requests were denied, and the American industry became increasingly frustrated.

In the five years 1954 through 1958, the U.S. Department of Commerce estimated total consumption, both domestic and export, of veneer-quality black walnut timber at 52.5 million board feet and total growth during the same period at 100 million board feet. Thus, the total inventory of black walnut timber was increasing in the late 1950s. In the five years 1960 to 1964, total consumption was estimated at 153.6 million board feet and total growth, during the same period, at 99 million board feet. In a ten-year period, the United States switched from building black walnut standing timber inventory to consuming it at a rapid rate. Exports in the first five-year period were 6.5 million board feet and the second five-year period rose to 52.6 million board feet. This was an increase of over 800 percent!

Foreign buyers were taking an increasing share of the veneer logs. One reason they could pay more was that they cut thinner veneer. Domestic companies were cutting veneer at a standard 1/28-inch thickness, while Europeans cut veneer for their customers at 1/42 or 1/44 inch. Thus, they got about 50 percent more veneer from a given volume of wood. To meet foreign competition, domestic buyers would have to be persuaded to accept thinner veneer. This was not easy.

ક

In 1963, the Southern Furniture Manufacturer's Association noted in a resolution as reported by Callahan:

> "The unprecedented export increases for the nine years since 1954 [and the] . . . annual cutting total considerably in excess of the annual growth increment threatens this valuable resource with extinction." The resolutions called for a reduction in standard veneer thickness from 1/28 to 1/36

inch in the interest of resource conservation and urged the Secretary of Commerce to "... assist in this conservation effort by imposing at once an embargo on further export of American Black Walnut Logs."

Export controls on walnut logs were imposed on February 14, 1964. Exports were limited to 7.3 million board feet and a " . . . new program is designed to minimize depletion . . . by reducing total annual consumption ... to 22.3 million board feet." This was intended to balance approximately the timber harvested with the estimated growth of the black walnut resource. In order to achieve this goal, the domestic industry was to limit its procurement to 15 million board feet through voluntary reductions in the total domestic cut of black walnut and through certain conservation measures. The most important of these was the manufacture of 1/36-inch veneer instead of the nominal 1/28-inch thickness, which had been accepted as standard. Theoretically, this change in thickness would result in about a 20 percent increase in yield from a given quantity of wood suitable for veneering purposes. (p. 259)

This "deal" did not last three months before the Southern Furniture Manufacturers requested relief, pleading problems associated with converting to thinner veneer. Also, problems were evident in administration of the agreement. There was "leakage" of walnut through the embargo in forms other than as logs. Domestic consumption exceeded the target by 4.5 million board feet. A decision to extend or end controls was necessary by February 14, 1965.

On February 12, 1965, the Secretary of Commerce announced that he would not extend export controls on black walnut logs. He cited the problems listed above and noted in his decision the following:

In conservation terms, the results of the first year of controls are quite disappointing. The excess of consumption over growth, instead of being six million board feet as originally allowed for the first year of controls, is more than 10 million board feet, or approximately 2/3 more than the total amount of growth.

The situation does not seem to involve the possible extinction of the walnut resource. On the contrary, walnut trees are constantly being planted and constantly maturing.

Among the important factors which could help to reduce domestic log consumption are not only price shifts, but shifts in consumer preferences and increasing use of substitute materials.

Even if technical difficulties were to develop in making the transition to use of other woods, it would seem preferable to try to ease these transition difficulties rather than continue export controls. For, while the controls may benefit log cutters and users, they also work to the detriment of the log growers and log exporters by restricting the marketing opportunities for their products. Moreover, controls on the export of walnut logs are clearly detrimental to our balance of payments position. (p. 262)

On February 18, 1965, Senator Hartke of Indiana spoke in the Senate and entered in the Congressional Record 100 letters and telegrams calling for export controls. Senator Bayh of Indiana spoke also and argued that some 60 countries controlled the export of their hardwood logs.

On March 16, 1965, Senator Hartke held hearings on export controls on black walnut logs. Nine testified for controls and three against, and the printed transcript of the hearings grew to 37 pages. The hearings were resumed on March 31, 1965, and recorded another 174 pages of oral statements and submitted materials. Paul R. MacLean, president of Wood-Mosaic Corporation, made the last statement. It was brief and prophetic:

> If the price exceeds market acceptance, then the users turn to other species. There is no reason to single out walnut for deification among woods. It is only since 1957 that it has assumed worldwide popularity. No one knows when this popularity will wane in favor of other woods as has happened so many times in the history of the veneer business. Frankly, I feel we have a tempest in a teapot. (p. 269)

Callahan comments on this statement:

> After the foreign and domestic mining of the veneer-quality black walnut resource had been nearly completed, the rush to exploit white and red oak began. Although MacLean dismissed the hearing as a "tempest in a teapot,"

serious questions about natural resource policy in the United States were raised as well as questions concerning what are the best interests of the country when given a choice of either exporting unprocessed or manufactured products. (p. 269)

The fight continued in Congress and in the Department of Commerce as more hearings were held and more petitions presented. On February 26, 1969, the American Walnut Manufacturers Association (AWMA) and the Fine Hardwoods Association (FHA) again petitioned for control of the export of black walnut logs. They cited consumption of walnut between 1964 and 1969.

In those six years, domestic consumption totaled 98.5 million board feet and export consumption totaled 99.9 million board feet. Thus, more walnut was being exported than consumed domestically and together the mining of the black walnut resource was nearly 80 million board feet *in excess* of the replacement growth rate. The American black walnut timber inventory was being consumed at a rate far above that at which walnut trees were growing.

Export consumption had risen from 9.6 million board feet in 1964, to 18, 12.7, 16.6, 21.9, and 20.8 in the following five years. Domestic consumption had declined from 17.6 million board feet in 1965 to 12.5 in 1969. The Secretary of Commerce refused to restore controls. The harvest of black walnut timber continued at a heavy and unsustainable rate. When would it end?

ੋ•

The export of black walnut logs declined in the '70s. After a peak of 23.6 million board feet in 1965, it gradually declined to 7.8 million board feet in 1974. Exports have since fluctuated between 4.6 and 8.0 million board feet per year. The inventory of black walnut suitable for veneer had been consumed, and the harvest of red oak and white oak have accelerated and replaced the black walnut in export volume. The industry, on both the foreign and domestic fronts, is now consuming the inventory white oak and red oak. Black walnut trees continue to grow, but the quality and quantity available for harvest is lower and will remain low until more trees mature.

So, the domestic veneer industry had won a battle, but it lost the war. The industry continued to lobby, but there has been no further embargo on the export of black walnut logs. The seeds for the virtual takeover of the American hardwood face-veneer industry had been sown. Foreign veneer companies, fearing another embargo, began buying domestic veneer companies. In 1960, there were no United States veneer companies with foreign ownership. In 1970, there were three; in 1975, there were six; in 1980, there were 11; and in 1990, there were 14. Of these 14, eight were German owned.

Foreign ownership may benefit the domestic veneer industry, as foreign investors bring capital and expertise. It matters little to a landowner who buys his logs. It matters little to the general employee of a veneer company who owns the company or who signs his paycheck. What matters to the landowner is that he has a good market for his veneer logs and what matters to the veneer company is a steady supply of quality veneer logs. The reduced supply of quality black walnut veneer logs has brought hard times to the entire domestic veneer industry.

The veneer trade associations have fallen on hard times as well. In 1971, the Fine Hardwoods Association merged with the American Walnut Manufacturers Association, and the resulting association was weakened, small, and stressed. On September 1, 1978, Larry R. Frye became executive director of this association, but in 1986, the two associations split into separate organizations again. They yet retain joint headquarters in Zionsville, Indiana, and Frye continues to head both associations. Larry Frye wears a third hat, since he is also executive director of the Walnut Council.

The Walnut Council is an organization dedicated to advancing knowledge of walnut culture, encouraging the planting of walnut trees, managing established walnut trees, and perpetuating the utilization of all walnut products. It began as a joint effort by walnut growers, industry representatives, state and federal government officials, and university researchers for the benefit of all who were interested in black walnut. The Council was founded in 1969, with 441 members.

By 1994, at the 25th anniversary meeting, the Walnut Council reached a paid membership of 1,000 in 43 states and four foreign countries. "Have You Hugged A WALNUT Tree To-day?" is the question emblazoned on bumper stickers of Walnut Council members' vehicles.

From his hardwood paneled office, which is adorned with magnificent displays of native hardwoods, art, and many black walnut objects, Frye directs efforts to promote interest in all aspects of black walnut and other fine hardwoods. His background as a forestry school graduate, timber buyer, and extension specialist has served him well in his difficult and challenging work.

I met with Frye in his office in June 1992. He arrived at our appointment nearly 30 minutes late. He appeared to be irritated and pressed for time. He said that he attended 20 association meetings a year and he was too busy to answer his mail. When I explained that I was writing a book about black walnut which, if successful, would further the goals of his Walnut Council, he said the Walnut Council was only a small part of his job and one he would rather relinquish. He said he only did it out of kindness, as no one else was available. He explained that it paid him virtually nothing.

It was obvious that Frye had been frustrated by the hard times his two associations had faced over the last 15 years. He had seen his office staff dwindle from 14 to three, and membership in both associations had declined as well. He said his budget was so limited he could do almost nothing to accomplish the association's goals. He had been fighting a losing battle for 15 years, and the fatigue and frustration of that fight showed.

Walnut has been displaced by cherry, oak, or mahogany as the favorite wood of furniture makers. Fifty percent of veneer-quality walnut logs continues to flow out of the United States. The domestic hardwood industry has become more and more foreign owned and dominated. The fight to limit the export of hardwoods has been lost again and again. But Larry Frye has not given up.

Most domestic walnut users, both foreign and locally owned, believe the export of hardwood logs in general and walnut logs in particular should be restricted. One veneer company executive told me confidentially that he would give his association a check for $500,000 the minute it had secured an embargo on the export of hardwood logs. When I shared this information with Frye, he laughed, and although I had not mentioned the name of the executive, he said, "He told me $1 million."

Any association with little influence in Washington does not attract great loyalty or great amounts of money. Frye explained that he was in the process of lodging yet another complaint with Washington about the export of hardwoods: a proposal to implement another embargo. It was his belief that preservationist interests, which are much larger in size and have more financial resources than he has, would eventually bring about the objective that he is seeking. At that time, it was his hope and intention to be in a position to broker between the preservationists and the timber owners to reach an acceptable compromise. Frye fights on hoping to win, in the end, some type of embargo on the export of American hardwood logs.

A successful embargo on the export of logs would be good for the domestic veneer companies, because it would increase the demand for their veneer and reduce competition for the limited supply of quality hardwood logs. Not only are about 50 percent of veneer black walnut logs exported, but about 60 percent of the black walnut veneer produced domestically is also exported. Together, about 80 percent of veneer-quality black walnut timber is exported. Eighty percent!

Without exports, prices of black walnut timber would be substantially lower, and timber owners would suffer. Further, those planting black walnut trees might be less likely to realize the economic gains expected from growing black walnut. Since the Walnut Council is composed largely of walnut tree farmers, Frye has a basic conflict between the interests of his two walnut user associations and the interests of the Walnut Council tree farmers. He seems to ignore this and most others have as well.

I could not help but wonder why the domestic veneer companies had allowed this situation to develop. Why did they not pay higher prices when the bidding for veneer-quality black walnut increased? Why did they let the foreign buyers outbid them? Why did they not cut and export thinner veneer, thus retaining the value added for the United States? Were they afraid that paying higher prices would forever "spoil" timber owners? Were they too weak financially to compete, or did they just lack the nerve? Surely with veneer mills in the backyard of the resource base, there are economic advantages to cutting and exporting veneer rather than logs? The weight and space requirements for shipping logs is far greater than for shipping veneer. Why did they go to the government for help rather than fight in the free market with their money and experience?

These questions remain unanswered. The domestic veneer companies failed to meet the challenge of foreign competition. In this, they are not alone. Many other American industries have been outhustled by aggressive foreign companies since WW II. As a result, domestic ownership of American veneer companies has been reduced and foreign ownership has increased. Logs were exported, and American jobs slicing veneer have been lost to workers in foreign veneer mills.

The tremendous inventory of second-growth black walnut veneer logs has been exploited. Now the red oak, white oak, and cherry timber inventories are being exploited while we wait for more black walnut trees to reach maturity. It will be a long wait.

Still, Frye is enthusiastic about black walnut, is growing some trees himself, and showed me, with pride, a three-drawer chest he had made from the lowest grade of black walnut lumber. The chest was beautiful (see photo section). It showed deep knots and defects and was obviously poor grade black walnut. It was made of a wood grade veneer companies would not use, and low-grade black walnut lumber that most furniture makers do not use either.

Of the chest, Frye said:

> I had to insist they make it. I said leave the knots in. Leave the defects in. Finish it naturally. Maple and walnut knots do not fall out. The knots of other woods fall out. They objected but made it for me. I took it into furniture stores and set it beside another finished the same way but made from better grade lumber without knots or defects. Sixty percent of the people preferred the one with all the knots. Of course you could not use knots in a load-

bearing leg, but I believe we are missing a bet in not using the lower grades of black walnut in furniture.

Frye reviewed his experience in growing black walnut:

In 1963, we had no information on planting hard-woods. Bob Burke went to Kentucky to plant black walnut in 1967, and was told to get out by a state forester. Plant-ing pine is easy. Planting hardwoods is not easy, but we are learning more and more all the time. We have 38 veneer mills in North America and they need raw material to operate. Veneer is better than solid wood. It will hold up longer and will not warp, cup, or sag.

I had the feeling Frye had just switched hats.

ã

During this battle for control of the black walnut re-source and the rapid consumption of the black walnut inven-tory, landowners realized higher prices and increased demand for their standing walnut timber. The price for prime black walnut sawlogs delivered to mills in Indiana gradually rose from under $200 per MBF (thousand board feet) in 1957 to almost $800 per MBF in 1990. The price paid for prime veneer logs *over 21 inches in diameter* delivered to mills in Indiana rose from $200 to over $6,000 per MBF in the same period!

Adjusted for inflation, prices rose faster than inflation until 1977, and then slower than inflation until 1985, when they again began rising faster than inflation. Unlike gold, silver, farmland, and some other "inflationary hedges," walnut did not decline sharply in price when inflation slowed in the mid 80s. The price of black walnut lumber has not declined since 1957, but has maintained a gradual rise for over 35 years. Standing black walnut timber has been a satisfactory hedge against inflation through the longest and most severe period of infla-tion in United States history.

Walnut timber has one major advantage over most other inflation hedges. Walnut trees grow. And bigger trees are much more valuable than smaller ones. The prices reported for the larger size classes of prime veneer logs were up substantially in 1989. The 1989 averages for the 16-17, 18-20, 21-23, 24-28, and greater than 28 inch were $2,836, $3,548, $4,206, $5,078, and $6,711 per MBF, respectively. Since there are many more board feet in a larger log, the value of a larger log is substantially more than a smaller one in both absolute terms and per unit of volume. Like fine wine, it pays to take no log "before its time." Patience, in Americans, may be rare, but in walnut timber owners, patience is rewarded.

Despite this obvious fact, the average size of walnut logs delivered to mills continues to decline. Since the standing black walnut inventory was largely consumed in the orgy of cutting, the annual maturation of large walnut trees has been unable to meet the demand. The scarcity of good-sized walnut trees has resulted in the pressure to cut smaller trees before they reach full, mature size. This premature harvesting may reflect greed or fear that the value of black walnut timber will decline.

In February 1965, the Secretary of Commerce announced that he would not extend controls and remarked, "The situation does not seem to involve the possible extinction of the walnut resource. On the contrary, walnut trees are constantly being planted and constantly maturing." This is true of course, but it takes 40 to 80 years to produce a quality black walnut veneer log. Some things cannot be hurried, and black walnuts are one of them.

è

Landowners in the United States have always been able to do about what they pleased with their land. Now, when they participate in government support programs, farmers are increasingly being told what they can and cannot do with their land. They are told what wetlands they can or cannot drain. In some cases, they are told they must practice certain conservation practices on land subject to erosion. Government-directed land management may be desirable for society, but it does represent some loss of freedom by the landowner.

Until recently, timberland owners have enjoyed similar freedom. They could cut timber, manage it, use it, or abuse it without government interference. However, the private property rights of timberland owners are under increasing government surveillance.

The Endangered Species Act of 1973 has brought attention to the northern spotted owl in Washington state, where 340,000 acres of private land are the subject of restrictive "owl memos." The last memo requires that the owners map owl habitat *at their own expense* and then use that data as a requirement for permits to apply forestry techniques. Should forestry be banned from endangered species habitats? Should landowners who lose the timber or use of their land in this process be compensated? If so, how much and by whom? Has society taken control of private timber without due process?

In the south, another bird flies. The red-cockaded woodpecker was the subject of a letter to *Tree Farmer* reprinted in the March/April 1992 issue. The letter from Ronnie A. Hartley, Macon Georgia follows:

> I am a Registered Forester in Georgia, and while working for a client, placed a small tract of timberland for sale. The tract was to be sold on a sealed bid basis. The highest bid was over $30,000 more than the next highest bid, and was submitted by a large corporation in the wood products industry. A contract was signed, and a 30-day closing was to follow a title search and inspection of the property for environmental hazardous materials.
>
> At the bid opening, one of the foresters mentioned that he had seen possible red-cockaded woodpecker holes in a few trees on the property. The company notified (the landowner and me, his agent) that they would like to bring in an outside expert to determine if there were, in fact, woodpeckers on the property. We agreed to this because we, too, were interested in complying with all regulations regarding endangered species.
>
> After the inspection by the outside party, it was determined that no current activity was involved and that previous activity was more than five years ago. Everything seemed fine. That was not to be. Even with a "clean" bill of health, the company cited that they "had enough birds to watch" on their own property holdings and needed no more. They resigned from the contract. The only thing we could do then was to sell the property to the next highest bidder for over a $30,000 loss.

What is evident here is that because of the Endangered Species Act, the landowner received a loss of monetary value for his timberland. This happened without government intervention. All that was needed was the vicious rumor of RCW's to frighten buyers away. (p. 8)

Another case of loss associated with the red-cockaded woodpecker was reported by Ike C. Sugg, in an article titled, "Ecosystem Babbitt-Babble," in the *Wall Street Journal,* April 2, 1993.

In Greensboro, North Carolina, Benjamin Cone is unable to harvest trees on 2,000 of his 8,000 acres because of the presence of red-cockaded woodpeckers, an "endangered" species. Mr. Cone has lost $2 million. "I cannot afford to let those woodpeckers take over the rest of the property," he says. "I'm going to start massive clear cutting. I'm going to a 40-year rotation instead of a 75- to 80-year rotation."

Mr. Cone is being punished for doing exactly what environmentalists want. Had he exploited his timber resources for a quick return on his investment, he would not have had the mature stand of trees that the woodpeckers prefer.

The issues involving endangered species, preservation and conservation of timber and timberland environments, exports of domestic hardwood timber resources, and preservation of domestic jobs will continue to be debated. These issues are complex, without easy solutions, and all involve the Eastern black walnut.

&

The rapidly rising prices for black walnut logs over the last 30 years, combined with the growing awareness of the scarcity of black walnut timber stimulated, in some, an increased interest in planting black walnut trees. The idea of growing black walnut trees in plantations was not new.

Around the turn of the century, it was not uncommon for walnut groves to be planted near prairie homesites in the Midwest to provide windbreak, nuts, and timber. Most were harvested for timber over the past 60 years. I recall seeing an entire walnut grove harvested for lumber south of Rossville,

Illinois in 1946. A huge grain crib was built from the walnut lumber. The crib burned two years later.

A few of these old walnut groves remain on the prairies of Indiana and Illinois and elsewhere throughout the Midwest. I visited two of these old black walnut groves in western Indiana, measured their area, and counted the trees. Each had over 140 trees on about 1 1/2 acres of prairie land. The trees were tall, clear of branches for some height and showed extensive signs of old age. Some were dead but still standing.

There was considerable walnut timber in both plantations in a small area, but the quality of timber was not high. It was obvious that these prairie trees were old, growing very slowly and so crowded that the rate of growth had slowed. It was also obvious that the groves had not been managed to improve the rate of growth by thinning when that would have been desirable. Livestock had been allowed into the grove in years past. Some trees had wire embedded in their trunks. Tractors had damaged some trunks when mowing between the trees.

Were these walnuts valuable? The examples from Chapter One might lead many readers to conclude that all walnuts are valuable. It is not so; all walnuts are not created equal. In 1993, the two groves described were surveyed and marked for auction by an experienced forester. Invitations to bid were sent to over 50 qualified timber buyers. Only two bids were received. The highest was for slightly over $11,000 for almost 300 old walnut trees. Not much for the total production of about three acres of rich prairie land over a period of what was probably over 100 years.

What went wrong? The wrong site, no care, no thinning, livestock grazing, machine damage, and waiting too long to sell after maturity probably account for the low value received for these old walnuts. When these old trees were cut, about 80 percent were hollow and rotten at the core. They would not make good firewood.

Prairie black walnut grove in western Indiana estimated to be about 100 years old and containing 142 trees on 1 1/2 acres.

Close up of the same grove as above showing size and spacing. These trees were sold at auction in late 1993, for about $5,500. When they were cut, about 80 percent were decayed and hollow.

Prairie tree stump from the same prairie grove showing decay and hollow center with nut shells left by red squirrels.

è

There is much yet to be learned about growing black walnuts in plantations. Conifer trees have been successfully grown in plantations for many years. Could black walnut be grown in plantations to produce a quality veneer log? It took 40 to 80 years or longer to grow a top-quality veneer log under natural conditions. Was it possible to reduce this growing time to 20 or 30 years?

At the same time, there was a recognized need for more knowledge about this uniquely American tree. Hybrid grain varieties had been developed that were far superior to natural varieties. Could the same be done with black walnut? If the world wanted American-grown Eastern black walnut, why couldn't good old American know-how deliver it? The push for more and better understanding of the black walnut was launched.

Before we look at what progress is being made to improve the species and the culture of black walnuts in Chapter Six, let's take a better look at black walnut wood, veneer, and nuts in the next three chapters. This should give us a better idea of why black walnut is so highly valued and why extensive efforts are devoted to improving and propagating Eastern black walnut trees.

3

BLACK WALNUT WOOD

ৼ

"Gentle to the touch, exquisite to contemplate, tractable in creative hands, stronger by weight than iron, wood was, as William Penn had said, 'a substance with a soul.' It spanned rivers for man; it built his home and heated it in winter; man walked on wood, slept in it, sat on wooden chairs at wooden tables, drank and ate the fruits of trees from wooden cups and dishes. From cradle of wood to coffin of wood, the life of man was encircled by it."

—Eric Sloane, *A Reverence for Wood*

American infantrymen carried black walnut gunstocks into every battle of every war until Vietnam. Black walnut formed the gunstocks of muskets in the Revolutionary War, muzzle loaders in the Civil War, the Springfields of WW I, the M1s of WW II and Korea, and the M-14s and the early M-16s of Vietnam. Later in the Vietnam War, the original M-16 was replaced with the M16-A1, which had a composition hard plastic stock. Walnut was too scarce, too expensive, or not good enough for the modern American infantrymen.

Yet today, United States Military Academy cadets, over 3,000 strong in a full Corps review, carry M-14 rifles with black walnut gunstocks on the West Point plain above the Hudson River where Lee, Grant, MacArthur, Eisenhower, Patton, Schwarzkopf, and others of the Long Gray Line once marched. Black walnut trees grow on the Military Academy grounds and squirrels harvest the nuts.

In the 17th century, French musketeers selected walnut for their firearm stocks, a preference that still prevails among U.S. makers of quality shotguns and rifles. Walnut wood machines well, does not break or splinter easily, has less jar or recoil, never warps or shrinks, and is very attractive. Some early long rifles made in Pennsylvania and Kentucky had curly maple gunstocks, but eventually nearly all were made of black walnut.

It is claimed that handling a walnut gunstock and carrying one for a long period of time will not irritate the palm because of its wonderful satiny surface. However, barn bedding containing walnut wood chips causes lameness in horses, but no one seems to know why.

The Pilgrims held their council meetings at a walnut table at Plymouth Hall. Aaron Burr composed himself over lunch at a walnut sidebar after killing Alexander Hamilton in a duel. Dolly Madison served tea from a walnut buffet to her husband and his generals while they talked strategy in the War of 1812. President Andrew Jackson's great black walnut secretary still can be seen at The Hermitage near Nashville, Tennessee. Daniel Boone, in anticipation of death, had a black walnut coffin built, polished it, and often practiced lying in it to the chagrin of his kin.

The president of the Sierra Club works in a San Francisco office behind an "imposing walnut desk." The ballroom floor of the famous Longwood Gardens Conservatory near Wilmington, Delaware is a hardwood puncheon parquet made from WW I surplus black walnut gunstock blanks.

When Lou Holtz and the Notre Dame National Championship football team visited President Ronald Reagan at the White House on January 18, 1989, they presented the President with a monogrammed sweater that in 1918 had belonged to George Gipp. Ronald Reagan, then actor, had played Gipp in the Hollywood movie *Knute Rockne: All American*. The sweater was enclosed in a carefully crafted black walnut case made near Notre Dame in Goshen, Indiana at Swartzendruber Hard-wood Creations.

Located in what had been and is now called The Old Bag Factory, Swartzendruber Hardwood Creations is the fulfillment of the vision of Larion Swartzendruber to bring together customers and craftsmen in the creation of fine custom furniture. Larion Swartzendruber was born and raised in Iowa as a Mennonite, educated at Hesston College and Bethel in Kansas, and taught industrial arts at Bethany Christian High School from 1970 to 1975. In 1971 he started building stereo cabinets out of black walnut and continued to make other fine furniture.

About 35 percent of the furniture from Swartzendruber Hardwood Creations is crafted from black walnut by 30 employees. In the summer of 1992, a beautiful executive desk of walnut with inlaid English and Eastern black walnut was offered for $5,997. A black walnut credenza with burled panels was priced at $8,397. In solid black walnut without the burled panels, the credenza was $6,897. A beautiful solid black walnut fireplace mantle was priced at $7,395. Black walnut furniture was priced only slightly higher than oak or cherry.

ﾞﾙ

The manufacture of fine walnut furniture in the United States has a long and distinguished history. During the 1700s and 1800s, walnut furniture was manufactured, in great quantity, in Chester County, Pennsylvania, from locally grown natural walnut. At that time, Philadelphia, only 20 miles east of Chester County, was the largest and most prosperous city in America. Many homes built during that period were filled with walnut chairs, tables, desks, spice chests, cabinets, clocks, beds, etc. Much of this antique furniture remains in homes of the Delaware Valley and can be seen on house tours such as the Chester County Day, held the first Saturday of each October to benefit the Chester County Hospital.

The classic Philadelphia Museum of Art displays a representative collection of Pennsylvania furniture from the 18th and 19th centuries. Nearly 80 percent of these pieces, made before 1750, was manufactured from black walnut. After

1750, mahogany was imported and used in addition to locally grown black walnut. Mahogany was more expensive but had become popular and fashionable in Europe. Now, black walnut is more expensive than mahogany and has become fashionable in Europe, but not yet in America.

On the west end of the Ben Franklin Parkway, the Philadelphia Museum of Art stands on a bluff overlooking the Schulkill River in Fairmont Park, which boasts several stately mansions of the early colonial period filled with black walnut furniture. At the opposite end of the Ben Franklin Parkway, which many believe is the most impressive avenue in any American City, the Fountain Room of the modern and expensive Four Seasons Hotel is paneled in richly colored and expertly matched black walnut veneer. On Walnut Street, The Walnut Street Theatre, which claims to be the oldest continuously operating theatre in the English-speaking world, displays chair arm rests and stairway hand rails of black walnut wood with a fine handrubbed patina. But, the fine restaurants on Walnut Street serve only English walnut desserts.

ೠ

Around 1800, Francois Andre' Michaux observed and wrote about black walnut in his book, *The North American Silva.*

On the banks of the Ohio, and on the islands of that beautiful river, I have often seen trees, (black walnuts) of three to four feet in diameter and 60 or 70 feet in height. It is not rare to find them of the thickness of six or seven feet.

Twenty or thirty years ago, before mahogany was imported in such abundance into Europe, Walnut wood was employed almost exclusively in cabinet making. In the country it is still in general use, and the furniture made of it is far from being inelegant especially pieces obtained from such old trees as bear small and thick-shelled nuts. It is preferred for the stocks of muskets; and in Paris and Brussels no other wood is used in the panels of carriages. The old trees furnish excellent screws for large presses. Great quantities of wooden shoes are manufactured of Walnut, which are more highly esteemed than others.

When the timber is freshly cut, the sap is white and the heart of violet-color, which after a short exposure to air assumes a more intense shade and becomes nearly black; hence probably is derived the name of Black Walnut. There are several qualities for which its wood is principally esteemed. It remains sound during a long time, even when exposed to the influences of heat and moisture; but this observation is applicable only to the heart; the sap speedily decays. It is very strong and very tenacious; when thoroughly seasoned, it is not liable to warp and split; and its grain is sufficiently fine and compact to admit of a high polish. It possesses, in addition to these advantages, that of being secure from worms. I have been assured that it makes excellent naves for wheels, which further proves its strength and durability. At Philadelphia coffins are very frequently made of it.

In the main lumberyards of Philadelphia, I have often seen it used for knees and floor timber; but in the vessels built at Wheeling and Marietta, towns on the Ohio, it constitutes a principal part of the frame. On the river Wabash canoes are made of it which are greatly esteemed for strength and durability. Some of them, fashioned from the trunk of a single tree, are more than 40 feet long and two or three feet wide. (p. 66, volume I)

Now, nearly 200 years later, black walnut wood is rarely available for common use. Most lumber yards do not carry it. It can be obtained, but at considerable effort and expense.

The antebellum homes of Natchez, Mississippi hold much lovely walnut furniture from Pennsylvania. In the mid-1800s, Natchez had more millionaires *per capita* than New York City, and was estimated by some to be the fourth wealthiest community in the United States, after New York, Boston, and Philadelphia. The homes of the Natchez elite were filled with expensive furniture transported up the Mississippi River before the Civil War. A lady of the south told me they still had this walnut furniture, because after the Civil War they were too poor to purchase "modern" furniture. This antique walnut furniture can be seen during the annual Spring Pilgrimage when 30 homes are open for tours. These impressive homes and their contents have become a major tourist attraction of the famous old city on the bluff overlooking the Mississippi River.

Biltmore House, the largest and most elaborate private home ever built in America, was completed in 1895, in Asheville, North Carolina. Richard M. Hunt, the architect who designed and built Biltmore House for George Vanderbilt, used red oak to panel most rooms and hallways. However, the library and master bedroom are of classical-baroque style, paneled in solid black walnut.

These two rooms display some of the most beautiful black walnut that can be seen anywhere. Two larger-than-life size carved walnut statues stand over the black marble fireplace of the library. They are Hestia, goddess of the hearth on the right and Demeter, goddess of the fruitful soil on the left. The fireplace mantle in Vanderbilt's master bedroom is of expertly carved, naturally finished, highly polished, solid black walnut.

Oblivion is a subtle and erotic carving from one solid piece of black walnut that stands over six feet tall and is over two feet in diameter. Created by Warton Esherick in 1934, *Oblivion* stands today in Esherick's former studio-home (now a museum) on Valley Forge Mountain, Valley Forge, Pennsylvania. The Wharton Esherick studio is filled with works of art and crafts by this extraordinary man whose work appears in the Metropolitan Museum in New York, the Philadelphia Museum of Art, and the Virginia Museum of Fine Arts in Richmond. He worked with all types of wood, but chose black walnut for this magnificent piece. He combined walnut with apple for the floor of his dining area and used black walnut extensively in the chairs and desks of his own studio. Much of the unusual and unique furniture he made was from black walnut.

ða.

By 1934, over 40 percent of living room and dining room furniture made in the United States was still made from Eastern black walnut. That percentage fell gradually to under 15 percent in 1955, and then rose back to almost 25 percent in the early 1960s. But after 1965, walnut steadily declined in usage. Today, less than two percent of living room and dining room furniture is made from black walnut!

Walnut wood became less readily available and more expensive. Tastes turned to mahogany, oak, cherry, teak, pine, etc. The overall use of walnut in furniture has declined, but some craftsmen still work in solid walnut.

The Irion Company, furniture makers of Christiana, Pennsylvania, is still devoted to recreating the natural beauty and design of furniture the way it was made 200 years ago. Employing 22 skilled cabinetmakers, the company combines rustic and modern techniques, securing locally grown logs, contracting for them to be sawn as they specify, kiln drying the lumber in their own kiln, matching boards and pieces from the same tree, and hand-carving delicate designs such as leaves, vines and ball and claw feet.

The Irion Company was founded in 1977, by Louis Irion III, his wife Wanda, and master cabinetmaker Chris Arato. The company began by restoring antiques and developed an impeccable reputation for restoration. Orders for custom-made furniture began filtering in and then began pouring in from all over the United States and Canada.

"We're flat out busy." says Irion. "People want quality. They want furniture that will last and last and last. They want something they can hand down to their children like they have inherited from their parents and grandparents. They're not antiques, but I think there is a spirit of revitalization going on. Something like the old days when you simply went to a cabinet shop to have your furniture made the way you wanted it."

Chris Arato says the company is not concerned with obtaining enough walnut for their needs. They are yet a small company and have two lumber yards and several loggers watching for walnut. They never buy standing timber, but wait until a log is cut and ready to saw.

When they buy a log and order it sawed, they assume a liability for any damage to the saw blade, which can run to a thousand dollars. Since many walnut trees grow in fence rows, in barnlots, and on suburban properties, the danger of metal embedded in the trees is high. To avoid this hazard, trees are often scanned with metal sensors, such as mine detectors.

While very large walnut trees are rare throughout the region, the company yet finds logs from which 30-inch boards can be cut for desks and tables. Chris believes that if a major furniture company wanted to produce walnut furniture, they would have a problem finding the wood. Chris believes over 95 percent of furniture made in Chester County in the 18th century was made of black walnut.

Chris said of black walnut, "I admire the tight grain and wonderful grain patterns of black walnut. I prefer to work with walnut over all other woods. But people do not understand black walnut. They believe it is not available. When they come in here asking for mahogany, I try to show them black walnut and explain its fine qualities. It really is necessary to educate them and I do it over and over again."

Another Pennsylvania craftsman who loves walnut is Jeffry D. Lohr of Schwenksville. Working alone in his cluttered shop on the second floor of an 1850s barn (framed in solid and heavy Eastern black walnut) Jeff strives for expression of his philosophy in his work. This 41-year-old bearded philosopher credits an article in *Fine Woodworking*, September 1978, with changing his life. This article about Greene and Greene craftsmen extolled the merits of superb craftsmanship and attention to detail.

Jeff abandoned his 14-year teaching career and set out to make fine furniture. Using walnut wood from trees cut from his own land, sawed with a friend, and dried naturally in his big barn, Jeff fashions solid walnut furniture with rounded edges, wooden pins and screws and no glue. Striving to express honesty and integrity in his work, Jeff rejects the lure of easy money in mass production of copies of the work of earlier craftsman. He gets more satisfaction from creating a unique and entirely new style of quality furniture from walnut.

Jeff believes only natural air drying allows the color of black walnut to show to its fullest. Kiln drying black walnut, he believes, saps the color and reduces the delicate shadings. For large logs he must wait up to five years for this unique hardwood to air dry. He believes waiting is worthwhile to get the full black walnut color.

Jeff had recently cut a large black walnut tree along the highway near his barn and together we inspected the big log. He said he had decided to cut it because a branch had begun to rot and he suspected the life of the big tree was endangered and decided to cut the tree to save the wood. The tree had been growing on the east side of a gradual slope in the roadside ditch and had plentiful moisture and good soil. The annual growth rings often were over a quarter-inch wide. I counted 70 annual rings, which was proof that the big tree was about 70 years old.

Jeff Lohr, furniture craftsman, stands beside a 70-year-old black walnut log.

North Carolina claims to be the furniture capital of the world, and it has held this position for the past 80 years. From Greensboro to Asheville, along Interstate 40, you will find the largest concentration of furniture companies and furniture showrooms in the United States. Hickory Furniture Mart in Hickory, North Carolina claims over ten acres of floor space and representation of hundreds of manufacturers. High Point, North Carolina claims to be the center of the center and the home of The Furniture Library, whose collection of over 6,000 books on furniture and design is the world's largest and most comprehensive.

Those who know furniture and want value shop in North Carolina. There they find the largest selections and the best values. Suggested retail prices for furniture are traditionally 240 percent over manufacturers' prices. Thus, an item priced at the factory at $100 would retail for $240 before discount. With a 40 percent discount the item would sell for $144, and the discounter would recognize a 44-percent markup. A 50-percent discount would bring the price to the consumer down to $120 and the markup down to 20 percent. People come from all over the United States and from foreign countries to see the large variety and to obtain discount prices. The Southern Furniture Market (the largest furniture display in the world) is held there each April and October.

North Carolina is the furniture capital of the world, but Virginia is the solid black walnut furniture manufacturing center. In Virginia, two companies manufacture solid black walnut furniture. The largest, Henkel-Harris, is widely known and highly respected throughout the furniture industry. It was founded in the 1940s by three people with a willing desire to produce quality furniture faithfully copied from 17th and 18th century English and American antiques. Carroll Hess Henkel, an engineer; his wife, Mary, a student of interior design; and a friend, John Harris, began cabinetmaking in historic Winchester, Virginia. Their first endeavor was a corner cupboard built in the basement of the Henkel home. The cupboard proved to be too large to get out of the basement.

Henkel-Harris works closely with the Society for the Preservation of New England Antiquities (SPNEA) in the authentic reproduction of noteworthy, but rarely seen, 18th century designs from the Society's collection. You can buy a new chair just like one built in Boston in 1740, a new sideboard exactly like one in Mount Vernon, or an exact replica of an 18th-century Philadelphia lowboy. The completion date and Henkel-Harris or SPNEA trademark are burned permanently (like a brand on a horse or cow) into a drawer interior or underside, or on the back portion of each piece of furniture. These trademarks are in the tradition of the 18th-century cabinetmakers who proudly placed their marks on everything they made as a promise of integrity and enduring quality.

Henkel-Harris now employs about 275 people. Many are fine craftsmen who have been with the company over 20 years. In a large single building, they begin with fine lumber at one end and ship "honestly made, genuinely reproduced" furniture at the other. They make furniture of walnut, mahogany, and black cherry, but walnut is a very small portion of their total production line, and they have been in and out of the walnut business two or three times in the last 25 years. The company uses solid black walnut lumber from Indiana, which is light in color and clear of defects. They had not bought any walnut lumber in 1991 or 1992, but had been consuming from walnut lumber inventory.

Black walnut furniture is now only about five percent of Henkel-Harris' total production, and I was told they may drop the walnut models entirely. The company continues to produce walnut only as insurance against the possibility that mahogany from South America may not always be available. Walnut wood costs somewhat more than cherry and mahogany, and Henkel-Harris prices walnut furniture 29 percent over cherry pieces and seven percent over mahogany. When I found two large furniture stores in the Philadelphia Main Line area with Henkel-Harris walnut furniture marked down over 50 percent and not moving, I understood the Henkel-Harris concern for the black walnut market. One fine furniture store had a walnut dining room set on the floor four years, now reduced 56 percent and yet unsold in January 1995.

Furniture fashions ebb and flow much like skirt lengths. Walnut has been in and out of fashion several times in the past 100 years. Mahogany and cherry compete with walnut for the favor of the consumer. Both can be stained to look much like walnut. But fine walnut has a luminescence and a grain pattern that make it unique. In walnut, you often see unusual horizontal streaks or patterns that are much like shadows running across the grain at intervals of an inch or so. I found no one who knew exactly what causes these horizontal shadows, but some believe they develop as winds rock and sway the tall trees in the deep forest.

ِ♣

Grayson E. Ferguson Jr. (Eddie) believes in walnut. When he was 13 years old, Eddie won first prize at the 1962 Virginia state fair with a stereo cabinet he had built. Eddie had a tough industrial arts teacher who demanded the best of him. Eddie credits this teacher with giving him inspiration and motivation toward his career in quality woodworking. "I really enjoy taking a tree and turning it into a piece of art." says Eddie. "It's the only thing I've ever done. Some say I'm lucky, but I don't believe in luck. Luck is when preparation meets opportunity."

In 1987, Eddie, along with two business associates, started Waterford Furniture Makers in an old, dirty building beside the railroad tracks across the street from a cement block company at the edge of Lynchburg, Virginia. Waterford makes *solid* black walnut furniture and uses no other wood but some aromatic red cedar in their cedar chests. *Solid* black walnut!

Eddie says, "At some point, veneer comes off. I make furniture to last centuries. I make furniture of solid wood, and you can refinish it as many times as you want and it will last." Waterford makes drawer bottoms, backs, everything but the solid brass hardware and the red cedar chest linings of solid black walnut. Henkel-Harris uses solid walnut, cherry, or mahogany *only* on the area you see and other wood in drawers or backs.

Eddie comes as close to turning sow's ears into silk purses as anyone I've ever met. Most black walnut he uses comes from within a 200-mile radius of Lynchburg. He keeps costs down by using only number one and two common grades of walnut, which are the lowest grades. His workers cut these ugly boards, which are sometimes warped and filled with knots, blemishes, scars, and other defects into various lengths. They cut out the defects without regard to length, but always looking for the longest piece of acceptable wood.

These various lengths, from 13 to 72 inches long, then drop to a revolving table, are sorted based on length, and stacked so that various lengths of boards that are acceptable are gathered together. Better-quality black walnut is used when needed for tops and large pieces. He does not cut to order, but looks at the cut inventory and picks out what he needs. Waterford sells the small lengths of walnut board, which result in excess of their needs, to another company that makes trophies and cutting boards of black walnut.

Eddie keeps costs down by hiring inexpensive employees. Waterford employs about 45 people. "High school graduates are the best value because, when they graduate, *they know everything,*" said Eddie. "Much of our work is repetitive and simple. I wanted to be a teacher and now I'm teaching these kids how to make fine furniture. I really enjoy showing them how to turn a leg or finish a cabinet."

As he showed me his production line, Eddie noted a flaw here and a design error there and vowed to correct these before the next run. He inspected the rejected knot and defect pieces where the boards are being cut and noted that some of those rejected pieces "looked pretty good." He noted a pile of metal duct pipe with welding equipment standing by it and a welder's goggles laying on the floor, but there was no welder. "He's got it pointing the wrong direction." moaned Eddie. "He's got to turn it all around." Eddie stayed to find the welder and correct the error while I went on. He was always teaching, teaching. He practices real hands-on management, which I suspect is rare.

According to Eddie, "We use all American black walnut and all American materials but for two brass items that come from Taiwan, and the locks, which come from England." Eddie does not waste money on equipment; he says, "Our most expensive equipment is our dust removal system, which is required by the law. All our other equipment is simple woodworking equipment like you would find in any wood-working shop." The company is contained in three separate buildings and is now expanding into the recently acquired third, which Eddie said was a "dirty mess filled with 40 years of dirt" when acquired.

Eddie says his favorite wood is walnut.

> We started with some cherry and mahogany but settled on walnut and now use only walnut. It is our niche. There is a lot of cherry and mahogany furniture out there, but we are the only company in the world making a full and complete line of solid black walnut furniture. We have grown every year for five years and now have a line of about 50 pieces of furniture and $1 million in furniture inventory. We can ship anywhere in the state for next-day arrival. Most of our sales have been in the East, but we are branching out and are negotiating a contract with a European firm. We will furnish them with walnut pieces for them to assemble and affix their own name.

Waterford furniture features dovetail drawer corners, dovetail parting rails, mortise and tenon joints, splined miter joints, tongue and grooved back paneling, full mortise and tenon door corners with wood pins, and mirror frame corner splines. The finish is a dark, moderate gloss. His square walnut wood pins are driven into round holes assuring secure fit. The beautiful chocolate color of the black walnut is fully revealed. Unlike Henkel-Harris' walnut furniture and other fine walnut veneer furniture, Eddie's furniture shows an occasional pin knot, worm mark and color shading, which would be rejected by veneer companies as a defect. Eddie takes pride in making something entirely different.

Both Waterford and Henkel-Harris use the lighter sapwood in their solid wood furniture. Veneer furniture companies reject this sapwood and trim it out. Waterford and Henkel-Harris stain just the lighter sapwood with darker stain so that it blends into the darker heartwood and can barely be detected. The sapwood has strength and durability characteristics almost equal to the heartwood, but the sapwood is lighter in color.

Waterford furniture is priced 15 percent below Henkel-Harris. It *is* real, it *looks* real, it *feels* real, and is *real heavy*. Waterford solid walnut furniture may restore chivalry. If she can't lift her chair, seating the lady for dinner may become more than an optional courtesy. Will the consumer buy this real, solid black walnut furniture? Only time will tell.

"Image is everything!" says Andre Agassi, professional tennis player, winner of the 1994 U.S. Open, and huckster for a camera company shown in TV commercials. The Agassi image, (unkempt, loudly dressed rebel with prominent ear ring), apparently attracts substantial interest from young, easily impressed females who scream and plead for his sweaty shirts after his tennis matches. In this age when gaudy plastic flowers "decorate" cemeteries and restaurants, when metal money no longer has real silver, gold, or value, when false eyelashes, false fingernails, false hair color, and silicone-enhanced bosoms are the norm, it does seem that "image is everything," and anything "real" is little admired, appreciated, or understood. Eddie is bucking this tendency to place image over reality, and he hopes consumers will want and buy real black walnut furniture. At least he hopes enough of them will buy to make Waterford a success.

Eddie said of walnut, "Walnut will fade, particularly if exposed to the sun. The rule is that darker woods get lighter and lighter woods get darker. Solid wood furniture does not respond well to wide swings in humidity. Since our furniture is solid wood, it expands and contracts with changes in moisture. All our furniture is designed with wood movement in mind. However, it should not be exposed to a humid area like a basement."

That is real, but will it sell? It sold me. I bought a solid black walnut end table for $407.55 with a suggested retail price of about $800. It is art, it is real, and it is solid Eastern black walnut.

ಶಿ

At the Amana Colonies in southeastern Iowa, three furniture shops offer handcrafted black walnut furniture produced by craftsmen who complete the entire construction of a piece of furniture without any help. Unlike most furniture made with assembly-line efficiencies, this furniture reflects the craftsmanship of one man who proudly signs each piece. The finishing is done by others who generally employ a natural finish (lighter than Eddie's) which clearly reflects the beauty of the locally grown black walnut. Iowa black walnut is lighter in color than Virginia walnut and is prized by veneer companies worldwide.

These shops also make furniture of cherry and oak, but 60-70 percent of their furniture is of black walnut; and, surprisingly, black walnut is priced the same as cherry or oak. They offer an impressive line of walnut rockers of various sizes and shapes, cradles, clocks, dressers, bed headboards, cabinets, bookshelves, desks, hutches, mirror frames, chairs, stools, and tables. They also do custom work and restoration, mostly in black walnut. (See Directory.)

Berea College in Berea, Kentucky, offers 1,500 talented youth of limited financial means an opportunity for education in exchange for 10-20 hours per week in Berea's labor program. About 200 students participate in the Student Crafts Program, which produces some very attractive black walnut furniture and novelty items. These black walnut items are offered for sale at retail outlets in Berea, Louisville, and Lexington. In addition, a crafts catalogue and woodcraft furniture catalogue offer black walnut items. (See Directory.)

Undoubtedly, there are others making fine furniture from black walnut; and I have no desire to belittle them by omission. These I do mention are just the only first-rate quality manufacturers I learned about in my travels.

A large amount of solid black walnut wood is used in what is called the novelty trade. Bowls, trays, candlestick holders, picture frames, clocks, sconces, plates, salad tongs, candy dishes, plaques, cheese boards, music boxes, etc. are all made of solid black walnut. Two large retail factory stores in Missouri offer these items; one is on Interstate 70 near Columbia and the other is on Interstate 44 near Lebanon. Both are owned by the Independent Stave Company, and they offer everyone a chance to have some black walnut wood at a nominal price. (See Directory.)

Lasercraft in Santa Rosa, California makes novelty items such as wall plaques, key holders, and music boxes by cutting a deep pattern into black walnut wood with a laser. Deep laser engraved patterns can be cut in this manner that are quite beautiful. According to Daryl Boyd, Purchasing Manager at Lasercraft, "Lasercraft is a manufacturer of solid Black American Walnut. The walnut we use is purchased from the Midwest, in states such as Indiana or Missouri. We do not use Eastern Black Walnut. We use approximately 200,000 board feet of lumber per year."

Humm. Very interesting. Actually they don't manufacture walnut, it grows. And they do use Eastern black walnut, which is the term that describes the species *Juglans nigra* growing east of the Rockies. American is sometimes added to differentiate *Juglans nigra* grown here from that grown in foreign countries. The American Walnut Manufacturer's Association promoted the name American Black Walnut for many years.

ᶻ▲

The Hartzell family has been sawing walnut logs into walnut lumber in Ohio since 1875. Located at its current mill in Piqua, Ohio, since 1900, the company still cuts walnut with a band saw. A process of steaming was developed by the company to turn the white sapwood of walnut to a uniform brown, nearly the same color as heartwood. This enabled the company to market sapwood, which was formerly worth much less. Steaming black walnut has become the standard industry practice.

In 1915, the company began slicing veneer. When a WW I embargo stopped walnut veneer production overnight, the company turned to production of walnut gunstocks and walnut airplane propellers for the military. The company branched into other activities and abandoned most. Now logs keep coming and the company keeps sawing, but fewer logs are black walnut.

Dick Elsas, superintendent of the Hartzell sawmill, has been with the company for 38 years. Elsas told his story:

> During WW II, every walnut log went into gunstocks. A government supervisor was here to assure that. I came after WW II and began as maintenance and have worked my way up to superintendent. We steam walnut lumber for 48 hours at 190 degrees to blend the color of the heartwood into the sapwood. We cut random widths and lengths for inventory based upon the orders we receive. The best logs are shipped to be made into veneer and we cut the remainder, which is graded twice as #2 common, #1 common, FAS (first and seconds), and FAS one face. We sell and ship from inventory to lumber yards and manufacturers in the United States and all over the world. We use the chips and sawdust as boiler fuel and the bark is sold for mulch.
>
> When I first came here, 100 percent of our business was black walnut. But now 50 percent or less is in black walnut. We saw a lot of oak now. The walnut logs we get are smaller and we get fewer of them. I would say it takes more like 100 years to grow a black walnut log. We are sawing white oak now but begin walnut on Monday. We'll go through seven or eight saw blades on Monday. You hit a lot more metal in walnut because of where they grow.
>
> We tried using metal detectors, but there was too much vibration here. The detector once rejected 25 straight logs. I sawed all 25 logs and never hit a thing. We quit using it. I've completely wrecked a saw on a small nail and sawed clear through a horseshoe and never hurt the blade. Blades cost $700 to $800, and we buy about six blades a year. If you hit something hard, you resharpen the blade and use it again.

Dennis Freeman was sharpening a saw blade that is 36 feet, six inches long and twelve inches wide with teeth on both sides of the circular steel band. "I once hit four horse shoes in one log and thought I would next hit the horse." said Freeman. He showed me a three-gallon bucket filled with metal that had been removed from logs. It contained nails of several sizes, insulators, bolts, a cutter guard from a mower sickle bar, an oil can, several horse shoes, other metal, and rocks. "We hit a lot more metal in black walnut than other logs." said Freeman. "If we begin cutting black walnut on Monday, I'll be busy sharpening blades."

At the Hartzell Walnut Mills in Picqua, Ohio, Dennis Freeman sharpens a 36-foot band saw blade that hit metal.

The band saw blade turns a 3/16 inch channel of fine hardwood into sawdust as it cuts each path through the log. This would have been six sheets of veneer if sliced instead of sawed. The system used at Hartzell is much like the one introduced over 90 years ago; the equipment and the building appeared old. It is a traditional industry and slow to change.

ॐ

Norman E. Hughes is owner and staff of Good Hope Hardwoods Inc., which he operates from a big red barn and adjacent building near the southeastern corner of Pennsylvania. Hughes takes time with his customers, working for almost two hours one day in February 1992 helping a customer select curly Eastern red maple and curly *Juglans hindsii* for her project of building six mirror frames. As rain fell and the chill wind blew through the unheated building, we talked and Hughes measured large pieces of wood three inches by nine inches and various lengths up to ten feet long while the customer selected wood based on color and pattern. Hughes shaved pieces with a hand plane to reveal the beautiful curly wood patterns he hopes to specialize in providing to appreciative customers.

The building had a dustless new cement floor. Hughes explained that he worked himself through the University of Delaware in Mechanical Engineering finishing cement, so he knew what he wanted, and he did not want dust. The building was filled with hardwoods along both ends up to ten feet high and piled on the center floor several layers deep. He had two kinds of walnut, butternut, myrtle, Eastern red maple, cherry and even osage orange, which he says finishes to a beautiful brown. Standing along the back wall were slabs of *Juglans hindsii* five to six feet tall, over three feet wide and two to three inches thick (see photo section). Hughes was saving these for a lady who was coming from Utah to look at them and expects she will purchase 250 to 300 board feet. In the far corner were several huge pieces showing interesting branching and knots.

Hughes worked for Hercules Corporation for almost 30 years but retired in 1991 to devote himself to providing specialty hardwoods to furniture craftsmen. While he admitted to being a bit nervous about being independent, he said, "I wish I'd quit sooner." Hughes had been working with fine woods for 30 to 40 years as a hobby and credits his interest to an inspirational shop teacher and to early exposure to his grandfather's shop where he recalls the fine aroma of woods. His grandfather was a cabinetmaker for the Pullman Company, which specialized in luxury railcars.

Hughes explained that the *Juglans hindsii* is called "claro walnut" and came from California where he had just been to buy two semi-trailer loads that would be delivered in a few weeks and that he would have sawed in nearby West Chester, Pennsylvania. He says the name "claro" was given to this variety of black walnut by the gunstock makers who prize it. About 20 percent of claro logs have the curly wood grain prized by furniture craftsmen and gunstock makers.

Juglans hindsii is native to Northern California and was planted for shade trees in towns such as Chico, California. The species has been used as root stock for grafting various English walnut varieties. Early grafts were often made six feet from the ground. So, the base of these trees are of the valued claro wood while the tops are of the less-valued English walnut. In the towns of California, many trees are dying now from street incursion, air pollution, and excessive pruning. Those in the walnut plantations are dying from salt buildup and high water tables.

Hughes explained that new English walnut trees are now grafted onto root stock of Eastern black walnut or a cross between the English walnut and the Eastern black walnut, which is called the Paradox or Bastogne variety developed by Luther Burbank. These resist moisture better, sprout less, and are now preferred to the claro. Norm said the English walnut has a small heartwood and large quantity of sapwood, which is very light and reduces its value. He explained that some sawmills steam the English walnut to extend the heartwood color into the sapwood, which raises the value of the whole.

Hughes and others are particularly interested in the curly patterns that appear in only about 20 percent of the claro walnut and less than one percent of the Eastern black walnut. Hughes speculated that nuts from curly trees might have curly offspring, but the catch is you don't know until you cut a tree if it is curly or not, and then where do you get the nuts?

Later, after Hughes had loaded $750 of curly pattern lumber into the customer's Nissan, we shared a cup of coffee over his solid curly black walnut kitchen table in his 1700s stone farmhouse. The modern kitchen had solid cherry floors, solid cherry trim and crown molding. The adjoining family room was paneled in solid cherry. The kitchen cabinets were yet doorless, but cherry doors are coming. Hughes confessed he finally hired them done because he is just too busy. The walnut table was fitted with expansion joints to adjust to changing humidity and was not glued. It was beautiful and not so smoothly finished so you could still feel the saw grooves, which were pleasing to the hand.

Hughes showed me his upstairs master bedroom, which has solid Eastern black walnut floors, solid black walnut paneling and window boxes. The window boxes frame the windows and are over two feet deep, because the walls of early Pennsylvania stone houses are mortar and stone and are two feet thick. He said he did all of the woodwork himself, and he showed me where the paneling has expanded and contracted with changes in humidity. This is an essential consideration when working with solid wood. Hughes said, "Walnut will get lighter with time, while other woods darken." He buys locally grown black walnut logs but gets the unusual curly patterns more readily and in larger pieces from California.

He said the claro walnut in California's walnut orchards are 50 to 60 years old and three to four feet in diameter. Larger trees can be found in some California towns. One of these city logs coming from California is 56 inches in diameter at the base, 50 inches in diameter at the top, and eight feet long. Hughes declined to reveal the name of the town. "It's my secret." he said. (See photo section.)

ತಿ

There may be some who believe that we live in the plastic age or the age of glass and steel, and that wood is an anachronism. Or, they may believe we can replicate wood using technology, which has made natural wood obsolete. But wood has properties or powers that cannot be quantified in scientific terms. These aspects of wood, without being well understood or even explainable, may well be among the most important and powerful.

In *Understanding Wood* (1980), Bruce Hoadley writes of wood's:

> ... *sensual properties*, where there is a close relationship to our senses of touch, sight, hearing, smell and taste. These properties include color, odor, resonance and so forth, and are in part explainable and describable in scientific terms. For example, the somewhat emotional reference to the warmth of wood is largely the physical reality that wood feels warm to the touch (especially when compared to ceramics and metals), which we understand scientifically in terms of dry wood's low coefficient of thermal conductivity. But there remains an aura of warmth suggestive of "friendliness." (p. 142)
>
> The psychological appeal of wooden objects develops through the interaction of two vital elements working together: nature and mankind. That wood is a direct and unchanged product of nature undeniably attracts us. In contrast, we bemoan the aesthetic loss in particle board and hardboard, or in products like rayon carpets or molded egg cartons, which are made of wood but are so transformed from the tree as to be unrecognizable. Subconsciously if not consciously, many people today resist being pushed gradually into a synthetic environment, further and further removed from nature, and they seek to retain every possible remnant of the natural world. (p. 143)

Hoadley describes an experiment he has conducted often with wood technology students at the University of Massachusetts.

> In our department seminar room we have a long walnut conference table. It is handsomely proportioned, with slightly bowed edges so the top is narrower at each end than in the middle. The table is expertly built, with a top of figured sliced walnut veneers, carefully matched. The ends and edges are neatly banded with deep strips of solid walnut, giving a plank effect to the whole.
>
> With a group of students seated around the table, I call attention to its features from the overall appearance and

design, the figure on the top and the well-fitted construction down to its general heft and resonance. I ask for a consensus on the table's merits, and the students enthusiastically approve. Then I ask, "If this is such a beautiful table, aesthetically pleasing and well crafted, does it really matter that it isn't real wood? You all *do* realize that it's actually plastic, don't you?"

The utter shock on every face reveals that indeed it does matter. The bewilderment deepens as I extol the sophistication of modern technology, which can precisely imitate the physical properties of the material, and of photographic methods capable of imitating the fine cellular detail of the wood. When I feel that the point has been driven home, I reveal my prank with the assurance that the table really is genuine walnut. After a short period of emotional confusion, the students forgive me when they realize the purpose of my deception. The group then agrees that "all things being equal" (as textbooks like to put it), there is indeed a difference between a real wooden table and a synthetic lookalike. That difference, whatever it is, is the mystique of wood. (p.145)

The mystique of wood is expressed with exquisite artistry at the George Nakashima Studios in the gently rolling hills near New Hope, Bucks County, Pennsylvania. Although George Nakashima, founder and philosopher, is dead, his wife Marion, his daughter Mira, son Kevin, and son-in-law Jon Yarnall continue the Nakashima tradition. Mira follows her father's groundbreaking design work and with fellow craftsmen transforms richly grained, rare hardwoods into expertly crafted fine furniture.

Although nearly a dozen of the world's finest hardwoods are employed in making these artistic creations, the vast majority of the wood used is walnut. Eastern black walnut (Juglans nigra), claro walnut (Juglans hindsii), and English walnut (Juglans regia) are featured in dining tables, coffee tables, end tables, chairs, rockers, benches, desks, wall cases, cabinets, lamps and accessory pieces. Often, slabs of these valuable and beautiful woods several inches thick and shaped as they come from the vertical sections of huge trees are displayed. Finished in a soft natural oil, the full lustrous beauty of these walnuts is revealed and can be compared.

Nowhere else have I seen such exquisite displays of these beautiful hardwoods. As I admired a large dining room table in natural light, I suddenly realized I was looking at nature's hologram. From various angles, the depth of view, shadings and lovely patterns shifted and changed before my eye. It was possible to look into the depth of the table top and from different angles it had an entirely different appearance.

Before he died, George Nakashima made much fine furniture but his crowning achievement may have been his Altar for Peace, which he created from a huge black walnut tree after the idea appeared to him in a dream while he was ill in the hospital. This 10.5 foot x 10.5 foot walnut Peace Altar can be seen in the nave of the Cathedral Church of Saint John the Divine, New York City.

A museum of George Nakashima's creations and showroom are open Saturdays 1:00 - 4:30. Items displayed for sale in the showroom in January 1995, included a walnut table 80" x 45" x 29" for $7,500, a small walnut Mira chair for $600, a conoid chair for $1,600, and a sled base coffee table for $2,600. Considering these as works of art and not just furniture, the prices did not seem unreasonable. Furniture is made by custom design as well. (See Directory.)

In 1988, in *The Soul of a Tree, A Woodworker's Reflections*, George Nakashima expressed his opinion of the merits of wood.

> A tree provides perhaps our most intimate contact with nature. A tree sits like an avatar, an embodiment of the immutable, far beyond the pains of man. There are specimens, like the Yaku *sugi*, a type of Japanese cedar, which in their single lives have spanned the entire history of civilized man. We woodworkers have the audacity to shape timber from these noble trees. In a sense it is our Karma Yoga, the path of action we must take to lead to our union with the Divine. Each tree, each part of each tree, has its own particular destiny and its own special relationship to be fulfilled. We work with boards from these trees, to fulfill their yearning for a second life, to release their richness and beauty. From these planks we fashion objects useful to man, and if nature wills, things of beauty. In any case, these objects harmonize

the rhythms of nature to fulfill the tree's destiny and ours. (p. xxi, introduction)

Nakashima also expressed his opinion on veneer.

> A basic decision faced by the woodworker is whether to work with solid wood or veneer. Good veneer is sturdy, light, attractive, and will not warp. Solid wood is heavy. It tends to split, shrink and swell. And it can warp.
>
> Even so, I use only solid wood, plain sawn. Why? Because for me solid wood is honest and real. The grain on the surface you see runs all the way through the wood. It isn't just glued on. Solid wood mellows with age. It weathers well. Scratches and scars can be sanded out. Indeed, marring often adds charm to a piece. Good solid wood has a permanent surface, not just a protective skin. Problems of splitting and shrinking can be solved by good design. Furniture, though heavy, need not look bulky if proper proportions are used. My choice must be solid wood over veneer, for the sake of honesty. (pp.113-116)

Honesty? Honesty preferred over the features of veneer extolled by Larry Frye when wearing his Fine Hardwood Veneer Association hat? Well, it is a free country and there is room for those who want solid wood and those who want the features offered by veneer. Would anyone want it differently?

≥▲

In Warsaw, Missouri, Reinhart Fajen Inc. employs over 65 craftsmen and manufactures approximately 60,000 gunstocks a year. The company was founded by Reinhart Fajen in 1951 in a small garage behind his house. While veneer companies may consider curly walnut a defect, Reinhart Fajen, George Nakashima, Norm Hughes, and many other woodworkers consider it a gift of God and highly desirable.

Reinhart Fajen buys all its wood in blank form, precut into specified sizes, from sawmills around a four-state area. Walnut logs less than 14" in diameter are not practical for gunstocks, because there is not enough dark wood between the usual 2" of cull wood of the heart (called juvenile wood) and the outside sapwood. The sapwood can be used in a gunstock, but is not as valuable as the dark wood. The wood of a walnut tree at ground level or below is sometimes very colorful, but it has very large pores and is generally brittle, so it is not used for gunstocks. Good gunstock blanks must air dry about three years before they are ready to be cut into gunstocks.

When a log is cut, it usually will develop cracks in the exposed end grain within hours if not sealed to prevent moisture loss. The cracks will go deeper as time goes on. Within a year an eight-foot log could be useless for gunstocks. A thick coating of paint, wax, or roof cement will prevent moisture loss and subsequent cracking from the ends. A log will also crack along the sides as time goes on and eventually make it unfit for gunstocks, especially if left exposed to sun, wind, or rain. When a tree is cut, the process of decay begins and it must be fought or the valuable log will become worthless.

The Reinhart Fajen illustrated catalog offers 11 types of grain and colors of American black walnut, nine of English walnut, four of Bastogne (Paradox) walnut, four of claro walnut, seven of maple, and seven laminated woods. With these woods they offer 70 different stock styles (see photo section). Each type of wood is carefully inspected and assigned one of seven grades. The grades are based primarily upon the amount of figure and beauty of the grain in the butt section of the stock. If the two sides of the stock contain substantially different amounts of figure, the stock is graded based upon the side opposite the cheekpiece side, which is the most visible. The extra fancy grade contains approximately 75 to 100 percent fancy figure in the butt section and costs over $600 for the custom fit and finished shotgun stock. That is for the gunstock alone!

Special selection gunstocks contain even more individual and unique patterns and are price quoted on an individual basis. In the American black walnut special selection category, Reinhart Fajen offers feathered crotch, stump, irregular stump or crotch, fiddleback, fiddleback curl, and broken fiddleback. These terms all serve to describe the patterns in the wood.

In the Reinhart Fajen catalog, feathered crotch is described as: "the result of nature's knitting together two forks of a tree to prevent them from splitting apart. The curl or hard cross figure usually forms a spreading feather pattern across highly colored grain." Fiddleback curl is described as: "containing a curl pattern which is usually pronounced and extremely bright. As the angle of light on the wood changes, deep reflections of light actually ripple beneath the surface." Pretty heady stuff, but correct. Nature's hologram.

Without doubt, the very best, most economical, rewarding and interesting way to see black walnut wood is to visit a Collectors Arms and Militaria Gun Show. These shows are numerous and widespread over much of the United States. Displayed at a good gun show will be rifles, shotguns, and handguns of all periods of history, and nearly all have black walnut gunstocks or grips. For a few dollars, one can see hundreds of the finest walnut gunstocks and the work of craftsmen over the past three centuries.

Composites and synthetics are being used as gunstocks on more weapons each year. These look artificial, and synthetics are black and unattractive. Eastern black walnut is no longer what the U.S. infantryman will carry. But still, American Eastern black walnut is prized by many who pay a lot for this work of Mother Nature as cut, sawed, dried, machined, sanded, etched, stained, sealed, and finished by the hands of skilled craftsmen.

4

BLACK WALNUT VENEER

è&

"Image is everything!"

—Andre Agassi

Most furniture made in America is veneer furniture. Very thin slices of a desirable and more expensive wood are assembled into sheets, held together with tape, and then glued under heat and pressure to a less desirable and less valuable material. The resulting "sandwich" is sanded and finished just as a solid piece of wood and great care is taken to avoid sanding through the thin veneer surface. Looking at the valuable walnut veneer surface alone, it is impossible to tell if the furniture is veneer or solid wood.

The word "veneer" is used as a noun, verb, and adjective. When furniture makers apply black walnut veneer to a cheaper, more plentiful or less heavy wood, they are veneering furniture that is then called veneer furniture.

Veneering is not a new technique. Veneered items have been found in the tombs of the Pharaohs of Egypt dating to 1500 B.C. In addition to wood, ivory, pearl shell, and tortoise shell, precious metals and precious stones have been used as veneers to cover cheaper materials.

Roman furniture was magnificent. Roman taste despised solid block pieces as being essentially barbarian and crude. Pliny, Rome's greatest historian, even went so far in his admiration of the veneerer's art as to denounce the over-use of gold and paint "because it covered up the beauty of the veneer."

In the period 1660-1668, oak was largely used for the base wood with walnut, then considered a semi-precious wood, used as veneer. Until the early 1700s, only the wealthy could afford pieces of veneered furniture. However, improved machines for cutting veneer and improved glues have made veneer furniture cheaper and increasingly popular. Ninety percent of furniture made now is veneer furniture, which ranges from the least to the most expensive furniture.

By using only a thin slice of the more valuable black walnut wood, black walnut veneer furniture can be manufactured at less cost than solid black walnut furniture. It is also lighter because of the lighter woods used under the thin veneer cover; the grand piano could not be constructed in any other way. Various woods can be combined to create interesting colors and intricate patterns. It has become fashionable to combine several types of woods to make dining room table tops and other furniture pieces, which offer a collage of several veneer woods. Walnut veneer is one of many woods used this way, and is often combined with unusual hardwood species from Asia, Africa, and South America.

ॐ

Beside the Blue Ridge Parkway, on a high meadow on the northwest edge of North Carolina, resides the town of Spruce Pine and the Henredon factory complex. Henredon is the largest maker of black walnut veneer furniture in the world. In Plant #6, 100 workers carefully cut, piece together, and tape several types of veneer wood into various patterns and shapes for further processing into table tops, desk tops, dressers, beds, stereo cabinets, etc.

Henredon buys veneer from veneer companies that specialize in slicing quality logs into long, thin sheets of veneer. One log 20 inches in diameter can furnish over 600 sheets of veneer 1/36-inch thick and the width of the log at the point from which it is cut. Henredon buys these veneer sheets in bundles called flitches from the veneer companies or from middlemen.

Henredon is using less black walnut veneer now than in the past. This is credited to fashion changes and the increased cost and reduced quality and availability of black walnut veneer. However, the cost of even the finest and most expensive veneer is a small fraction of the total cost of a piece of fine furniture.

Henredon makes some of the more expensive furniture in substantial volume and is respected throughout the furniture industry for style, design, and craftsmanship. Henredon recently offered four complete lines of black walnut veneer furniture. Two of these lines have been discontinued and the company is making less black walnut furniture now than in earlier years. Henredon still makes the Pierre Deux French Country line, which features "naturally finished black walnut veneers in an attempt to capture and reveal all the beautiful colors and patterns of black walnut." This line consists of about 50 different pieces of furniture and "replicates some of the most exquisite furniture from 18th century France."

However, another Henredon line using black walnut veneer is not recognizable as black walnut. The Versailles line is described in the company brochure as:

> French court furniture . . . brought home with the lyrical power of poetry . . . designed to give ceremony to the everyday . . . creating dazzling realms that engage the imagination. This is Henredon's Versailles, Louis XV furnishings for dining, bedroom and accent.
>
> Versailles offers the familiar French silhouettes dressed in newly confident finishes. Walnut veneers are treated to a medium dark sherry and to a light bisque - the bisque clearly exploiting the natural luminosity of the grain. Both finishes are aglow in the warmth of walnut, a wood worthy of the aristocratic designs.

The color bisque, it is red-yellow or cream. Sherry is dark maroon. The brochure continues:

> At Henredon finishing a fine piece of wood furniture is an art involving many hand operations. Our craftsmen stain, pad, antique, highlight and shade—all by hand. And while we are very careful to formulate each finish and

apply it to exacting standards, variations in color will occur. Woods vary in their acceptance of finishing materials. Hands vary in their touch.

Baker Furniture of Grand Rapids, Michigan has used walnut veneer, off and on, for 50 years. Less than 10 percent of their line is in walnut at the present time. The reason they gave for this small percentage was that, "the fashion for the last 10 years has been heavily weighted to mahogany, consequently that has been our major usage. There is a fair amount of walnut veneer exported to Europe as European walnut has become very scarce and consequently very expensive."

The Karges Furniture Company, Inc. of Evansville, Indiana, has made beautiful and expensive veneer furniture for 150 years. With only about 100 employees and emphasis on design, the company won the American Society of Interior Designers Product Design Award in both 1988 and 1989. A Karges brochure states:

> The world offers up a bounty of lumber with romantic names like Tulipwood, Bubinga, Avodire, Cocobolo, Paldao and Purpleheart. These and many others provide inspiration for Karges cabinetmakers. Wood's inherent beauty can be lost in mass production. But when each piece is crafted individually, a skilled finisher can accentuate grain pattern with glaze or padding . . . giving full play to qualities unique to the figure of that particular wood. The process of bringing wood to its greatest possible beauty cannot be hurried.

Natural is not good enough. *Enhancement* is needed. Pliny might object, but Andre Agassi would love this. "Image is everything."

But Henredon and Karges are not alone in "improving" on the color of natural black walnut. Steelcase, the largest maker of *office* furniture in the United States does so as well. Despite the misleading company name, Steelcase branched into making office furniture of wood and wood veneer in 1972. They have become the largest maker of wooden office furniture in the industry.

Steelcase Woods Products Division is located south of Asheville in Fletcher, North Carolina. Unlike Henredon and

Karges, Steelcase does not assemble and glue their own veneer faces but buys them already assembled from veneer companies and middlemen who furnish Steelcase with specified faces in about 20 sizes. Over 40 percent of its wood office equipment is finished with black walnut veneer. White oak, cherry, and mahogany make up the remainder in nearly equal amounts. Steelcase is the largest consumer of domestic veneer faces in the nation.

Steelcase produces black walnut veneer office furniture in red, black, green, or any other color the consumer wants. This furniture is not recognizable as black walnut veneer, but it is. Thus, the customer can have walnut, which has long denoted status and authority, in the color of his choice. "Image is everything." But what does it say about taste? Is red- or green-stained walnut really black walnut? If you want red or green furniture, what difference does it make which species of wood is stained?

A Steelcase executive showed me a door that from a distance appeared to be wood, but upon closer inspection proved to be a composite material made of wood. It was to wood what hamburger is to steak. "We can turn out thousands of those and they will all look *exactly* the same." he boasted. "If the price of veneer gets too high, we can make this and won't need veneer. We can use nearly any kind of wood in the composite and make it look like walnut or whatever you want. We can produce the type grain we want and the color we want and it will have the texture and feel of real wood." Isn't modern technology wonderful?

The business executive may want black walnut for the status and authority it denotes, even if it is red or green, composite or veneer, but the preferences of some homeowners are even less precise. Many consumers are confused about wood.

❧

Francis A. Bishop, of O'Neill and Bishop, a fine furniture store in Haverford, Pennsylvania, is now 80 years young. He has sold furniture along the Philadelphia Main Line since 1925. Bishop said:

To most people, wood is wood. I've seen very little black walnut lately. It is scarce and expensive. We have a Henkel-Harris secretary in solid black walnut reduced 50 percent and have had trouble selling it. They may have the wrong finish, but people see it as a dirty chocolate. They haven't heard of black walnut. People know very little about furniture and buy what is available, what is presented, and what they hear about from friends.

At O'Neill and Bishop, each piece of furniture had a hand-written tag indicating the type of wood. In North Carolina and in most furniture stores this is not done. In many cases, you cannot tell one wood from another. Bishop attributed this failure to specify wood type to the Federal "truth in advertising laws." He said they could not call veneer furniture "walnut" any longer, when only the veneer was walnut. After all, only a small percentage of the entire piece of black walnut veneer furniture was real walnut. For that reason and others, wood type is no longer emphasized. Design, color, and manufacturer are featured.

Bishop said, "When you go to buy a suit, you don't go looking for a wool suit, but for color, style, maker, etc. The type material and wool content will be secondary." But by law, clothing does carry a label indicating the percent of each type material included. Furniture does not.

Looking at a piece of furniture from a distance, it is often hard to identify the type of wood used. Various stains are available that can give almost any wood the color of walnut. Cherry and mahogany can be finished to look like walnut, and walnut can be finished in several shades and will often look much like cherry or mahogany. Carefully finished natural walnut has a luminescence and grain pattern that is unique, beautiful, seldom seen, and little appreciated.

Since 1934, the Fine Hardwoods Veneer Association has conducted a furniture woods survey at the biannual North Carolina Furniture Show. In 1934, over 42 percent of the furniture was black walnut. Twenty years later, in 1954, walnut was only 14 percent of the total. Walnut rose to almost 30 percent from 1959 through 1964, and then began a long, steady decline. By 1971, it had dropped below 10 percent, and by 1992, it was 1.3 percent.

In 1971, the Fine Hardwoods - American Walnut Association conducted its annual survey of bedroom and dining room furniture. They identified seven finishes on black walnut: dark, walnut brown, fruitwood brown, light brown, grey-brown, tan, honey, and red-brown dark. Walnut came in any finish you wanted, except the bisque, red, green, and black since developed by Henredon and Steelcase.

In 1971, of the various woods used in dining room and bedroom furniture, walnut was 9.5 percent, mahogany 2.7 percent, cherry 7.9 percent, maple 10.2 percent, oak 11.1 percent, butternut .1 percent, pecan 14.2 percent, birch 1.9 percent, pine 5.9 percent, prints and plastics 22.8 percent, painted 9.7 percent, other solids 1 percent, and other veneers 3 percent. Twenty percent of *other woods* were finished in walnut brown, and 56.3 percent of the walnut was finished in walnut brown.

In the 1970s, to promote black walnut and combat the finish confusion, the American Walnut Manufacturers Association was issuing and promoting two tags for furniture. One tag said "SOLID WALNUT," and one said "all veneers and solids of GENUINE WALNUT." Fighting imitations, the association issued many tags, but often they disappeared when they reached the retail level. The tags are no longer issued, and as Bishop says, "Wood is wood."

By 1992, walnut furniture was only 1.3 percent of the total, when it had been 42 percent in 1934, and perhaps 85 percent in the 1700s. Was the age of black walnut furniture in America over? Would black walnut return? Tastes and fashions change constantly.

To American consumers, black walnut may be out of fashion, wood may be wood, and style and image may be more important than substance, but in Europe and Asia, black walnut is in great demand. About half the veneer-quality black walnut logs harvested in America are exported as logs. Of veneer-quality black walnut logs cut into veneer in this country, about 60 percent are trimmed for export. Together as logs or veneer, about 80 percent of top-quality American black walnut timber is exported. On a percentage basis, black walnut may be the most successful United States export!

Atlantic Veneer Company in Beaufort, North Carolina, is probably the largest veneer company in the United States and the world. Atlantic has 600 employees in a huge plant on the Atlantic Coast, larger plants in Brazil and others in Europe. The company both slices veneer and exports logs.

Al Huff is Vice President and head log buyer for Atlantic and has been for the past 18 years. Huff explained his business.

> Our plant runs on red oak. We cut about three to four percent black walnut and prefer quality black walnut trees 26-27 inches in diameter. Trees 90 years or older make the best veneer. We prefer trees from Indiana and parts of Ohio and Iowa. We rarely buy walnut from other states because of bird peck and color. I have a load of logs here now from Indiana, but they are Kentucky walnut. I've phoned my buyer who is flying down. I want to point out to him why these are not Indiana logs. If you can't tell the difference between Indiana and Kentucky black walnut logs, you shouldn't be in this business.
>
> We hear about black walnut by word of mouth. You can spot them driving the back roads. If the owner will not sell, that is O.K. We wait. The owner will eventually die and the heirs will sell. We don't want curly black walnut, but clear, straight grain and the right color. The furniture people want thousands of duplicates. When they put out a catalog, they want all the pieces to look like the pictures in the catalog.

When I commented that uniform veneer, as he described, would be easier for imitators to replicate artificially, he agreed. But, he said, "They always need something to compare it to. There will always be people who want the real wood."

Obviously, Huff enjoyed his work and was a storehouse of interesting stories. He said:

> In 14 years of buying logs, I've only been taken one time. A seller offered a lot of trees. We bought and began cutting. We had five trees down and a guy wanted to know what we were doing. A lawyer in Nashville owned them. I sent our lawyer to see him, offer three times their value and settle. Now! He accepted the value

we said. The original seller, who did not own the logs, got eight years for larceny.

Huff started his work life in the Tulsa oil business, then ran a sawmill in Iowa for 17 years. One day while watching television in Iowa, he noticed they had had 45 days of below zero weather.

"Why am I here? I don't have to do this," he thought. He dreamed of an island in the South Pacific where he had been in WW II. He found an 11-page booklet on Western Samoa that had copra and cocoa beans; Robert Louis Stevenson was buried there. He went to Western Samoa and stayed five years. After two weeks, he was bored. He went to Potlatch, (a wood products company) told them of the hardwoods in Samoa, and together they built and operated a sawmill. "When you get sawdust in your cuffs, you can't get it out." said Huff.

Mr. Huff explained that they want veneer strips 7' 4" for doors and 8' 6" for panels, which are big production items.

> We buy more eight, nine, and ten foot logs than any other lengths. Europe is our biggest customer now. I don't have a timber buyer with a forestry degree. It takes at least four years' experience to make a good buyer. Most of my buyers have little or no college education. In school they do not spend enough time in the woods. Ninety percent of the time we can detect log rot or defects in standing walnut. We use metal detectors to look for metal in logs on the site and here in our mill.

Huff had known about some big walnuts in New York state near the state forest and finally got a call four years ago to go bid on them.

> Ah ha! Finally got them, I thought. I flew up personally to see them. The owner was 72 to 73 years old. The trees were three to four feet in diameter. The owner told me he was only selling five. What? Only five! Yes. His wife had complained about the nuts staining the driveway. He was retiring. His sons and daughters did not need the inheritance, so he had given the rest of the trees to the New York State Forest.

In another situation in Iowa, a large parcel of walnut was offered in a river bottom.

It was a good area. Fifty miles south and it would have been no good. The trees were well walked around indicating much interest, but only two companies had the money to buy the parcel, which would require almost $500,000. I was asked by the owner of Atlantic, 'Do we need it?' No. But if Atlantic doesn't buy it, I will. And I won't sell it to Atlantic Veneer. We bought them.

Huff said he did not believe in the importance of genetic inheritance in black walnut.

The most important thing is soil and climate. We (Atlantic Veneer) don't buy land or plant trees, but we should encourage more tree planting. Everything we do is wrong. We are a backward industry. When we go, our knowledge goes with us. Many in this industry want to keep what they know a secret.

Huff was deeply concerned about the threat of the gypsy moth to hardwoods.

The gypsy moth kills trees. They have killed more in the last 10-15 years than all our industry. I looked at aerial photos of Pennsylvania. It is awful, and last year they sprayed only 9,000 acres. West Virginia sprayed the whole state. The problem is only half-heartedly addressed. The caterpillars ride in here on logging trucks. We've trapped several moths in this area.

ॐ

In June 1992, north of Asheville on the Blue Ridge Parkway, caterpillars of the gypsy moth were everywhere, feeding on oak trees, crawling on the highway, dropping their waste onto picnic tables, and quickly defoliating the trees. Shreds of oak leaves blew across the road as if it were autumn. I decided to look into the gypsy moth situation. Did they defoliate black walnuts too?

I spoke with Dr. Max McFadden, U.S. Forestry Service who explained the history and progress of the gypsy moth.

In 1869, they were introduced into Massachusetts and since then have been increasing their range by about nine to 15 miles per year. You saw the gypsy moth caterpillar front moving along the Blue Ridge in North Carolina. They do not kill the trees but defoliate them and stress them. Subsequently, the tree may die from drought or disease. Gypsy moths also artificially spread by riding on vehicles such as campers or log trucks. There have been outbreaks in Oregon, Washington, and Idaho. The front now is roughly along the Western Pennsylvania-Ohio state line. We spray and try to eradicate isolated outbreak and are spraying to slow the advance to one to two miles per year.

The gypsy moth caterpillars will feed on black walnuts, but prefer oaks and other species. As the front passes, the oaks die and their population may drop by 30 percent or more. The total volume of timber does not decrease, but other species supplant the oaks. Red maple and cherry fill in the spaces left by the dead oaks.

Huff has reason for concern since his mill "runs on red oak."

In Pennsylvania, in the spring of 1992, $3.6 million in federal, state, and local funds was spent spraying 205,000 acres in 42 counties. In 1991, more than 1.2 million acres of trees in the state were defoliated, according to the state Department of Environmental Resources. In New Jersey, nearly 26,000 acres were sprayed at a cost of about $279,000. Huff again seems to be largely correct; these are only token efforts. At a cost of $10-$15 per acre, there is not enough money to spray all the forests of the northeast. Spraying only reduces the number of caterpillars and slows their spread, it does not stop them. Nothing has.

ક

Huff gave me a complete tour of his veneer mill. To produce veneer, logs are first cleaned of bark and dirt and inspected for metal and defects. Metal "S" shaped devices may be driven into the ends of the logs to prevent splitting. Logs are then immersed in huge concrete vats in very hot or boiling water to soften the wood so it will slice easier and to bring out the best color. Each different type of wood has a different *cooking* schedule. Cooking starts at about 125 degrees F, and the temperature is increased five degrees per hour until the required temperature is reached.

One recommended cooking schedule for Eastern black walnut is: 12 hours at 140 degrees F — 12 hours at 160 degrees F — 12 hours at 180 degrees F — 12 hours at 212 degrees F. Then cool for at least 48 hours and cut at 130 degrees F anytime thereafter. Often companies will cool the logs under canvas to slow the process and improve the color. This entire cooking and cooling process takes at least four days.

Worker cleans a log taken from the soaking tank at the rear prior to slicing at the Hoosier Veneer Company, Trafalger, Indiana.

Next, the logs are ripped down the middle from end to end like a banana is cut for a banana split. Lastly, each half is securely fastened into the carrier of the slicing machine at the fresh center cut. At Atlantic, ten slicing machines in a long row were slicing veneer from seven log species. The prewarmed, razor sharp, 17-foot blade is held solidly in place and the log moves up and down against the blade slicing a 1/36-inch long slice at speeds up to 100 slices per minute. It takes a solid, well-built machine to move a huge log up and down, accurately advancing it 1/36 inch each stroke at speeds of up to 100 strokes per minute.

Sliced veneer comes from the slicer one sheet at a time.

These slicing machines, and most throughout the veneer industry, are made in Indianapolis by the Capital Machine Company. Capital has been making slicing machines since 1887. Jack Koss, president of Capital and grandson of founder Louis F. Koss, was justifiably proud of Capital. He expressed his feelings this way.

> We've come a long way since our founding in 1887. But some things haven't changed at all . . . like our emphasis on quality. From the beginning, our philosophy has been to build the best . . . solid, dependable equipment, to provide the latest technology to the extent that such equipment can be serviced in remote regions, and to ensure that our dependable equipment will do the job right through years of service. And we have succeeded. Today, Capital machines as much as 90 years old are still in operation all day, every day. Our commitment to quality continues. In veneer-making machinery, we build it to last.

When I visited the Indianapolis plant of the Capital Machine Company occupied since 1904, Koss gave me a tour. The plant employs 25 skilled machinists and produces up to six veneer slicers a year. Prices begin at $200,000. Veneer slicers weigh over 56,000 pounds, and each machine is handcrafted to the specifications of the buyer. Koss explained his business:

> We like to say we have veneer machines on every continent but the Antarctic. We have about 500 slicers and staylog lathes working in the field. We've had bad times. When Dad died, we had $100 in the bank.
>
> We developed a way of heating the blade so that the initial slices would not be stained. This patented, exclusive blade temperature control reduces waste substantially. We also developed a slicer with dual independent flitch tables so that two flitches can be sliced simultaneously with thickness accuracy to 1/1000 inch with up to 80-85 cuts per minute. We also make dryers, trimming systems and a complete inventory system including hardware, software, training, and supervision.

Those who believe the United States cannot compete with foreign companies should visit Capital Machine Company. This company combines the proven methods of the past with the modern developments of today, and maintains the best of quality standards and service in the process. Koss said his friend John Grunwald at David R. Webb veneer company was Hungarian and quoted Grunwald who had said, "You could tell a man was a Hungarian if he started through a revolving door behind you but came out first on the other side." Koss said, "John thinks I'm probably Hungarian."

Koss insisted I visit Curry-Miller Veneer Company only a few blocks from his office and one of only two veneer companies remaining in Indianapolis. Of course they used Capital Machine Company veneer slicers and are so close to the source they can save on maintenance personnel. Capital Machine Company can have a repairman report to solve a problem for them in ten minutes. It may be the same man who built the slicer.

Bill Miller, president, said the company began by slicing nothing but black walnut but, like other veneer companies, was now slicing other hardwoods. He said they began slicing only for domestic consumption but now sliced for export as well. Times change, and you either adapt or die. Curry-Miller has a reputation for producing some of the finest black walnut veneer produced by any company in the trade. Their facilities were immaculate. They intend to survive, but regret that so many black walnut logs are exported.

As I left Capital Machine Company, I noticed a quotation by Robert Louis Stevenson displayed in the reception area, "Judge each day, not by the harvest you reap, but by the seeds you plant." A creed by which an admirable company has survived and served the veneer industry through four generations and for over 100 years. It is a good creed for tree farmers, too.[1]

ॐ

Back at Atlantic Veneer Company in North Carolina, the very thin sheets of veneer from the Capital Machine Company slicer enter a drying machine in exact order. In the dryer, controlled drying and sometimes pressing removes excess moisture and controls warping or rolling of the paper-thin sheets. Still in order, the veneer sheets are stacked into complete flitches and crated or bound with bands for domestic sale or further processed by trimming and bundling for export sale.

Sheets of sliced black walnut veneer being fed into a dryer at The Hoosier Veneer Company, Trafalger, Indiana.

---

[1] *Mr. Jack Koss passed away November 9, 1994, of cardiac arrest at his office, one day short of his 70th birthday. His son, Bill Koss, is the company's fourth-generation president.*

Foreign buyers want veneer trimmed of defects and sap-wood and banded in neat rectangular bundles that each contain the same number of pieces. They look at each bundle of the entire tree. The product they want requires more processing and is closer to the way it will finally be used than that preferred by domestic buyers. Since there is more processing and waste in preparing veneer for export, the price charged is higher per square foot of veneer.

Flitches of dried veneer ready for further processing at The Hoosier Veneer Company, Trafalger, Indiana.

The fact that domestic and foreign veneer buyers have a different veneer requirement immediately complicates inventory problems for a veneer company. Once veneer is processed for the foreign market, it is not suitable for the domestic market. Since about 60 percent of black walnut veneer is exported, domestic buyers see only about 40 percent of the total veneer cut in the United States. And since half the walnut veneer logs are exported, domestic veneer buyers see only 20 percent of the total veneer-quality black walnut timber.

Domestic buyers look at three sample slices from an entire flitch that may consist of several hundred slices, and will buy or not based on these samples. Some buyers visit the veneer companies, which display the three sample slices of each flitch. In an hour, a skilled buyer can reject or buy the veneer of a hundred trees. Samples may be sent to a central location such as High Point, North Carolina in the heart of the furniture makers. The sample will be displayed there for local buyers by a middleman who may represent several veneer mills. Buyers are skilled in detecting defects and are looking for the particular color, grain pattern, length, and price their company wants.

Veneer is priced based on the square feet of face. This is calculated electronically as the flitch slices pass under an electronic eye linked to a computer. The price varies with the quality of the wood and the supply. Buying veneer is an acquired skill, like many others in the entire process from forest to furniture buyer.

The Atlantic Veneer Company further processes much of its veneer by cutting and gluing slices to cheaper materials to make wall panels, door panels, and various specialty pieces. Some veneer companies do this, and others only produce veneer.

Sheets of taped veneer form a sunburst pattern in one step toward a table top.

John C. Callahan's excellent book, *The Fine Hardwood Veneer Industry in the United States 1838-1990*, published by the National Woodlands Publishing Company in 1990, describes the history of the veneer industry in great detail. After long and careful research and interviews with many still active in the veneer industry, Callahan described how this small industry of never more than 50 firms began, evolved, and survived the many economic and social vicissitudes that have occurred since 1838.

Callahan describes the evolution of the veneering process, the pioneering East Coast veneer mills, the development of coastal mahogany mills from Pennsylvania to Louisiana, Indiana's early veneer mills from 1850-1920, Indiana veneer firms established after 1920, veneer firms in other states, the veneer mills with foreign investors, the battle for control of the American black walnut resource from 1950-1970, and the veneer trade associations. It is an excellent source for anyone who wants to learn more about the veneer industry.

There are approximately 38 veneer companies still active in the United States. Each is somewhat different, but all depend heavily upon the hardwoods of the northeastern United States for their raw materials. Those hardwood raw materials are a renewable resource, but the quality and quantity of veneer logs of all species have been declining. To keep the slicers running, smaller and smaller logs of lower quality, and species formerly spurned are being consumed. If the veneer industry were an engine, you might notice it coughing and belching smoke to show the effects of running on a poor grade of fuel.

This decline in log quality and quantity became most obvious in the harvested Eastern black walnuts. By the 1960s, it was apparent that something had to be done. More and better black walnut trees were needed. Much was known about growing black walnut and the federal government had been encouraging reforestation for years, but the results were hardly noticeable. The quantity of black walnuts from plantations was tiny and the quality suspect. In addition, establishing hardwood timber stands was harder and much less assured than the successful experience with evergreen species.

The Eastern black walnut produces a rare hardwood that is valued for its color and properties in furniture, gunstocks, veneer making, and novelty items. In addition, it produces a nut with a delicious meat and a shell that is the black diamond of the organic world. Before we look into what has and is being done to produce more and better trees, we will review walnut nuts. Many people are nuts about black walnut nuts.

5

NUTS, HUSKS, SHELLS, AND MEATS

ða

In Pittsburgh's Schenley Park, a squirrel was seen regularly to reach a forepaw up into the back of an outdoor vending machine, pull out a candy bar, and run away and eat it. (He preferred bars with nuts.)

—*Squirrel Book*, Eugene Kinkead

I once read that General George Washington, while drinking in a pub, would entertain friends and demonstrate his digital strength by cracking walnuts between the fingers of his bare hands. Although I've never seen this specified, surely these must have been English walnuts. Perhaps he was making a political statement. I doubt that even General Washington could have cracked an Eastern black walnut with his bare hands. They are truly hard nuts to crack, as was Washington.

In less happy times, on December 19, 1777, after losing the battle at Brandywine Creek to the south, and control of Philadelphia 20 miles to the east, both to the British) General George Washington pitched his campaign tent (marquee) under a big black walnut tree at Valley Forge. At Valley Forge, Washington's discouraged men fought the elements, sickness, and hunger for six months. They survived, and the army was reborn.

One of General Washington's campaign tents can still be seen at the Valley Forge Visitor's Center and Museum, but the original black walnut tree is gone. In 1975, to commemorate the bicentennial event, the Valley Forge Signal Seekers planted, at the original tent site, another Eastern black walnut tree which, in the fall of 1994 was 7.5 inches DBH and about 30 feet tall. The walnut tree was reborn, too. At the tricentennial in 2077, the walnut tree should be nearly as large as the original under which Washington pitched his tent.

&

Most walnut nuts sold retail in the U.S. that are called walnuts or light walnuts are English walnuts and are products of the California nut industry, which produces 99 percent of the industry total. A few English walnuts are grown in Oregon and Washington, but most come from the San Joaquin and Sacramento Valleys of California. These English walnuts are actually *Juglans regia* L., also called Persian walnuts, because they originated in Persia (now Iran). A frost-tolerant strain of *Juglans regia* was found in the Carpathian Mountains of eastern Europe and is grown throughout the range of the Eastern black walnut. It is called the Carpathian walnut.

Nuts moved from Persia to Greece and then to Rome, where they became known as "Jovis Glans" (Jupiter's acorn, or nut of the Gods) and the term "Juglans" is derived from this Roman name. The term "English" applied to the Persian nut came about from use of English trading ships to transport the nut in commerce around the world. Introduced into England around 1562, the nut was referred to as "wahlnut," an old English word for "Welsh-nut." Welsh was a term used to indicate a person not of Saxon origin— hence, "wahlnut" or foreign nut. England never developed a nut industry, but America did when the nut was introduced into California around 1770 by mission fathers.

Historically, the most important native walnut species in America was the *Juglans nigra* L. or Eastern black walnut (sometimes called American black walnut) native east of the Rocky Mountains. It was frequently found near pre-Columbian camps. It was perhaps planted but undoubtedly harvested by native Americans for centuries.

Archaeological finds in the Great Lakes region indicate that Indians there ate walnuts 2,000 years ago. The kernels were extracted, dried, pounded into a powder as fine as flour, and mixed with water to form a delicious and nutritious "milk." Black walnuts, chestnuts, and hickory nuts were an important part of the pre-Columbian diet and were stored in quantity for winter use.

Early immigrants from Europe found and used the Eastern black walnut in the "New World." Donald Culross Peattie, in *A Natural History of Trees of Eastern and Central North America* (1963), describes early nutting parties.

> In a more innocent age, nutting parties were the most highly prized of children's festivities in autumn throughout the eastern forest belt, and though butternut, hickory nut, hazel nut, chestnut, chinquapin and even beechnut and king nut were gathered, walnut was the favorite. The charm of the nutting party, of course, did not depend solely on the subsequent pleasure of cracking the rough shell and extracting the delicious, oily sweet kernel from its intricate walls. It derived much from the tingling autumn airs, the flaming forest leaves, the wild telegraphing calls of the crows, and the shouts and games of the other children. (p. 122)

Also native to America was the *Juglans hindsii* (Hinds black walnut), found in a few scattered groves in Northern California when white settlers arrived and which was used extensively in the English walnut industry as rootstock to graft English walnut cultivars.

Other native walnut species in America are *Juglans californica* (California walnut), the native southern California black walnut; *Juglans microcarpa* (Little walnut), native to Arizona, New Mexico, and Texas; *Juglans major* (Arizona walnut), native to New Mexico, Arizona, and Colorado; and *Juglans cinerea* (butternut or white walnut). These are of minor commercial interest.

ॐ

The *Juglans* family is an ancient family. Remains of walnuts have been found in geological deposits of the Cretaceous period, which places walnuts on earth nearly 100 million years ago. In a 1912 issue of *The Plant World*, reprinted in the *Annual Report of the Smithsonian Institution*, 1913, Edward Berry documented the history of the walnut family through study of geological deposits. He wrote:

> It is readily apparent that the modern segregated species of *Juglans* are isolated remnants of a once world-wide distribution and that the glacial epoch was an unimportant incident in their history on the North American continent, while in Europe it greatly restricted the range of *Juglans regia* and altogether exterminated one or two additional species of the walnut. From the Upper Pliocene of Germany, nuts have been collected in the lignite deposits, which are exactly like those of the existing American species *Juglans nigra*.
>
> The genus *Juglans* is apparently one of the earliest of the still-existing dicotyledonous genera to appear in the fossil records, leaves suggesting it having been found in the Middle Cretaceous. It is well represented in the fossil flora from the base of the Upper Cretaceous to the present, the former horizon furnishing at least seven species. There are about 25 Eocene species of walnut well distributed over the Northern Hemisphere. *Juglans nigra* has been found in the late Pleistocene in Maryland and in the Pleistocene river terraces of Alabama.
>
> We should not forget the sentiment which attracts to a family of such magnificent trees, a family with an ancestry, as we have just seen, extending back millions of years to a far-off time when the dominant animal population of the globe was the uncouth reptiles of the Cretaceous, a time when the evolution of the mamilia had not yet been wrought out, and when man was a far-distant promise, not even hinted at in the teeming life of that age. While we can never hope to bring back the primeval forests of our ancestors, we can use the intelligence which has been slowly acquired through the ages in conserving these magnificent tree relics of bygone ages. (p. 331)

ۿ

In October, during the 1940s and 1950s, when I rode a school bus in Indiana, young boys would often board the bus with fingers yellowed as if from a serious nicotine habit of at least two packs a day. They had been picking up walnuts, and yellow-stained fingers were the sure sign of it. The nuts were run through a hand-cranked corn sheller, washed, and dried. The nuts were then cracked and the meats selected to provide handy snacks and flavor for baked goods.

It has become the custom in many churches to hold a short Children's Worship before sending the younger congregation to Sunday School. Children are called to the front of the church where the minister teaches them a short lesson. At one such service, the minister began, "What is it that lives in the woods, climbs trees, and has a soft, furry coat?" No answer. He continued, "I'll give you a hint. It also has a large, fluffy tail and likes nuts for breakfast." No answer. He tried again, "Surely someone knows." Finally a small girl responded, "Well I know the answer must be Jesus, but it sure sounds like a squirrel to me." And, to me too.

Squirrels are nuts about nuts, but how do they locate them? When a walnut falls from a tree in the fall, it quickly goes dormant in response to fall temperatures in a process called stratification. During stratification, the nut meat changes from large-celled storage tissues to metabolically active densely-packed tissues. Live, moist walnuts emit metabolites that squirrels locate by smell.

Here in Pennsylvania, I have placed a fresh can of walnuts on my workbench at the back of my garage, left the garage door open, and returned 30 minutes later to find a squirrel on top the workbench in the can of nuts. I can only conclude that a squirrel can smell metabolites from a walnut at a distance of at least 25 feet. When I have walnuts in my garage and the door is down, they gnaw away the rubber strip at the bottom of the door to get in. Squirrels are quickly drawn to walnuts.

Professor Walter F. Beineke of Purdue University related an incident in which he had gathered black walnuts in the bed of a pickup truck and driven onto the campus in West Lafayette, Indiana, where he had not noticed squirrels. He parked the truck and returned 30 minutes later to find three squirrels enjoying a party in the bed of his truck.

Squirrels are the most intelligent of rodents, as anyone with a bird feeder will attest. If you have squirrels and a walnut tree bearing walnuts and you intend to pick up walnuts, you must be fast, or you will be last. Squirrels (much like self-employed people with large mortgages) work long, hard days starting at first light and ending at dark. They even work in bad weather and have been observed to bury over ten nuts in an hour, each in a separate hole. Working steadily at this rate, a squirrel can bury several thousand nuts during the three-month nut season. Considering the number of squirrels at work and the number of nuts they can bury per day, the annual number of nuts buried beneath the soil is mind-boggling.

Squirrels will carry a nut farther than a city block, but usually they stay closer to the tree. Except for squirrels and man, the only other force that moves walnuts is water. Walnuts that fall into water with husk intact may float and be carried downstream by currents. When the husk is removed, a good nut will not float. When the husk rots, good nuts do not move, except with the assistance of squirrels and man. This accounts for the small, tightly packed groves of black walnut trees, their frequent location near stream beds, and the limited natural distribution of the tree.

The question of which came first, the chicken or the egg, continues to stump most of us. Berry, quoted earlier, proved that the walnut came before the squirrel. Since walnuts were on earth long before squirrels, it is a mystery to me how they were dispersed over much of the Northern Hemisphere millions of years before squirrels evolved. What force moved the nuts? Was it one of the "uncouth reptiles" Berry mentions? Did they just move gradually over millions of years by the breadth of branch spread? Does the unbelievable hardness of the walnut shell have something to do with this? Why did the shell of the walnut evolve such extraordinary hardness? Darwin argued that natural selection was the cause of diversity, and we can conclude that natural selection influenced the black walnut toward very hard shells, but why?

Perhaps it was to allow the nuts to survive some creature that ate them—such as turkeys. Turkeys? In 1992, while driving along the banks of the Mississippi River, I stopped for coffee and began talking with a gentleman who told me there were many wild turkeys returning to the area. He said they ate acorns and I agreed. He said they ate hickory nuts and I thought—maybe. He said they ate black walnuts and I was very skeptical. Turkeys eat black walnuts? Come on!!

Well, maybe they do. Scott Weidensaul has written more than 20 books on natural history and in *Mountains of the Heart, A Natural History of the Appalachians* published in 1994, he wrote:

> We humans are poorly fitted for converting mast to meat, but other animals excel at the task. Wild turkeys swallow walnuts and hickory nuts whole, the nuts pass to the powerfully muscular gizzard, where they are crushed as easily as a child crumples a wad of paper. The power of a turkey's gizzard is remarkable. In one experiment, a turkey crushed metal tubes that required five hundred pounds of vise pressure to collapse; in another, an eighteenth-century Italian scholar fed surgical scalpel blades to captive turkeys. The blades were reduced to harmless steel filings in sixteen hours with no ill effects on the turkeys. Turkeys will scratch up enormous patches of forest floor seeking mast, their work looking like that of children armed with rakes. (p.60)

Like coyotes, beaver and deer, wild turkeys are returning to the range of the black walnut. They may pose some threat to walnut reforestation but turkeys are not the only threat—or the first.

A creature called *Purgatorius* lived 70 million years ago and was a contemporary of the dinosaurs. It was one of the first mammals (it descended from the reptiles), and some believe it gave rise to a line of creatures that would slowly lead to a new and unique species: *Homo sapiens*. Reconstruction of the few remains found of *Purgatorius* indicates a kind of small rat with a long tail that lived in the trees and ate leaves, bark, and grains. Perhaps it ate walnuts! Some drawings of *Purgatorius,* which are of course subjective, closely resemble our squirrels.

Squirrels do not venture far from trees unless they are very brave or very hungry. A squirrel in open ground is unable to outrun a coyote, fox, or dog, and is vulnerable to these predators. A walnut tree isolated and remote in a field or pasture and far from other trees will be the last to attract squirrels. If you find no nuts under walnut trees in deep woods, you will have a better chance under remote trees.

Usually, the first thing a squirrel does when he picks up a nut is remove the husk by biting it off in small pieces and leaving them in a pile. He may eat the nut promptly or set off with it in his mouth looking for a place to bury it. After finding the perfect spot, the squirrel digs a small hole about three inches deep while holding the nut in his mouth. He rams the nut into the hole and roots the dirt back into place with his snout. Then he covers it with grass or leaves and pats it down, much like a dog hides a bone or a cat his — well, you know. Like you, squirrels prefer to dig where it is easy and love flower beds and compost piles.

After a squirrel has buried a walnut, he may have trouble finding it. If it is a good nut emitting metabolites, he will have a better chance of finding it. One farmer planted walnuts in a field and spread walnuts on the surface of the ground around the field for the squirrels. In the spring, the planted walnuts were gone, but the walnuts spread on the ground were still there. It is probable that the nuts on the ground dried out in the sun, killing the embryo, so no further metabolism occurred. The buried nuts continued to be metabolically active all winter, producing volatile metabolites that the squirrels used to locate them.

The local population of squirrels fluctuates widely over time. In May 1990, alarmed at the number of squirrels in my fruit orchard, and knowing a squirrel will eat several peaches a day, I decided to trap and transport some to reduce the excess population at my home in Wayne, Pennsylvania. With a Have-a-Heart trap I began trapping squirrels under a bird feeder. I baited the trap with sunflower seeds and began trapping on May 25. I caught two the first day, ten the second, and six on the third day. Each squirrel was transported in the trunk of my car about three miles away across a rather wide river and released with instructions: "And, don't come back!" To return, they would have had to swim the river, which was about 100 yards wide, or cross a highway bridge.

I maintained accurate records and recorded each catch. After the first three days, during which I had caught 18 squirrels, the daily catch dropped to about two a day, but some days was as high as four. On some days I did not trap. In less than 60 days, I had caught and transported 62 squirrels all from under a single bird feeder. I quit trapping in July and we enjoyed peaches. Before winter, we had more squirrels. In the summer of 1992, I caught and transported 20 in one month and gave up. They seemed to get around a lot, and the supply clearly was endless.

Squirrels have been a "problem" in Pennsylvania since the 1700s. *Pennsylvania Agriculture and Country Life 1640-1840* by Stevenson Whitcomb Fletcher, printed in 1950, relates the following:

> About every seven or eight years, or whenever the acorn and nut crop was scanty in northern and central counties, squirrels migrated to southeastern counties in search of food. They traveled in armies numbering many thousands, devastating all grain fields on the line of march. In 1796 it was reported, "During last week several hundred squirrels per day crossed the Susquehanna from Cumberland County into Dauphin County. Some of the inhabitants who live near the banks of the river have been enabled to salt barrels of them for winter's use."
>
> Unlike other wildlife, squirrels seemed to increase rather than decrease after settlement began, since farm crops were added to their bill of fare. The General Assembly authorized counties to offer a bounty of three pence a head but this did little to check them. In 1749, the sum of 8,000 pounds in Pennsylvania currency was expended as bounties on more than 640,000 squirrels. This exhausted the treasuries of a number of counties. The minutes of the General Assembly for 1750 record, "The farmers com-

plained this year that the bounty given for squirrels had tended to their injury, for the laborers, instead of helping them with their harvest, had taken up their guns and gone to hunt squirrels, as they could make more by squirrel scalps than by wages of day labor."

Large hunting parties were organized to reduce the squirrel population. In July 1830, one such party in Crawford County killed 891 squirrels in Randolph Township. (p. 74)

Many of these were black. In one hunting party, "About 95 percent of the squirrels were jet black." Black squirrels seem to be more rare now than in the past. In 17 years, I have never seen a black squirrel in Eastern Pennsylvania. Black squirrels still live in substantial numbers in Detroit, Michigan; Blair, Nebraska; Goshen, Indiana; Bryan, Ohio; and probably elsewhere. Black squirrels are a melanistic phase of the gray species and seem to be increasingly rare. Even more rare is the albino squirrel, which is pure white and which I have never seen.

Throughout the natural range of the black walnut, there are two major squirrel species. They are the fox squirrel (*Sciurus niger*), which is often called the red squirrel, and the gray squirrel (*Sciurus carolinensis*), which will occasionally be black or very rarely white. The gray squirrel is smaller than the fox squirrel, and the two species rarely live together peacefully. Anyone interested in learning more about the habits and unusual antics of squirrels will enjoy *Squirrel Book* by Eugene Kinkead published in 1980 by Elsevier-Dutton, New York.

Despite a tremendous population of active and hungry squirrels, some walnuts and acorns buried by the squirrels escape detection through the winter and come up each spring in my flower beds and compost pile. If there is a large crop of nuts, more than the squirrels can eat, or the squirrels die, or the nut is not found for some reason, or is not eaten by a worm or consumed by rot, the nut will probably sprout and become a living tree. A hungry squirrel may dig up the nut of a sprouting tree and eat it, which may or may not kill the young tree. Although people plant some walnut trees each year, still more walnut trees result from the efforts of squirrels. It is Nature's way of looking out for squirrels and walnuts.

ঌ

Walnut trees are most visible in the fall. The leaves color earlier than most other trees and turn a distinctive light yellow. Walnut leaves often drop before the leaves of other trees, and the leaves of the walnut often drop before the nuts. A walnut tree without leaves, but bearing nuts, looks as if it has been decorated with green balls. In Pennsylvania, walnuts often begin to color and lose leaves before the end of August. In any area, not all walnut trees color or lose their leaves at the same time. This difference may be important.

The longer the walnut tree holds color in its leaves and holds the leaves, the longer the production of nutrients and the more growth of wood and the fatter the nutmeats. Some believe a tree that loses its leaves before it loses the nuts may have nuts that do not fill and meats that are shriveled and unfit to eat. Purdue University studies, however, showed no correlation between the length of time the leaves stayed on a tree and the quality of the nutmeats.

Since walnut trees are selected both for their production of valuable wood and for nuts, the length of growing season reflected by the length of time they hold green leaves still may be a valuable selection criteria. Hugh Pence of Lafayette, Indiana, has learned that applications of large amounts of nitrogen fertilizer keep leaves green and on black walnut trees longer. Does this endanger the buds when frost comes? Does rapid growth stimulated by nitrogen increase risk of damage from wind or ice? Perhaps.

ঌ

Many individuals harvest black walnuts for personal consumption, but no one knows how many individuals or how many nuts. Individual techniques of harvesting vary, but any technique involves some hard manual labor that can only be partially mechanized.

Nuts are gathered in the fall, and it is best if you do not delay, or squirrels or other people will beat you to them. Delay in harvesting may also result in meats that are discolored. Nuts are mature when pressing the husk with a finger leaves an indentation. The husk starts out green, turns yellow and then black as it gradually decays and exposes the black shell.

Husks should be removed from the shell as soon as possible. Husks left on the shell too long will cause the nutmeat to become dark and less flavorful. A good nut will separate easily from the husk, but if the husk holds tightly to the shell inside, the nut is probably unfilled and worthless.

Charles Richcrick of York, Pennsylvania, is husking walnuts with an electric-powered corn sheller.

Husks can be removed by hand, with a hand-cranked or powered corn sheller, with a cement mixer, by driving over the nuts with a car, by rolling under the foot, etc. Charles Thatcher, a chemical engineer who has grown black walnuts for 60 years, advocates leaving the husks under the walnut trees because they contain trace elements that are needed by the tree for growth and nut production. His studies indicate that constant removal of the husks from beneath the trees reduces nut production and nut quality.

Joel F. Salatin, organic farmer, in Swoope, Virginia, uses walnut husks as organic fertilizer on his perennial forages. He spreads 10 to 15 tons of fresh husks per acre on his pasture. He obtains these husks from black walnut buying stations and believes the husks stimulate earthworms, which in turn aerate and rejuvenate the soil, increasing the calcium one and one-half times, magnesium three times, nitrogen five times, phosphorous seven times, and potash 11 times.

Salatin maintains that decomposition of the husks gives off carbon dioxide, which plants require to breathe. When carbon dioxide contacts water in the soil, it forms carbonic acid, the most efficacious reagent that can be used to break minerals out of rock. Salatin says, "Many farmers experience soil nutrient deficiencies because their practices discourage an active decay, or decomposition cycle, in the soil, thereby precluding the microorganisms' ability to extract nutrients from the soil."

No matter what method is used to remove husks, gloves should be worn because the brown stain in the husks is strong and persistent. In addition, a powerful chemical called juglone is found in the husks, and juice from the husk may cause dermatitis in some people. The husk juice should be avoided, then, especially on hot, humid days. Wear gloves and a long-sleeved shirt. If you get husk juice on the skin, wash as soon as possible.

Walnut husks hold traces of a natural sedative called ellagic acid. Native Americans used walnut husks to stupefy fish. In Mississippi, where that trick has lingered, a state law bars using walnut, dynamite, or gunpowder to fish. Liquid from the husks has a remarkable effect upon earthworms. When husks are soaked in water and this water is poured into the soil, earthworms come quickly to the surface. This beats digging, and no law protects the earthworms from fishermen.

Walnut husks have long been used to form a dye to color wood, hair, wool, linen, and cotton. In earlier times, a cap of walnut husks was sometimes worn to keep hair from turning gray or to restore it to a darker color. The green husks provide a pigment that is still used in brown hair dyes.

During the Civil War, uniforms for Virginia soldiers were dyed with brown stain of the black walnut hulls. This dye did not destroy the cotton and was a fast dye. In addition, the color blended well with the landscape and provided camouflage. Tents were also stained with this dye. The dye is a "boil fast" dye, and is still used when making some homemade quilts and blankets and to demonstrate methods of early colonial life.

Walnut bark and husks help stop the flow of blood and were used for this vital purpose during the Civil War. The oil from the nutmeats was thought to stop the pain of toothache, and salves made from the oil and from the leaves were not uncommon. Juice from the husks was sometimes rubbed on the skin to cure skin infections and ringworm, and it was believed that leaves spread around a house would repel fleas. Tea made from walnut bark peeled from roasted branches was thought to remove bile from the intestines. It probably did!

Husks may contain husk maggots, which are white. These maggots increase the rate of decay of the husk. While the maggots are revolting, they do no harm to the nuts if the husks are removed promptly and the nuts washed soon after.

After the nuts are husked, they should be washed. Nuts can be washed in a bucket in small quantities or in an old washing machine when larger quantities are involved. Nuts that float can be discarded, because the kernel will be shriveled and worthless. *A good nut will not float.* This test gives you an early check of the quality of your nuts and will indicate if continued husking and washing is worthwhile. A large percentage of nuts should sink in water, or you are wasting your time. Thorough washing and stirring will clean the shells and give you an attractive walnut.

After they are washed, nuts should be dried in a shaded and well-ventilated area for several weeks. After drying, nuts should be stored in a cool, dry area until ready to crack. It should be noted that after nuts are allowed to dry and cure, they *will not germinate if planted*. If you plant old dry nuts saved from last fall, they will not grow, because the embryo has died.

Just before cracking dried nuts, soak them in hot tap water for 24 hours, drain the water off, and soak them again in warm water for a minute. Then dry and crack quickly. This soaking will soften the kernel, reduce shattering, and make kernel extraction easier.

After husking, Charles Richcrick washes the black walnuts.

Black walnuts are the hardest of all nuts to crack, which limits their appeal for many people. Some standard nut crackers will caution, "Not for use with black walnuts." Walnuts can be cracked with a hammer or in a bench vise. But with either it is difficult to crack the nut and not smash the meat.

With a hammer, if you do not strike hard enough, the hammer will merely bounce into the air, and the nut will remain intact. Strike too hard and the meat is mush. Since nut shells vary in hardness, cracking black walnuts with a hammer is very difficult and hard on nerves and fingers. After cracking, kernels are removed with a pick or by cutting the shell away from the kernel with a pair of small end nippers or diagonal pliers. This is tedious work.

ᴥ

Recognition of these problems has stimulated the development of many specially designed mechanical black walnut nut crackers. These crackers offer speed and reduced damage to the kernel and your fingers. Three black walnut crackers stand out from the many.

"The World's Greatest Nut Cracker" was invented by Lawrence Hunt of Hartford, Iowa, who patented it in 1982 for a fee of $400. Hunt was cracking black walnuts one day with a hammer and hit his thumb (a common problem with the hammer method) and resolved to do something about it. Despite being limited to a fourth grade education, Hunt began studying the cracking of black walnuts and decided the secret was to stop the cracking at just the right moment to avoid crushing the kernel.

Using an old bottle capper as a model, Hunt designed a device that allows the nut to be held firmly in place by two beveled surfaces. These beveled surfaces place pressure on the thinner side walls before putting pressure on the ends of the nut. Also, no matter what the size of the shell, the crushing movement is limited to only 3/16 of an inch and no more. This, he claimed, would allow the user to crush the shell but not the kernel and would deliver 90 percent of the kernels in whole quarters.

Hunt had iron castings for his Hunt's Black Walnut Nut Cracker manufactured of malleable cast iron in lots of 50. He maintained accurate sales records in this manner. In ten years, he sold 4,150 of these hand-operated devices, which weigh 15 pounds and were priced at $45.75 each. Later, he introduced an electrically powered nut cracker, which was poorly received. He made three and only sold one. He said the price of $185 "turns people off."

Black walnut nut cracker invented and patented by Lawrence Hunt, Hartford, Iowa.

Hunt received radio and television coverage in Iowa for his invention and was the subject of several magazine and newspaper articles. When the story of Hunt and his nut cracker was aired on television, the station received over 1,000 telephone calls. As a result, he received three packages of letters and sales rose sharply. Hunt advertised in the *Walnut Council Bulletin* but said, "There is no substitute for free publicity."

At the end of the year in which his story was reported on TV, Hunt's story ranked number one among the year's top news stories in Iowa. As a result, he was given more coverage and appeared on other TV stations as well. Later, he was at the Iowa State Fair selling nut crackers when he was again interviewed and given more publicity. Hunt said, "You have to have something good to sell. People will come to you." In Iowa, people take their walnuts seriously.[1]

---

[1]*Mr.Hunt passed away in 1993 at the age of 85. Three of his grandchildren continue to offer his nutcracker (See Directory) now priced at $67.50.*

ঌঌ

Gaston G. Fornes of Charlottesville, Virginia, was 84 in the fall of 1992. He remembers his boyhood in eastern North Carolina when he began cracking black walnuts with a hammer on a rock at the age of five or six. "Hands and clothes were stained and the kernels were in tiny pieces. Lots of time was needed to get a cup of kernels for fruitcakes and cookies."

Fornes related the story of how he came to invent and patent his "Squirrel Tooth" custom-built *Nut Kernel Extractor*, "Conqueror of the Black Walnut."

In my adult life I became a mechanical engineer and majored in machine design with skills in machine shop, die-making, drafting, welding, mechanisms, etc. I moved to the University of Virginia's Engineering School as Professor of Machine Design. Here gray squirrels and black walnut trees abound.

When I first studied engineering, I told my father that I was going to be able, one day, to design machines and he said to me, "If one day you can design a device, hand-operated, that can shell the black walnut, then I will say that you are a real machine designer." After coming to Virginia, I began to design and build rough models each fall. Over a period of 20 years and eight experimental models the *Extractor* was worthy of its U.S. Patent.

A squirrel can "extract" the entire walnut kernel by making only four small holes in the black walnut shell. One fall morning I was riding by the edge of one of Charlottesville's city parks and saw a fresh-killed, very large gray squirrel. I tossed the dead squirrel into my trunk and later dissected the head of the squirrel. I measured the bite opening of the teeth and the dimensions of the cutting teeth. The cutting teeth, two upper and two lower, are kept sharp with the upper tooth sliding across the lower tooth. As the gnawing proceeds, the teeth are sharpened. The teeth would grow too long if the squirrel could not cut (gnaw) hard-shelled nuts, wood, bark, roots, etc.

The *Extractor* design used these findings in sizing the *Extractor*; and the tooth shape in sizing the nippers. A squirrel's tapered tongue is over one inch long, and the squirrel can curl the tip of the tongue to extract bits of the nut kernels. The *Extractor* is hand-operated, is made of aluminum and alloy tool-steel. It weighs about 1/2 pound and will fit inside the pocket of a work coat. It has a scoop-pick and a pencil housed in the hollow handles. It has a safety-ring and Neoprene handguards together with a sliding pin-lock to hold the nippers closed when not in use.

With the *Extractor*, I can shell a well-prepared black walnut in 15 to 20 seconds and extract the kernel in five large pieces — one heart and four lobes. The shelling is usually done in my den where I can listen to the radio or T.V. and the shell-bits do not mingle with the kernel pieces at any time. There is very low noise and one hand applies the shelling force. I provide an instructional manual that explains the new process. This is a precision device and is custom-built for persons who greatly enjoy a hand-tool that helps overcome a difficult task. It permits a high-grade, high-quality product worth about $8 per pound free from nutshell bits.

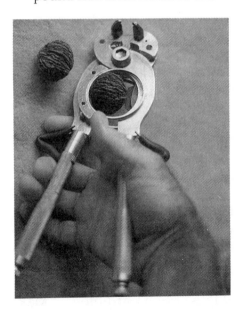

Black walnut "Extractor" invented and patented by Gaston G. Fornes, Charlottesville, Virginia.

Fornes' *Extractor* is different from Hunt's nut cracker in that it does not crack the nut, but cuts or shears the shell much as a squirrel does. The nutmeats are removed in whole sections and the shell reduced to carefully cut sections that could be reassembled.

Fornes sells his *Extractor* for $150 plus $3 shipping and handling. The 19-page instruction manual contains 13 carefully drawn diagrams and helpful hints on proper use of the device. Both *Extractor* and manual are unique.

The Missouri Dandy Pantry of Stockton, Missouri, offers a "Get Crackin' Nutcracker" for $30.95, which they recommend and say, "needs no adjusting, is free standing and of all-steel construction." Walnut nut crackers are many and diverse, but these three are unique. (See Directory.)

꜅

Dry nuts may be stored in a cool, dry place for a year. (Remember that they won't grow.) Eventually they will turn rancid. Rancidity is potentially one of the more serious quality problems facing any item with a high oil content. The precise cause of rancidity is not understood, but it appears to involve reaction to oxygen in light. Nutmeats stored in plastic bags or glass containers and frozen will keep at least two years without loss of quality.

Walnuts are high in protein and fat when compared to other nuts. Black walnut nutmeats contain 20.5 grams of protein and 59.3 grams of fat per 100 grams of nutmeat. They are concentrated energy with 628 calories per 100 grams, near the highest of all nuts.

Studies have shown that eating a handful of nuts daily reduces the chance of both fatal and non-fatal heart attacks. A six-year study of diet and fatal coronary heart disease among 34,000 California members of the Seventh-Day Adventist Church found that nuts were the only food item that provided significant protection. "Compared to a person who never ate nuts, a person who ate them at least once a day had only 47 percent of the risk of fatal heart attack," said Dr. Gary Fraser, co-author of the study presented at the International Conference of Preventive Cardiology. "Making this even more significant is that a year ago we looked at non-fatal (heart attacks) and got findings that were similar," said Fraser.

The results of this study were reported in *The Nutshell*, the quarterly newsletter of the Northern Nut Growers Association. Nut growers are not an unbiased or disinterested group of readers when it comes to nuts, but perhaps they are onto something. Nuts have a lot of fat, but the right kind, or "good" fat. "They are relatively fatty, as vegetables go, but they have much more polyunsaturated fat than most of the fatty foods one could eat," Dr Fraser said.

Walnuts contain 63 percent polyunsaturated fat, which is the highest percentage of the good fat of all the common nuts. Other studies have shown that polyunsaturated fats tend to be less likely to cause coronary disease than saturated fats.

In February 1993, the *New England Journal of Medicine* reported the results of a study financed by the California Walnut Commission which demonstrated that men who got 20 percent of their calories from walnuts had cholesterol levels that were 12 percent lower. Even bigger declines of 16 percent were reported for the so-called "bad" cholesterol known as LDL. Volunteers ate three ounces of the nut per day in three one-ounce servings, either as a recipe ingredient or straight from the shell. Researchers cautioned that the walnuts were used as a substitute for other sources of fat and calories. People who add lots of walnuts to their regular diet may simply gain weight. It should also be noted that this study was made with English walnuts.

ﻸ

The *quantity* of nuts produced by a single Eastern black walnut tree varies across a wide spectrum. Studies have documented the poor yields and severe biennial bearing patterns of walnut trees. Dale T. Lindgren reported the results of one study in the *81st Annual Report* of the Northern Nut Growers Association. Information from a single 70-year-old black walnut tree near North Platte, Nebraska, recorded from 1982 through 1989 revealed the following total nut harvest each year: 9,488; 500; 1,554; NA; 0; 19,625; 130; and 440. Thus, in the eight years of observation, the annual nut harvest varied from 0 to 19,625.

Archie Sparks of Beaver, Iowa, has proposed a method to judge nut yields so that black walnut trees can be compared. He recommends that nut yield be expressed as pounds of hulled nuts per *square inch* of trunk. Trunk measurement should be made 4 1/2 feet from the ground at what is commonly called diameter breast height (DBH) by foresters. Nuts should be harvested soon after maturity, cleanly hulled, and weighed. If sufficient data is collected over many years, a yield efficiency curve for each walnut tree or cultivar (cultivated variety) could be constructed. But what about nut *quality*?

All black walnut trees are not alike, and the nuts are not alike either. Nine states (Pennsylvania, Ohio, Indiana, Illinois, Kentucky, Missouri, Iowa, Kansas, and Nebraska) have fairs or nut shows in which black walnut nuts are judged. Judging methods vary between states, but the basic nut quality parameters are the same. These are: nut seal, appearance, usability, size, percent kernel, percent kernel in large pieces, light kernel color, and absence of kernel defects. Surprisingly, taste is not judged in most states, but it is judged in Nebraska. A dark nut that would be rejected as unfit for consumption could still win if high in other factors. A uniform nationwide judging system for black walnut nuts has yet to be devised, but steps are being taken toward that end.

The *81st Annual Report* of the Northern Nut Growers Association (NNGA), published in 1990, carried an article by Cyril Bish, Chairperson, NNGA Evaluation Committee, titled: "NNGA Nut Evaluation: 1989 Nut Crop." Evaluated were nuts of 45 different cultivated varieties (cultivars) totaling 92 samples of Eastern black walnut nuts submitted from seven states and nuts of 41 seedling black walnut trees submitted from eight states. The formula used was: [(percent kernel) / (nut weight + seal + appearance + usability + separation + pieces + kernel size + color + veins + shrivel + taste grades)] x 100 = Final Score.

The cultivar Elmer Myer placed first with a score of 259.14, second was Emma Kay with 248.13, and third was Sparks-147 with 236.35. The scores tailed off to the cultivar Card, which was 92nd with a score of 76.30. This evaluation clearly proved that all nuts are not created equal. This is the result of only one year, and cultivar scores often vary from year to year. In choosing a cultivar, perhaps one should use the results of several years.

In the seedling category, the highest score was from a sample from Pennsylvania, which scored 233.30, and second was from Iowa, which scored 217.06. The scores trailed off rapidly to the 41st entry, which scored only 67.83. The next chapter will look at how black walnut cultivars are selected and propagated in an effort to obtain superior walnut trees that will yield better quality and a greater quantity of nuts.

ᶻᵃ

The commercial processing of Eastern black walnut nuts is now largely confined to one company. The Hammons Products Company, of Stockton, Missouri, has grown from the dream of Ralph Hammons. Hammons was released from the U.S. Navy in 1945. In 1946, he was running a small grocery, feed, and produce business in southwestern Missouri and recognized that there was an abundant crop of black walnuts in the area. He purchased three million pounds of hulled black walnuts in bags and shipped them by rail to a processing plant in Stanton, Virginia. The freight alone was several thousand dollars. The Virginia facility was closing, and he bought some of the shelling machinery which came to Missouri along with some of the people from Virginia to help install it.

R. Dwain Hammons, Ralph Hammons' son, is now president of the family owned and managed company. Dwain Hammons related his first experience in the walnut business.

> I was 12 and shoveled, washed, and cleaned the old shells we had bulldozed over a hill in Virginia. It was not cost effective, but we had found a use for the shells. They were ground into powder and sent to the Atlas Powder Company, Hercules, and DuPont, where they were used as filler in the manufacture of a slow-burning time fuse. That was the first use we found for the walnut shells, and we had only one size: 30 openings per square inch. We had no sizing then. Now we have hundreds of uses for the shells and many sizings to specification.

The first recorded commercial use of black walnut shells was probably for making charcoal. The charcoal from black walnut shells was of a superior quality, especially for use in gas masks during World War I. Since there were no commercial shell processors at that time, the government asked all farmers and roadside nut stands to save their shells for this use.

Walnut shell flour was used in the middle 1930s as a carrying agent for various insecticides, and in 1938 a patent was issued for the use of certain sizes of ground shells in cleaning furs. Walnut shells have also been embedded in rubber to recap tires, because the shells increase wear and traction on ice or snow.

The Hammons Company's spacious and pleasant offices in Stockton, Missouri, are paneled in a rich, dark-colored imitation black walnut Masonite. When I suggested to Hammons that he should have the real thing, he said, "When we get rich enough, maybe we'll repanel in real black walnut." Throughout the Midwest, very little of the real walnut wood is used as paneling. In the heartland of fine hardwoods, plastic imitation wood abounds in stores, restaurants, and offices. The real thing goes to offices in Chicago or the East. It goes to the homes of the rich or is exported to Europe or Asia. Those who appreciate fine hardwoods and have the money to pay for them get the real walnut wood paneling.

Hammons explained how they use black walnut shells.

> The shell weighs about eight times as much as the nutmeat. We've found numerous uses for the ground shells because they are very hard, light and exhibit many unique properties. They are the perfect media for cleaning jet engines, electronic circuit boards, ships, and automobile gear systems. We used to sell a lot to the automobile industry to clean pits and blemishes from metal before it was electroplated, thus reducing the need for chrome, but that market has gone along with the chrome. Other markets have replaced it. Eastern black walnut shell is nontoxic and dust-free, and it can be used on plastic, aluminum, and soft alloys. Used as an abrasive, it leaves the surface smooth without scarring.

Another market which uses our shells is the oil well drilling business. Our *Oil Patch* is used widely in oil well drilling for lost circulation material in making and maintaining seals in fracture zones and unconsolidated formations. The paint industry uses Hammons' Eastern black walnut shell for new plaster-effect paint. Paint contractors report that paints and varnishes mixed with this light-bodied agent are far superior to ordinary sand paints. It covers plaster, wallpaper, brick, and wallboard, where it conceals surface cracks and gouges. The paint goes directly over taped and filled joints, and the surface can be repainted with flat wall paint if desired.

And, black walnut shell is still used to manufacture explosives as a filler in dynamite. It is compatible with other materials and works well in this application. The shells are used in glue and wood cements. Last, but not least, blackwalnut shell is ideal as the gritty, rough agent in soap, cosmetics, and dental cleansers. All this from the *waste material* father had shoved over the hill in Virginia in 1946.

⅋

Technically, black walnut shell has so many uses because it has a very high modulus of elasticity. That is, it resists deformation. The elasticity (capability of a strained body to recover its size and shape after deformation), of Eastern black walnut is phenomenal. Measured in pounds per square inch, the modulus of elasticity of black walnut shells is 170,000. That compares to only about 10,000 for pecan shells, peach pits, cherry pits, olive seeds and coconut shells.

Black walnut shell is an extraordinary product of nature. How it evolved to be so hard through natural selection is a mystery, but Hammons is glad it did. What was a waste product in 1946 has become a large share of Hammons' business. In fact, it probably is the margin of profit, without which the whole commercial black walnut nut business would fail. Without the value of the shell, commercial nutmeats for candy or ice cream might not be available.

Hammons buys nuts from wild Eastern black walnut trees growing in 24 states. The vast majority of nuts are bought in only ten states: Missouri, Kentucky, Tennessee, Virginia, Ohio, Indiana, Illinois, Iowa, Arkansas, and West Virginia. It is not yet feasible to harvest the wild black walnut nut crop mechanically. Thus the company depends upon many individuals picking up walnuts under wild trees in competition with local squirrels. Yields per tree are often low, the annual production from any one tree variable, and the total annual nut crop dependent on weather and other factors. So, it takes a huge effort on the part of many people and some luck for Hammons to obtain the large volume of nuts the company requires each year.

Tom Rutledge, a sincere and earnest young man, manages the nut harvest for Hammons. Rutledge covers 24 states and bought 12 million pounds of hulled walnuts in 1991, 18 million pounds in 1992, and wanted more in both years. The 1992 crop was the third scant year in a row. Hammons needs nuts. Rutledge explained:

> This fall, in order to meet our demand for nutmeats during the holiday period, we may have to dry mechanically nuts of the 1992 season. You can't buy nuts if there are none. We had our best year in 1982 when we bought 50 million pounds.

Rutledge explained how he gets 12 to 18 million pounds of black walnuts.

> We survey the area in June and July to estimate the size of the walnut crop. It seems to depend a lot on the amount of rainfall in both the current year and the preceding year. With the sales department, we determine what we will pay and sign contracts with about 400 collection agents in the 24 states.
>
> There once were five companies buying walnuts for commercial processing, but we are the only one left. We deal with middlemen, such as feed mills, lumber yards, hardware stores, and grain elevators, who collect walnuts for us from clubs, schools, and individuals. We own about 400 patented mechanical hullers, which we deliver, service and maintain for the middlemen. They collect the walnuts, hull, and bag them in bags we furnish. We pick up hulled nuts or pay freight to deliver them here to

Stockton, Missouri. We paid $8.00 per hundred pounds of hulled walnuts in 1991 and will in 1992.

Hammons sold nearly all the 1992 black walnut crop before the summer of 1993. In 1993, with a goal of buying 30 million pounds of nuts, Hammons raised the price paid for hulled black walnuts 25 percent to $10.00 per hundred pounds. They also hired a promotion company, raised their advertising budget, and increased the number of hulling machines and buying stations. It worked, and in 1993, Hammons bought 32 million pounds of walnuts.[1] In 1994, they bought only 21 million pounds.

On the west coast, a large crop of English walnuts was bringing $40.00 per hundred pounds at buying stations. However, the English walnuts are much lighter, and a buyer gets more nut meat per pound.

To Hammons, all walnuts are created equal and worth $10.00 per hundred pounds hulled. However, the hobbyists who grow the superior cultivars know all walnuts are not equal and believe they should be paid more for superior nuts. Most will not sell their superior nuts to Hammons for $10.00 per hundred pounds. Occasionally, Hammons pays up to $12.00 per hundred pounds for nuts from a black walnut plantation. Better nuts should bring a better price.

Grain, eggs, milk, and most commodities are graded and a higher price paid for a quality product. Why should superior walnuts not receive a higher price than average walnuts? If Hammons could develop a walnut grading system which was acceptable to these hobbyists it would encourage them to grow and furnish better walnut nuts to Hammons and further the development of a domestic Eastern black walnut plantation industry. Hammons has been unable to obtain all the black walnuts it wants from wild black walnut trees and has planted a plantation of its own. Paying a premium price for premium black walnuts would encourage more planting of cultivars in plantations.

---

[1] *Economists will recognize this as an example of "elasticity of supply." When price was raised 25 percent, the supply of walnuts rose by about 100 percent, i.e. the supply was "price elastic."*

The price of $10.00 per hundred pounds barely compensates for the labor of picking up "free" nuts. The landowner or plantation owner receives nothing for his product. A higher price for walnuts may be required before walnut plantations of size are planted to grow nuts.

Tom showed me one of the hulling machines developed by Hammons. Painted bright yellow and about a five-foot cube, it was a heavy-gauge steel wire cage in which a knobby rubber tire driven by an electric motor rotates. The walnuts rub against the tire and the steel wire, with the husks going one way and the cleaned nuts another, where they are bagged and ready to ship to Missouri.

Bagged walnuts under cover can be stored for over a year or until the squirrels get them. Even though 1991 was a sparse nut year, Hammons still had bagged walnuts stored under cover to be processed when I toured the facility in March 1992. Red squirrels were raiding the storage facility and seemed enthusiastic in the activity. Squirrel heaven is in Stockton, Missouri.

ò▲

The shelling plant reminded me of a feed mill. A truck load of bagged walnuts was being delivered and fed to the cracker. The noise of cracking walnuts was substantial. Walnuts are bought at about 30 percent moisture and cracked at about six percent. If they are too high in moisture, they must be dried first. When Hammons buys walnuts they buy a lot of water, which they don't want. Hammons pays the same price without regard to moisture, and this is another area where grading could be beneficial to all.

Nuts are cracked mechanically in a rolling mill by forcing the nuts between steel rollers. Then the meats are separated from shells. Currently Hammons uses a device that holds the meats on metal pins and releases the shells. Hammons purchased an electronic technique from Indiana Walnut Products, West Lafayette, Indiana, when that company went bankrupt. That technique uses an ultrasonic sound system to separate the meats from the shells. Hammons has not used the electronic technique but continues to use the metal pins. The separation of shells from meats is one of the most difficult and important steps in the processing of black walnuts and one where more technology may eventually be applied.

The separated shells may be ground immediately for one of their many uses or stored in a large warehouse pending later grinding. Walnut shells can be inventoried almost indefinitely. Shells are ground into several grades of fineness, sometimes mixed with pecan shells or apricot pits and bagged in 50-pound bags for shipment.

The nutmeats are segregated by size into five groups by running them over sizing screens. Then, nutmeats are sent single-file between rubber rollers through an Ultra-Sort 800 machine, which studies each nutmeat with an electronic eye and based on darkness decides if a kernel passes or fails. The lighter colored nutmeats are selected and the darker nutmeats rejected by a puff of air. Poof, poof, poof, at high speed, the nutmeats are sorted. Black walnut nutmeats in five-gallon buckets are everywhere being moved from place to place and machine to machine as they proceed from cracking, to separating, to sizing, to selection for darkness, to visual inspection and then to the bag.

The rejected dark nutmeats become animal feed. Mixed with other ingredients and pressed into pellets, this feed is marketed to cattle and hog feeders. Chicago meat packers were said once to use all of the hog but the squeal. Hammons has learned to use all of the nut but the husk, and they are working on that. Another company collects some of the husks at the time the walnuts are husked and squeezes out the husk juice for further processing, primarily into dye.

The next step for the sized and electronically selected light nutmeats is a visual inspection by up to 17 workers who feed the nutmeats over a belt they speed control. These workers make the last inspection for shells among the meats and for dark-colored meats that did not get a "poof." If you have ever bitten into a walnut shell when eating a piece of candy or cake, you know how important it is to segregate the shells from the nutmeats. That super modulus of elasticity plays havoc with bicuspids and dentures. After this last human inspection, nutmeats are bagged and ready for shipment to walnut retailers, ice cream makers, bakers, candy makers, or to you.

ॐ

Donna Hammons, wife of the company president, manages Missouri Dandy Pantry from a small retail store, office and shipping location handy (next door) to the offices and processing facilities of Hammons Products Company. Responding to an increased demand for black walnuts by mail, the Missouri Dandy Pantry was formed in 1979. The Pantry offers a large selection of nuts, candies, and black walnut wood products. They publish several catalogs annually and a book of black walnut recipes (see Appendix II and Directory).

When Donna learned that I was from Wayne, Pennsylvania, she remarked that she had just received over a hundred calls from Pittsburgh. The Pittsburgh newspaper's food section had carried a recipe that required black walnut nutmeats, and gave the Missouri Dandy Pantry phone number. It pays to get free publicity, just as Lawrence Hunt had learned in marketing his nutcracker.

Brian Hammons, lawyer, son of the company president, and company nutmeat sales manager, explained how the company markets nuts.

We only sell five percent of our volume through the Pantry, but it is growing. We sell about 25 percent through retail stores and 70 percent to industrial users such as bakeries and ice cream makers. Ice cream is a big item. I've heard black walnut ice cream is a top flavor in Birmingham, Alabama, and Kansas City, Missouri. The taste seems to be regional. People who like black walnut *really* like it. It has a full, rich, aromatic flavor that stands up well. *Everyone* likes chocolate-covered black walnuts.

Rebaggers buy from us and repackage with their own names. If you buy black walnuts from a retail outlet, no matter whose label is on the package, we probably processed them first.

Brian showed me several packages of walnut meats and explained that they were attempting to determine which package had the greatest appeal. He seemed to be leaning toward a package with a black border with BLACK WALNUTS in large black letters. Brian continued.

Our biggest demand period is the Thanksgiving and Christmas holiday season. Some stores feature nuts in the produce section and these bags are designed for them. You may find nuts in the regular nut department but you could also find them at times in the produce section as a special. We would like to have more nuts. We'll have trouble meeting the demand this holiday season.

&

I later found some black walnut ice cream at a Baskin Robbins retail outlet in Danville, Illinois. It did have big pieces of black walnut and a full, rich, aromatic flavor. But the flavor was *not* available at my local Wayne, Pennsylvania, Baskin Robbins. Why not? I wrote the company to find out. Kathie Bellamy, Baskin Robbins consumer affairs representative replied.

Although we're known as the home of 31 flavors, we actually have more than 650 flavors in our flavor library! It's a real challenge for us to rotate flavors in and out of our stores so everyone's favorites are available from time to time. Black Walnut is a rotating flavor on a national basis for at least two months a year. However, it is a special regional flavor in our Mid-American area and more likely to be found there year around.

In December 1992, I found some black walnut ice cream at a Baskin Robbins retail outlet in Freeport, Bahamas. I asked the dipper if they always had black walnut. "Yaaas maaan. We always have it, but not all the time." He understood Baskin Robbins.

Meadow Gold Dairies Inc. makes black walnut ice cream in Des Moines, Iowa, which is distributed to stores in the Midwest. I tasted some at Amana Colonies, Iowa, and it was good stuff. Edy's Grand Ice Cream of Oakland, California, produced some black walnut ice cream on a limited basis in 1992, and distributed it in the Midwest and East coast areas. I was surprised to find some in Lake Worth, Florida. But sales were discouraging and Edy's has discontinued the flavor. In Nashville, Indiana, a homemade black walnut ice cream was offered, but it was a bit heavy on the ice and light on the cream. If you like black walnut ice cream, check often with your Baskin Robbins outlet, move to the Midwest where black walnut ice cream is popular and available, or make your own. If you want to make your own, there is a recipe in Appendix II.

❧

Steve Rutledge, brother to Tom, has been with the Hammons Products Company ten years and manages the walnut shell marketing activity.

We have found many uses for the shells and keep finding more. As a non-pitting abrasive, walnut shells can't be beat. The secret is that when they are ground they have a diamond shape no matter what size and they hold that shape. They were used to clean the Statue of Liberty several years ago and have been used to clean many monuments and statues. (In 1993, the statue of Freedom atop the United States Capital was removed and cleaned with black walnut shells.)

The walnut shell does not scar, pit, or scratch due to its hardness and weight ratio, and it is non-absorbent. We've found it can be used to separate crude oil from water. There are many uses in the adhesive industry. It is used as an extender in wood glue, in particle board and wafer board. Some manufacturers use walnut shells to make novelty items in a molding process that produces an effect that looks very much like real carved wood.

Our biggest customer is the General Supply Agency for the U.S. Navy. They may have six coats of paint on a ship and six colors. They can blast down to the color they want with black walnut shells. I've heard it saves up to $150,000 per ship or submarine. NASA uses walnut shells to clean exterior surfaces of space shuttle solid rocket boosters. In tumbling applications, walnut shells are used to polish ink pens, jewelry, shell casings, and nails.

Jim Jones manages the Hammons Products Company's black walnut plantations. Jim is a tall, rangy product of an Ozark farm 100 miles south of Stockton, Missouri. There were 28 in his 1960 high school class. He studied engineering and forestry at the University of Missouri and joined the

Peace Corps to spend two years in western Venezuela. You immediately know when speaking to him that he is a sincere man with a purpose and that he wants to do something worthwhile. His office at Hammons is filled with books, and the floor is piled high with the materials of his trade. It is a working office. Jim is a farmer — a farmer of trees.

Jim Jones, in Hammonds Products Company's Sho-Neff Plantation, Stockton, Missouri. Note spacing of trees and compare with Pierson-Hollowell plantation shown on page 207.

For 18 years Jim has worked to develop Eastern black walnuts in plantations that will yield superior walnuts on a more predictable basis than the wild natural walnuts that are the erratic and unpredictable source of Hammons' raw material. Jim has proceeded steadily and methodically toward this objective and has accomplished much, but is not yet finished.

The Hammons Products Company's Sho-Neff Plantation is northwest of Stockton. The farm consists of 790 acres of which 380 acres have been planted to over 50,000 Eastern black walnut trees rowed 20 feet x 40 feet and pruned free of lateral branches to a height of about 10 feet. Two tall towers hold instruments connected to computers that record wind speed, wind direction, temperature, humidity, and other factors. This data helps Jim determine the effect of these weather factors on nut yields.

The yearly record of walnuts collected from each tree has confirmed the lore of walnut collectors. Some trees do consistently yield more than others and some yield nothing. Some have not yielded one nut in 18 years. A few are averaging over 300 nuts per tree over a five-year period. Nut quality is evaluated along with quantity.

From his records on 1,800 trees, Jim has selected 27 worthy of further consideration. These 27 walnut trees are being propagated by grafting to ensure genetic continuance and are then planted in Hammons' plantation. Hammons is in the process of obtaining patents on their first selections. It will take eight to 10 years for these trees to yield their first nuts and the nut crop will be light for several more years. Black walnut cannot be hurried and the time required for production exceeds the patience of most humans. Jim is a patient and persistent man.

Jones also oversees the Forestry and Land Management Division of Hammons Products Company, which planted, under contract for others, 450 acres to trees in 1992. Much of this is Conservation Reserve Program (CRP) land for which landowners will receive financial assistance from the Department of Agriculture for taking the land out of conventional agriculture production and planting trees. The service Hammons offers includes planning, establishing and caring for new plantings, as well as improving existing wild groves. The Hammons division works with various state and national agencies in conducting research to improve knowledge about black walnut trees, and it conducts educational workshops and seminars to pass along that knowledge to landowners for practical application.

Jim has done extensive research on agroforestry, which is the growing of trees and an agriculture crop on the same site. Black walnut trees have been grown on a wide spacing with crops of wheat, corn, milo, soybeans, or orchard grass and red clover grown between the rows. This system permits more efficient use of high-value land while waiting for walnut trees to grow and lowers the market risk through diversification. It also offers earlier cash flow while the young walnut trees are growing and before nuts are ready to harvest. As the trees mature, the nut yield should increase, but shade will reduce the ability to grow other crops.

Attempts at economic analysis of black walnut plantation enterprises have been frustrating. One major problem is the large number of assumptions about costs and revenues and the long time frames over which these assumptions must act. The lack of examples and concrete evidence of success have delayed and slowed any movement to plant large acreages of black walnut plantations.

Hammons conducts a pioneer effort on faith and goes where others fear to go. Jim Jones and Hammons have made a major investment of time and resources toward advancing the knowledge of black walnut plantations. It remains to be seen when or if their investments will pay.

ও

In addition to squirrels, individuals for personal use, and Hammons Products Company, tree nurseries need walnuts each year to plant for seedlings. Tree nurseries get the majority of their nuts from the same source and thus compete with the others.

The Illinois Department of Conservation has two tree nurseries. One nursery is near Topeka in Mason County, and the other is in the Anna-Jonesboro area of Union County. At these two tree nurseries, they produce seedlings for private and government reforestation projects throughout the state of Illinois. Because the number of commercial seed sources was limited and the cost of nuts high, Illinois developed a program to buy nuts from individuals.

At 23 district offices of the Division of Forest Resources, net bags are furnished to collectors who return the bags filled with unhusked nuts and receive 10 cents per pound (in 1990). Each bag holds an average of 300 unhusked nuts and weighs 35 to 40 pounds. Thus the state buys about 300 nuts for $3.50 to $4.00 or an average cost per unhusked nut of $.0125.

In an article titled, "Walnut Man," reprinted in the Summer 1991 issue of the *Walnut Council Bulletin*, Fred Tetreault described "the undisputed champion of Illinois walnut seed collectors." This collector, Glenn Lentz of Knoxville, Knox County, had gathered about 90,000 pounds of walnuts for the Illinois Department of Conservation since

1969 — 44,000 pounds since 1982. Lentz had retired because of age, but had his best year in 1983. That year, he gathered more than 12,000 pounds. His production that year stands as the program's all-time record among collectors. In 1983, the department was paying $.04 per pound, and Lentz received his largest check ever: $484.00.

Collecting nuts in such volume is not an easy task. The work is arduous, hard on the back, and monotonous. In a good year, a large tree can yield 875 to 1,000 pounds of nuts. But often trees will go several years without substantial production. In some years nuts are very scarce on all trees. When production is heavy and undergrowth sparse, nuts can be raked and picked up from piles, but when nuts are fewer or ground cover is heavy, they must be picked up individually, which is a back-breaking chore.

The Indiana Department of Natural Resources also operates two tree nurseries. In March 1992, I visited the Vallonia Nursery about 100 miles south of Indianapolis. The nursery supervisor, James R. Wichman, sat at his desk in a coat in his very cool office going over shipment records. He described nursery operations.

> We buy seed from the public and pay $2.50 per bushel unhulled. We have a Hammons hulling machine they have loaned us. After hulling the walnuts, we float them and plant them. Floating nuts (about 20 percent) are rejected because they are unlikely to grow. We want sinkers.
>
> The Conservation Reserve Program (CRP) has been a big factor to increased demand. We are operating at capacity, and this year demand will exceed supply. We furnished about 300,000 black walnuts a year until the late 80s. One year we did one million. Now we are back to about 450,000 at both nurseries.

Paradoxically, the CRP program may have had the effect of reducing the number of Eastern black walnuts grown at the Indiana nurseries. Wichman explained.

> The CRP program has stimulated demand for all species of trees. Much of the land being planted is wetlands and the demand for suitable species has reduced

our ability to grow enough black walnuts. We produce about 30 species of trees and five million trees between the two nurseries. We try to maintain a balanced inventory. In 1993, we will allocate black walnut seedlings on a lottery basis. We will have about 328,000 black walnut seedlings, and many more will be requested. Our price for walnut seedlings will be $.13 each.

The two Indiana nurseries shipped 5,193,268 trees in 1991, and of those, 563,075 were black walnut seedlings. The nursery operates at a break-even cost/revenue basis by statute. That means the revenue that comes in covers all the direct costs going out. The number of trees they are able to grow each year depends upon the allocation of funds from the Indiana State Budget Agency.

The tricky part with all budgets is who or what covers the overhead and long-term investments that are required. It is difficult and costly to expand and/or contract production. If the CRP program were to end, the demand for many species would be reduced but the production of Eastern black walnut seedlings could expand.

Walnut seedlings growing in Ohio State Nursery near Zanesville, Ohio.

Of all the seedlings bought at Indiana state nurseries, 78 percent are planted by private landowners, 20 percent are planted by industry and two percent are planted by public agencies on public lands.

Still, the squirrels plant more. Only a small percentage of the annual walnut nut crop is harvested by man, and the remainder is left to the squirrels. Many suburbanites look upon the nuts as a nuisance in their lawns or driveways. They rake walnuts, pick them up, and throw them away. Then, they drive to their local grocery and buy packaged English walnuts, which are considered by many to be inferior in taste and nutrition to the Eastern black walnuts.

If squirrels had cars and money, they might do the same. The English walnuts are easier to crack, have a higher meat-to-shell ratio, and are heavily advertised. Squirrels would become spoiled by the easier-cracking English walnuts. They might become fond of chocolate chip cookies and glazed donuts. They would grow fat and lazy, and their teeth would grow long. They would probably stop eating the harder-to-crack Eastern black walnuts and then stop planting them. Eventually, there would be no more black walnuts and squirrels would be dependent on West Coast suppliers for their nuts. Sad for squirrels and black walnuts both. But that is about what we humans have done.

We have become more dependent upon the English walnut growers and less reliant on our native Eastern black walnuts. English walnut growers often call their nuts walnuts as if there were no other nut called walnut. Many people do not know the difference between an English walnut and an Eastern black walnut. Many do not know what they have falling onto their own properties. Squirrels know.

And the people of Spencer, West Virginia, know as well. Spencer, in Roane County, is home of the West Virginia Black Walnut Festival, which began in 1954. That year, Henry Young's sale of two million pounds of local black walnuts provided incentive to celebrate the bountiful black walnut harvest. The festival (celebration begins on the second Thursday in October) has grown from a one-day event that drew an estimated 15,000 people, to a four-day event that welcomes approximately 75,000 people and now includes a parade, live music, entertainment, band and majorette competition, carnival, arts, crafts, agricultural exhibits, gospel music, antique car show, black powder shoot, 5K nut run, football game, and the all-important Black Walnut Bake-Off. The baking contest features cupcakes, candies, or cookies in alternating years. *The Black Walnut Festival Cookbook* features prize-winning black walnut recipes from the festival's founding in 1954 through the 1991 event. (See Appendix II & Directory.)

·

Despite the enthusiasm of the people of Spencer, West Virginia, the number of companies processing Eastern black walnuts for commercial sale has declined to only one. Black walnut nutmeats are not easy to locate in many local grocery stores. Products containing black walnut are rare outside the Midwest. Many people have never experienced the taste of Eastern black walnut and some are being fooled.

In January 1994, in Santee, South Carolina I found a chain store offering "Chocolate Black Walnut Fudge." When I commented that I was surprised to find black walnut fudge in South Carolina, the clerk said, "Well, we use only black walnut flavoring and English walnuts. Do you know how much black walnuts cost?" "As a matter of fact, I do," I said. I elaborated and obtained the address of the home office in Michigan. I later wrote the company to tell them such false advertising and misrepresentation was unethical. They did not reply. Why could they not use the real thing? Why fool people with ersatz black walnuts?

People who have never tasted real black walnuts are the poorer for never having done so. The squirrels benefit from our ignorance and neglect, but we benefit from the trees they plant.

Some hobbyists appreciate the Eastern black walnut and have been working to improve the quality and quantity of nuts walnut trees produce. Others understand the value of black walnut wood and veneer and are striving to improve the growth rate and form of this most valuable native American timber tree. Can only God make a tree?

6

CAN ONLY GOD
MAKE A TREE?

ஃ

*The greatest service which can be rendered any
country is to add a useful plant to its culture.*

—Thomas Jefferson

In *The Harvest of the Years* (1931), Luther Burbank with
Wilbur Hall described the impact that the work of Charles
Darwin had on Burbank's thinking. Burbank wrote:

> I have in mind the influence on me of the greatest
> scientific thinker of our age—the man who changed the
> whole meaning and language of science, Charles Darwin.
> In Lancaster I had got hold of a book of his: *The Variation
> of Animals and Plants under Domestication*; it opened a new
> world to me. It told me, in plain simple sentences, as
> matter-of-fact as though its marvelous and startling truths
> were commonplaces, that variations came from cross-
> breeding, and that these variations seemed to be suscep-
> tible, through selection, of permanent fixture in the indi-
> vidual. (p. 22)

Luther Burbank was one of the earliest and most successful plant breeders to apply Darwin's discoveries to im-

provement of plants in an effort to improve their quality and value to man. He foresaw the need for better trees. He subsequently wrote:

> Plant improvement can only be done by a man with a vision and a purpose. The principal source of man's wealth, health, pleasure, and happiness is the plant life of this planet! (All animal life depends upon it.) It must be plain that in neglecting study and culture and invention and creation in this realm we are defrauding ourselves of untold billions of wealth and untold measures of satisfaction, beauty and utility.
>
> We need trees that grow very rapidly — more rapidly than those we have now. We need those that produce lumber — durable lumber, and lumber for different uses, whether for building houses or making ax helves. There are various uses for very strong and fine lumber, increasing all the time. (p. 35)

Working in California, Burbank developed improved varieties of flowers, plums, apples, tomatoes, and many other fruiting and ornamental plants. In 1893, Burbank published a catalog entitled *New Creations in Fruits and Flowers*. Of this catalogue he wrote:

> The list began with the hybrid walnut, which I called the "Paradox," because it was a paradox that a hardwood lumber tree could be produced to grow so fast as the most rapid-growing and short-lived variety. The catalogue said of this tree: *The first and one of the most interesting of the hybrids produced among walnuts. Budded trees six years of age are fully twice as large, broad, and tall as Black Walnuts at ten or Persian Walnuts at 20 years of age. The leaves, which are from two feet to a full yard in length are clean-cut, glossy, bright green, and have a surpassing sweet odor resembling that of fragrant apples and as powerful and peculiar as that of roses and lilies.* (p. 73)

It sounds magnificent, and it was. It was a cross between the *Juglans hindsii* of California and the *Juglans regia* or Persian walnut, and is still used as rootstock for grafting English walnut for nut production. Although it is relatively fast growing and vigorous, it is not known to be very frost hardy or a good nut producer. It did not solve the need for a fast-growing, improved Eastern black walnut. This was, and is, a need that Burbank had identified but never filled. The words of Burbank remain true today. Much has been done, but much remains to do.

꙳

In August 1924, The U.S. Department of Agriculture published Farmer's Bulletin No. 1392 entitled *Black Walnut for Timber and Nuts.* One of a long series of government publications on this topic, the bulletin sold for five cents and reported the progress in selecting and grafting superior nut-producing black walnut varieties. The bulletin explained the term "variety" and mentioned by name six varieties offered by various nurserymen. It stated:

> The term "variety" is used here in the only sense in which it may properly be applied to cultivated fruits or nuts. It does not refer to seedling trees but only to those which have been budded or grafted. The significance of the term "Thomas," with reference to the black walnut, is relatively the same as that of "Baldwin" with reference to the apple, "Elberta" to the peach, or "Washington Navel" to the orange.

The term "cultivar" has come to be used for "cultivated variety," meaning a clone produced by some type of grafting. "Seedling" refers to progeny grown from seeds. The seedlings of nuts from cultivars are grown and studied to obtain improved selections that are reproduced by grafting and called cultivars. In this constant process of seedling selection and cultivar growth, the Eastern black walnut tree has been under improvement by hobbyists and nut growers since the first selection of the *Thomas* variety near King of Prussia, Pennsylvania, in 1881.

The 1924 Farmer's Bulletin stated:

> A considerable number of black walnut varieties have been propagated during the past years, although not many are available at any given time. Probably more were available from the nurserymen during the period

1915 to 1920 than at any other one time. Fewer varieties are being propagated now than then, not wholly because of proven superiority of some over others, but partly because of the cost of producing the trees in the nursery and the consequent high prices charged by the nursery-men, partly because of the hesitancy of many agriculturists in taking up new lines—particularly when the product is one right at home, and partly because of established records of production and profit.

Generally, this remains true today. The bulletin is describing varieties that are "discovered" among the natural black walnut population and then propagated by budding or grafting. That means all trees of a "variety" would be of the same tissue and genetic makeup *above the graft* as the "discovered" original. They would be genetic clones.

Mentioned in the 1924 Bulletin are: the "McCoy" discovered, in 1917, by R.L. McCoy in Spencer County, Indiana; the "Miller" also from Indiana; and the "Ohio" from a tree near McCutcheonville, Ohio, first propagated in 1916, by J.F. Jones, Lancaster, Pennsylvania. Also mentioned is the variety "Peanut" from Ohio, and "Stabler" from a farm in Howard County, Maryland. Of "Stabler," the Bulletin says, "It is regarded as being one of the most promising of any known variety."

Finally of the variety "Thomas," the 1924 bulletin says:

> This variety is doubtless represented by more old bearing trees in various places throughout the country than any other. It was called to public attention during the early nineties (1890s), by J.W. Thomas & Sons, King of Prussia post office, Pennsylvania. For more than a decade it was the only variety of black walnut to be propagated or disseminated to any extent. Many planters still regard it as among the leading varieties.

Seventy years later, this is still so! The Thomas cultivar was represented by six of 92 total walnut samples submitted to the Northern Nut Growers Association (NNGA) Nut Evaluation: 1989 Nut Crop. However, the highest place the Thomas variety reached was 29th. Of the other cultivars selected for mention in the 1924 bulletin, only Stabler was represented by two samples in this nut evaluation, and Stabler placed 80th.

At the 1990 Pennsylvania Farm Show, Thomas nuts were one of five cultivars named for consideration. The other four were Elmer Myers, Ohio, Stabler, and Vandersloot. At the 1993 Pennsylvania Farm Show, seven cultivars were named. These were again Thomas, Elmer Myers, and Vandersloot plus the addition of Hare, Farrington, Rohver and Sparrow. Ohio and Stabler have been dropped. Many walnut hobbyists believe other newer varieties are superior to Thomas. However, Thomas has remained prominent for more than 110 years, and more walnut trees growing in suburban areas are probably Thomas or seedlings of Thomas than any other single variety.

After more than 110 years, the Thomas variety is still one of only two black walnut cultivars (grafted trees) offered by Stark Brothers Nursery in their Spring 1992, 175th Anniversary Catalog. Of the Thomas Black Walnut, Stark says:

> This grafted tree is noted for its hardiness and abundant crops of thin-shell nuts that crack easily with plump kernels that can be removed in quarters and halves. Growing to about 65 ft., often bearing its first crop in two to three years after planting. Needs to be pollinated by another black walnut variety. Zones 5-9. Shipped after November 15th or in Spring. Two feet and up. $16.95.

Stark's other black walnut cultivar is called "Stark Kwik-Krop Walnut," which is a Boellner cultivar with the trademark name Kwik-Krop. Stark's catalog says of it:

> This grafted black walnut often produces bountiful crops of easy-to-shell nuts in only two to three years. Tree reaches 40-60 ft. For bigger crops plant with another black walnut. Zones 5-9. Shipped after November 15th or in Spring. Two feet and up. $16.95.

Two samples of Kwik-Krop were submitted to the NNGA Nut Evaluation: 1989 Nut Crop and the highest placed 35th. This evaluation was only of nut quality and not quantity.

Stark's third black walnut offering is a native American seed-grown tree that, "offers abundant, delicious crops and valuable timber grown in temperate North America. Black Walnut is trouble-free and grows rapidly, reaching heights of 60 ft. $9.95."

In fine print, Stark warns, "Many other plants, including fruit trees, may not grow if planted within 50 feet of black walnut trees."

Stark also offered black walnut seedlings for larger plantings and of these says:

> Planting native seedgrown black walnut trees is the perfect solution for unused acreage. These beautiful shade trees are valuable for lumber when grown. Select walnut logs sell for thousands of dollars. Grown trees also yield large crops of nuts. Plant them on unused portions of your land or in a row along the edge for a growing investment. Complete planting instructions come with our husky 12-18" seedlings. Bundle of 10, $24.95; bundle of 20, $44.95; bundle of 40, $79.95.

Since 1881, when Thomas was first selected and propagated, over 750 cultivars of the Eastern black walnut have been selected and named. In October 1988, William Reid, in his paper "Eastern Black Walnut Potential for Commercial Nut Producing Cultivars" submitted at the First National Symposium on NEW CROPS in Indianapolis, Indiana, wrote about these cultivars:

> For the most part, these cultivars were selected by amateur nut growers from the native population solely on the basis of nut quality characteristics. Although black walnut is not a new crop, *the growing of walnut trees solely for nut production remains the passion of backyard enthusiasts.* The commercial production of black walnuts from orchards of superior nut producing cultivars is nonexistent.
> *Black walnut is an under-exploited crop. The potential for genetic improvement in nut yield, percent kernel and kernel quality is great.* Even under the low level of selection pressure applied by amateur nut growers, cultivars have

been identified that exhibit one or more of the important genetic traits needed for further crop improvement. Genetic traits that would lead to advances in a tree improvement program include: lateral bud fruitfulness, late leafing, resistance to the anthracnose fungi, productivity and improved nut quality. (Italics added)

As to nut quality, Reid wrote:

Nut quality characteristics have been the primary focus of the evaluation of black walnut cultivars. Over 400 cultivars have been named and their nuts evaluated for nut weight and percent kernel. Nut samples are evaluated annually by many State nut growers associations. (Nine) Results from 28 years of nut evaluations in Kansas are summarized for selected cultivars in Table 1. (See below)

Table 1.
A sample of black walnut cultivars exhibiting genetic traits important for future crop improvement and their nut quality characteristics.

Cultivar	State of origin (1)	Percent kernel (2)	No. nuts per kg (2)	Notable genetic traits
Bowser	OH	30.7	65.6	High kernel quality
Clermont	OH	35.5	59.0	Productive
Cranz	PA	31.4	71.9	Lateral bearing
Emma K	IL	35.3	62.0	Thin shell
Football II	MO	30.0	43.1	Lateral bearing
Kwik-Krop	KS	31.5	58.1	Precocious, productive
Ohio	OH	26.7	64.7	Anthracnose resistance
Sauber	OH	34.1	65.6	Thin shell, kernel quality
Sparks 127	IA	31.5	64.0	Lateral bearing
Sparrow	IL	28.7	58.3	Productive
Thomas	PA	24.0	51.9	Anthracnose resistance

(1) All cultivars listed were discovered as chance seedlings of unknown or questionable parentage.

(2) Means of data collected in the years 1959-1987 by the Kansas Nut Growers Association.

Reid continued:

> Shell thickness and structure are the most important determinant of percent kernel and nut crackability. The highest quality walnuts have a thin outer shell with no internal convolutions producing into the nutmeat. The inner shell partition between kernel halves should be very thin to allow easy removal of kernel pieces. Most thin- shelled black walnut cultivars yield over 30 percent kernel. The heritability of a thin shell has not been studied for black walnut but in Persian walnut, heritability for shell thickness is high.
>
> Kernel quality and plumpness is strongly influenced by tree care and harvesting practices, but with trees receiving optimum care, wide differences in kernel quality still exist between cultivars. High-quality walnuts have light colored kernels with an absence of kernel veins. Dark colored or strongly veined kernels are associated with rancidity by consumers. Kernel color and veination are under a moderate level of genetic control in Persian walnut and a similar level of heritability should be expected for black walnut.
>
> Several currently available cultivars deserve further evaluation for their potential as commercial orchard trees. Cultivars that bear nuts on lateral branches and produce nuts with more than 30 percent kernel are the primary candidates for commercial plantings. These cultivars include, 'Cranz,' 'Football II,' and 'Sparks 127.' 'Clermont,' 'Kwik-Krop,' and 'Sparrow' have been noted for their consistent productivity and should be evaluated further. Black walnut cultivars are not widely available from commercial nurseries and initial trials will most probably be developed by *field grafting seedling rootstocks.* (Italics added.)

Note that Reid suggests "field grafting seedling rootstocks." How does one do this? Where does one go to learn more, get scionwood, or purchase young cultivars? Who and where are the experts?

Archie Sparks lives in Beaver, Iowa, and is a former two-term president of the Northern Nut Growers Association. In August 1992, he was awarded the prestigious Achievement Award at the Walnut Council Annual Meeting at Amana Colonies, Iowa.

Beaver is a small town on Route 30 in central Iowa. Like many rural Midwestern towns, Beaver has seen better days. Archie, over 75 years young, has acquired the abandoned school and grounds, several vacant homes and lots, and has planted most of these properties to black walnuts. Also, Archie is mayor of Beaver.

Archie and his son, Brian, plant the nuts of cultivars and select seedlings that show promise and reproduce these selections by field grafting. Those that perform well are given numbers and become numbered/named cultivars. It is a slow and time-consuming process that easily takes a lifetime. It is a labor of love.

Archie has been actively involved with black walnuts for over 30 years and has the trees to show for it. His Sparks #127 and Sparks #147 are only two of his selections that have consistently ranked high in nut evaluations. His numbering system is simple. The #127 is his first selection of 1972. The #147 is his first selection of 1974. He selected these specific seedlings from many others 20 years ago and has waited patiently for them to gain the recognition he believes they deserve.

Archie believes strongly in field grafting on already established rootstocks. Field grafting means it is done *in place*. He field grafts in the spring using buds selected from the variety he wishes to propagate. He starts when the terminal buds break and has a two- to three-week window of time before he stops. One disadvantage of field grafting is that it often is done in cold, rainy spring weather under difficult conditions. Timing is important.

Archie attaches a bud to a one-year rootstock (seedling) and grows a three- to six-foot tall tree in one year. He has a one-year top on a two-year root. These can be transplanted bare rooted the following year or left in place if the tree is where he wants it.

Bench grafting can be done inside a greenhouse or other building and consists of grafting scion (pronounced sign) material to rootstock, which is then planted in a pot to grow. Bench grafting may be more comfortable for people, but is harder on walnut trees.

People who bench graft don't get as cold or wet and can sit down, but the tree suffers a double shock. It must accept the graft and recover from root pruning when placed into a small pot and is at a disadvantage rootwise in growing and accepting the graft.

Archie believes his field-grafted trees will outgrow the potted bench-grafted trees in a three- to five-year period. He believes the bench-grafted trees growing in containers produce very little root growth and take two to three years to recover when transplanted to the field. Field grafting avoids this shock and the slow recovery.

Bench-grafted trees have proven to be less winter hardy than field-grafted or budded trees. Young trees protect themselves from freezing temperatures by a process called "hardening off." They harden off by returning sap, which contains a high percentage of water, downward and into the tree's root system. Bench-grafted trees have callus cells that join the rootstock to scionwood near the ground. These cells obstruct the flow of plant liquids into the ground. Bench-grafted trees may pool plant liquids above the graft where they can freeze resulting in death or injury to the young tree. Field-grafted trees have a higher graft, less plant liquid *above the graft*, harden off better, and have higher survival rates when temperatures drop quickly.

Grafting superior scion material *in place* onto superior seedlings avoids transplanting, reduces losses to freezing, should be less expensive, and should outgrow trees of other grafting methods. Nuts would be drilled or planted three to six per location but at least three inches apart. The following year, the best seedlings of the group would be chosen to receive the graft of the selected variety. Later, the most successful cultivar would be saved in place and others could be transplanted or destroyed.

I asked Archie how scion material would be managed. He wrote:

> If a nursery were to pick a tree to market, it would establish a scion bank orchard. This would be close spaced in a high-security area convenient to the nursery. These trees would be severely cut back yearly, and once started, one acre would no doubt supply more wood than is currently used. More scionwood could be cut from only

five acres than the world could use. Just to illustrate, this year I put five to six buds on one tree. I roughly measured the growth this year, and I could cut over 25 feet of wood from it with approximately five buds per foot or enough wood to bud 100 trees. The next year, it would produce as much. A tree if topworked 12 feet high has more growth than this.

I asked Archie what the rate of field grafting would be and how it should be done. He wrote:

The only figures I have on my budding was that done in 1988. Ward Mally and I, each of us 70 years old at that time, worked eight hour days for one week. We averaged one bud every three minutes. I always thought a young, vigorous,dedicated person could do one in 1 1/2 minutes. In commercial practice in the field, the most skilled person would only place the bud and tape it briefly in place to be followed closely by a taper and a third person to tie. This would result in higher percentage takes and probably fewer man hours.

Archie wrote that timing the bud grafting is very important.

Start when terminal buds break. You should be working with vigorous stocks. When about one foot of growth occurs, stop. This allows about a two week to three week period of budding in the field. When it is time to bud, get to work.

The problem commercially with field budding is our variable spring weather. In a nursery where seedlings are growing to be transplanted later, that could be solved with a cheap hoop house using plastic that need be up no more than three weeks. If you were to do trees in a field plantation, it would take a little longer because you would be moving through a larger area and climatic control would be more difficult and costly.

If I were to start a plantation for myself, I would plant three seeds in each place I wanted a permanent tree, bud graft each vigorous tree the next year, and fill in any blank spaces by transplanting from any place where I had more than one successful cultivar.

It never ceases to amaze me how gullible people are today. They seem ready to part with fairly large sums of money to people who are promising more than can be delivered. Why people do not do the ground work to become familiar with the subject is beyond me. It seems the more educated and more intelligent people are, the least likely they are to do the groundwork.

I am basically a researcher and do not propagate for sale. Because of the regulations, I do not advertise and do not ship. I dispose of surplus at my site. Here at my place, I have named five of my favorites for nut production. They are Sparks #127, Sparks # 147, Hay, Cranz and Davidson (Iowa 629). I want a tree you have difficulty seeing through. If the foliage is dense and healthy, that is an indication you have a vigorous tree.

Archie had a cut leaf Eastern black walnut that I had never seen before. It had unusual foliage much like a Japanese maple. In addition, he had several selections growing that he hopes will produce curly black walnut when cut for lumber or veneer. If so, cultivars of these will be popular with those interested in growing valuable timber. It will be a few years yet before these trees will be large enough to cut to evaluate the wood grain they produce.

Brian and Archie Sparks of Beaver, Iowa, and some of Archie's selections of Eastern black walnut.

The Northern Nut Growers Association (NNGA) has over 1,500 members (about 500 more than the Walnut Council) in 48 states and 14 foreign countries. The association is

60 years older than the Walnut Council. Nineteen papers were presented at the 1992 NNGA meeting, and none were on the Eastern black walnut. The NNGA has much interest now in chestnuts and filberts. Black walnuts are only part of the association's concern. In past meetings, much more attention was devoted to black walnut.

A joint meeting of the NNGA and the Walnut Council is planned in Indiana for 1997. Joint meetings have been held before, but members found they had too little in common. One individual who is a member of both told me the NNGA was composed of mostly retirees and hobbyists who operate on a limited budget while the Walnut Council was composed of more professional and institutional people with more money, and the two groups could not agree on either agenda or lifestyle. It seems unfortunate that the two groups cannot work more closely together to further the cause of the black walnut, even though one is interested in nuts and the other primarily interested in timber for wood or veneer.

Despite broad interest in all nuts, some NNGA members grow and select cultivars of the Eastern black walnut. These hobbyists are the source of over 750 black walnut cultivars that have been selected for various desirable characteristics over the last 110 years. Some sell or trade their cultivars.

ð

A. W. Heiman, Jr. lives in a suburb of Anderson, Indiana where most residents mow grass, but Heiman doesn't. Bill, as his friends call him, has planted his lot to persimmon, apple, walnut, and ornamental trees, and grows a small garden so there is no room for grass. Like many retirees with an active mind and many interests, Bill has more to do than time to do it. He was an automotive engineer with General Motors until recently and worked about 2,000 hours a year. Now he finds that he works over 4,000 hours at his interests and hobbies. Walnuts are only one of his interests.

Bill is a former president of the NNGA, current editor of *THE HOOSIER KERNEL*, which is the quarterly publication of the Indiana chapter of the NNGA, and was bestowed the title of "The Big Nut" at the annual NNGA meeting in Corvallis, Oregon in 1991. With the title goes a crown and necklace that are made of nuts. The crown is passed on each year from the previous year's winner when the award holder circulates among the banquet tables, sneaks up behind the nominee and places the crown upon his head. It is a light-hearted event, but being named "The Big Nut" requires years of outstanding service to the organization.

When I called on Bill in 1992, he was repairing his bicycle which, since 1970, he had ridden over 5,000 miles each year commuting from his home to his tree farms. Bill was growing black walnuts and other trees on several farms he had acquired and like most who grow trees found them to be demanding. Bill does not select superior varieties but collects the varieties of others and grafts scion material of these. Abraham was his favorite variety, but he had a large collection of black walnut varieties and a record of 482 named and described black walnut varieties in his personal computer.

What did he have in his computer? In his second floor office, Bill cleared a place for me to sit and showed me. He records the name given to the selection, the nut size, cracking difficulty, production, and comments such as place of origin and year selected. The information he has on each nut is sparse, stated in general terms, and is not precise. However, it probably is more than can be found anywhere else. Much of his information was obtained from Ray Walker of St. Louis, Missouri, who is deceased. Bill says his reason for keeping this information was a "thirst for knowledge."

ঽ

While nine states have black walnut nut evaluations, the method of evaluation is not identical, and there is no comparative record kept of the annual results, which would not compare scientifically anyway. So, what does one do if one wants to obtain and plant a superior black walnut variety to grow nuts? It isn't easy.

If a person goes to one of the major nurseries, such as Stark Brothers, he will be offered Kwik-Krop or Thomas,

Indiana Pioneer Mothers' Memorial near Paoli, Indiana.

Two of the last great black walnuts remaining in Cox Woods, Paoli, Indiana.

TYPES OF WOOD

AMERICAN BLACK WALNUT

American Black Walnut is certainly the most popular and widely used wood for gunstocks. It is exceptionally strong for its weight, and is hard enough to allow intricate carving and checkering. Best of all, it offers a wide range of different types of grain and colors to choose from.

(Edge Grain)

(Flat Grain)

Utility, Supreme & Supreme Deluxe

The above pictures fairly represent all three grades of straight grain American Black Walnut. All three grades are available in either Edge Grain or Flat Grain, as pictured. If neither is specified, we will ship Edge Grain.

Semi-Fancy

Fancy

Extra Fancy

Special Selection

Feathered Crotch

This type of figure is the result of nature's knitting together two forks of a tree to prevent them from splitting apart. The curl or hard cross figure usually forms a spreading feather pattern across highly colored grain.

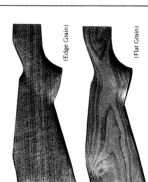

Stump

This type of figure is highly colored, with irregular streaks or large spots of curl or wave which add flowing depth to the finished wood.

Irregular Stump or Crotch

This type of figure is highly colored, with slashes and spots of figure or curl. Many unusual and beautiful pieces develop, with no common pattern.

Fiddleback

This type of figure is one of the most beautiful available, and is generally achieved by quarter sawing the log.

Fiddleback Curl

This type of figure contains a curl pattern which is usually pronounced and extremely bright. As the angle of light on the wood changes, deep reflections of light actually ripple beneath the surface.

Broken Fiddleback

This type of figure contains offset fiddleback, which forms a wide shadow stripe effect.

(Photo courtesy of Reinhart Fajen Inc.)

THE FAJEN SHOWCASE

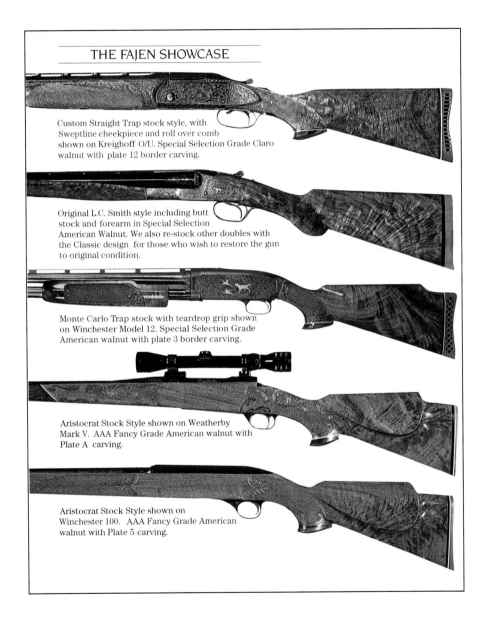

Custom Straight Trap stock style, with Sweptline cheekpiece and roll over comb shown on Kreighoff O/U. Special Selection Grade Claro walnut with plate 12 border carving.

Original L.C. Smith style including butt stock and forearm in Special Selection American Walnut. We also re-stock other doubles with the Classic design for those who wish to restore the gun to original condition.

Monte Carlo Trap stock with teardrop grip shown on Winchester Model 12. Special Selection Grade American walnut with plate 3 border carving.

Aristocrat Stock Style shown on Weatherby Mark V. AAA Fancy Grade American walnut with Plate A carving.

Aristocrat Stock Style shown on Winchester 100. AAA Fancy Grade American walnut with Plate 5 carving.

Examples of Reinhart Fajen Inc. gunstocks. Claro walnut is at the top and the others are all Eastern or American black walnut. (Photo courtesy of Reinhart Fajen Inc.)

Craftsman and fine hard-
woods dealer Norman
Hughes and a slab of
Juglans hindsii. (Photo
courtesy of Norman
Hughes.)

Black walnut chest
made to order for
Larry Frye from low-
grade lumber. Note
knots and defects
normally rejected by
craftsmen.

Examples of quality solid black walnut furniture manufactured by the Waterford Furniture Company in Lynchburg, Virginia.

Black walnut in a variety of finishes displays a wide range of color, grain, and shade.

Sheets of black walnut veneer ready for a buyer to inspect.

Stored flitches of white oak and black walnut veneer awaiting shipment at the Hoosier Veneer Company, Trafalger, Indiana.

Processing black walnut nuts at Hammons Products Company. (Photos courtesy of Hammons Products Co. of Stockton, Missouri.)

Larry Owen, Dave Mercker, and Bob Chenoweth planting trees in Illinois, May 1989.

In May 1994, Bob Chenoweth stands in the former woods pasture. Over 300 young black walnuts 3.5 inches DBH and larger have come in 18 years through efforts of squirrels. The large black walnut in the background is 59 inches DBH.

which we have noted are good, but no longer the best. Gurney's Seed and Nursery Co. of South Dakota grows and sells only native black walnut seedlings and no cultivars. Henry Field's Seed & Nursery Co. currently sells only seedling black walnuts. The only cultivar in their scion bank is Thomas and they have not produced any Thomas cultivars for several years. The limited selection of black walnuts offered by the larger nurseries reflects the decline of interest in the Eastern black walnut by their customers.

If a walnut lover wants a better black walnut, he will need to hunt out a specialty nursery or a hobbyist. The December 1994 issue of *The Nutshell*, which is the quarterly newsletter of the Northern Nut Growers Association, lists nearly 20 companies or individuals as sources of black walnut seedlings and/or cultivars.

Two specialty nurseries stand out. One is Ken Asmus', Oikos Tree Crops in Kalamazoo, Michigan, who offers butternuts, buartnuts, English walnuts, heartnuts and several cultivars of the Eastern black walnut. Asmus offers Lambs, which some believe will yield a curly grain pattern in the wood.

Another specialty nursery, established in 1985, is Nolin River Nut Tree Nursery in Upton, Kentucky. Owners John and Lisa Brittain offer 27 cultivars of the Eastern black walnut. They sell about 500 grafted black walnut cultivars each year and offer Beck, Boellner, Clermont, Emma Kay, Football #2, Ridgeway, Rowher, Sauber 1 1994, Sparrow, Surprise, Thomas Myers, Vandersloot, Baker, Baker's Ohio, Burton, Cutleaf, Davidson, Elmer Myers, Farrington, Harney, Lamb's Curly, Schrieber, Sepic No.2, Stabler, Ten Ecke, and Thomas. This is the largest selection of black walnut cultivars offered for sale from one source.

The Nolin River Tree Nursery catalog warns:

> We make every effort to supply true-to-name nursery stock. However, since we obtain some scionwood from other sources, there is a very slight chance that a small percentage of such wood could be mislabeled. Any nursery stock sold by this nursery and later found not to be true-to-name will be replaced free of charge, plus packing and shipping costs.

Proper identification of plant material is a problem with Eastern black walnut cultivars. There is no simple or easy way to tell one young walnut cultivar from another. DNA analysis of plant tissue is possible, but it is very expensive and impractical for most purposes.

Another source of superior black walnut trees is one of the hobbyists who will sell cultivars. The NNGA would be a good place to start looking for one of these hobbyist nurseries in your area. Most hobbyists offer a larger selection of black walnut cultivars than the big professional nurseries. And, a hobbyist in your geographical area should have trees that should adjust well to local climatic conditions.

૨**

When Kenneth Dooley returned from WWII in 1946, he purchased 20 acres of land in Marion, Indiana, from his father and began planting apple trees. He later planted black walnuts, pecans, hicans, hickory trees, etc. He has a large collection of trees of many varieties. Dooley, like Archie Sparks, believes strongly in the importance of rootstock, and argues that no tree is any better than its root. A superior cultivar grafted onto an inferior rootstock will not produce a superior tree. Too little emphasis is placed on selection of superior rootstock. *Field grafting onto vigorous seedlings is the only effective way of selecting superior rootstock.* If a seedling is vigorous, it has a strong root.

Dooley has a cut leaf black walnut that is 30 feet tall and bears no nuts. He says he bought it from a nursery many years ago. The one I saw in Beaver, Iowa, that Archie Sparks had, may have been reproduced from scion material from Dooley's tree.

Dooley is a modest and quiet-spoken man with a large collection of walnut cultivars. He showed me a number of trees that were crosses of black walnut and butternut or black walnut and English walnut. None of them have produced superior nuts. It is the dream of black walnut enthusiasts that a black walnut will be found, selected, and cultivated that has the thin shell of the English walnut and the flavor of the black walnut. It hasn't happened yet.

ﻬ

Scionwood is available from the Nebraska Nut Growers Association, and scionwood and grafted trees are sold and traded among NNGA members. Black walnut cultivars that have desirable characteristics get around within this small community. The nine state nut evaluations each year highlight those walnut cultivars that produced better nuts.

However, there is no way to guarantee that a cultivar is authentic, and errors do occur. Scion material may become mislabeled, a graft may be mislabeled, or a tree may die and resprout unnoticed from the root, producing a tree of different genetic material. There may be many "Thomas" cultivars that are actually not Thomas, but something else. This may be true of any of the named cultivars.

Maintaining genetic authenticity is complicated by the length of time between grafting and nut production, which tends to verify the authenticity of the tree. Some nuts have distinctive shapes and other characteristics, and a true expert can sometimes identify a parent tree by looking only at the nut. There do not seem to be many true experts.

Despite over 110 years of selection, the perfect Eastern black walnut has yet to be selected. The ideal is a tree that produces heavily every year nuts with a thin shell that cracks easily and yields a fat, delicious meat. Some selections have some of these characteristics, but not one has them all. And, some trees do well in one geographic area and poorly in others.

With the exception of Kwik-Krop and nine Purdue University walnut selections to be discussed later, these trees are not patented. Once a person has living material, he can reproduce it, grow it, sell scionwood, or sell grafted trees or seedlings from it. There are few rules, and because the demand volume is low, not much money is made in grafting and selling black walnut trees. There has been no incentive to refine or improve the system and no way to guarantee that one gets what one pays for when buying a cultivar. Still, these specialty nurseries or hobbyists are the best place to get Eastern black walnut trees if one wants to grow a tree to produce superior black walnut nuts.

ða

Charles Richcrick lives outside York, Pennsylvania on four acres he acquired in 1974. Richcrick gardens and grows a wide range of fruits, vegetables, and nut trees. When I visited him in October 1992, he was busy harvesting, husking, and guarding black walnut nuts from chipmunks and squirrels. However, he was not too busy to share his knowledge and enthusiasm for the Eastern black walnut. Richcrick grows 10 cultivars of the black walnut and enters his nuts in the Pennsylvania Farm Show each year where he has often won. With skill, hard work, and some luck, he could win first prize in seven cultivar classes and total prize money of $49. He advertises and sells black walnut cultivars, but not many.

Richcrick credited George Webber, who died recently at around 90, with giving him a start with walnuts. Richcrick confirmed what I have found to be common visiting with these hobbyists. All have had a mentor who gave them instructions in grafting and scion material to begin their hobby. Also, all are men of advanced age who have turned to this hobby after other work and have found it expands and enhances their later years. All seemed to be vigorous and in relatively good health. Outdoor exercise, walnuts, and an interest to keep the mind active seem to promote longevity.

Richcrick had no younger person working with him. Unfortunately, this also seemed to be common. How sad that so much knowledge and experience could be gained from him or other hobbyists by a younger person who would show interest and willingness to learn. Only Archie Sparks has a son who is working with him and shows an active interest in black walnuts.

Luther Burbank commented upon this in *The Harvest of the Years:*

> I have spent a lifetime scratching at the surface of this illimitable field; out of more than one hundred thousand separate, costly, and often bold experiments I have added more than I can count in numbers and more than I can estimate in value (new wealth) to the gardens, fields,

and orchards of the world. This is not written boastfully, but in the hope of encouraging others to enter this poorly explored and sketchily mapped territory of applied science. If I could stir even half a dozen young men or women (for it is a field in which women could compete with an equal chance and equal credit and equal achievements with men), I would feel that I had done even more than I have thus far in actual creations and discoveries. (p. 115)

ॐ

Jay Book was a school administrator who now lives on the edge of the Pennsylvania Turnpike near Hershey, Pennsylvania. In fact, I have parked my car beside the turnpike and climbed the fence into his plantation to admire his trees. He has some magnificent old black walnut trees and many young cultivars he is propagating. Book gives lessons on grafting to other members of the Pennsylvania Nut Growers Association. He sells walnut and hickory nutmeats and grows and sells cultivars of these trees. His hobby took a lot of time and has developed into a business now that he has retired from school administration.

ॐ

Charles Thatcher went to Alaska in search of adventure and gold in the 1930s. Now, he mines gold in the form of hickory nuts and black walnuts in the rolling hills south of Pittsburgh. He does not sell nutmeats or trees but showed me the most perfect nutmeats of hickory and black walnut I have ever seen. Thatcher's favorite cultivars of the Eastern black walnut were Hoffeditz, Rowher, Clermont, and Hare. His black walnuts placed very high in the 1989 Nut Crop Evaluation held by the Northern Nut Growers Association.

Thatcher and I agreed that hickory nutmeats are superior in flavor to black walnuts, but even harder to obtain. His favorite hickory cultivars are Yoder and Seas. He gave me some nuts that were delicious. Hickory nuts are rarely offered for sale at retail. No commercial firm, such as Hammons, processes hickory nuts. In March 1993, I found some hickory nutmeats labeled "shellbarks" at the IGA Shady Maple Farmers' Market near New Holland in

Lancaster County, Pennsylvania. These were offered at $5.99 per pound, which was the same price at which they offered black walnuts. I considered this a bargain. I suspect the nuts of these two species were gathered and cracked by the small fingers of Amish or Mennonite children.

&

Far away in Birch Run, Michigan, Dr. Richard Goldner has an 18-acre grove of grafted black walnuts containing about 20 different cultivars that are 30 years old and over 30 feet tall. Dr. Goldner said, "Black walnuts have no great popularity in Michigan. I have no problems with hardiness, but don't always have a good nut crop. I raise seedlings for sale and some grafted cultivars, but demand in this area is limited." Dr. Goldner mentioned the varieties Bowser, Patterson, Kwik-Krop, Emma Kay, Sparrow, Clermont, El-Tom (Elmer Myers x Thomas) and the inevitable Thomas.

&

It seems strange that Hammons Products Company began their 380-acre Sho-Neff black walnut plantation from the nuts of wild, naturally growing black walnuts, rather than with cultivars from these hobbyists who have been selecting and growing cultivars for over 110 years. Hobbyists have made substantial improvement in nut quality and quantity. Rather than start from this already-superior group of black walnut cultivars, Hammons elected to plant ordinary wild black walnuts. In effect, they have started over and disregarded over 110 years of selection and experience. Why?

In answer to this question, Jim Jones of Hammons Products Company of Stockton, Missouri wrote:

> There is a relatively long list of Eastern black walnut cultivars. However, one must be very cautious in selecting one for a commercial planting. Many cultivars have been selected with a very narrow list of selection criteria. Many have been selected for individual nut quality characteristics as opposed to a selection based on quantity of

quality nutmeats produced per land area. The latter is paramount for commercial application. I know of no older plantations of any variety other than Thomas.

Much remains to be learned about the Eastern black walnut, and plantation nut production has only just begun. It is not too late for anyone to begin this interesting hobby.

୬

Nearly all the named selections from native wild walnut trees and the named grafted progeny from them, were directed toward improving walnut nut quality and quantity. To hobbyists interested in producing nuts, the wood of the black walnut was a sideline. Several told me they wished they had pruned their trees higher to increase the timber value. This was hindsight after they had realized the value of black walnut timber. Normally, nut trees are pruned less than timber trees and tend to branch lower to the ground and have shorter trunks, which are not what timber buyers want.

Nut growers and timber growers have different objectives. Black walnut trees, which leaf and bloom early in the spring, are exposed to the risk of early frost and loss of the nut crop. Nut growers prefer later blooming spring trees, but timber growers want early leafing and long growing season trees. Timber growers believe longer season trees will produce more wood, because the leaves capture light and produce food for the tree for a longer period each year. Those interested in producing timber want nuts only to grow more trees. Large nut crops may reduce wood production. An all-purpose tree, designed to meet the needs of both nut growers and timber growers, would be hard to produce. Efforts to breed cattle for both milk and meat have been of only limited success. The *all-purpose* black walnut tree may be only a dream.

୬

Luther Burbank successfully crossed two *Juglans* species in California and identified the need for improved black walnut timber trees. However, serious work toward improving *Juglans nigra*, the Eastern black walnut, for wood or timber did not begin until the 1960s. It began in two places: West Lafayette, Indiana, and Carbondale, Illinois.

In 1967, a black walnut tree improvement program was initiated at Purdue University. Techniques of superior tree selection, grafting, controlled pollination, close spaced progeny testing, and early second-generation selection were developed. Professor Walter F. Beineke, Department of Forestry and Natural Resources, headed this program. He decided to "focus" on black walnut when he found it too difficult to work on numerous species at one time. Like Burbank, Beineke recognized the need for better black walnut trees.

The problems encountered in initiating a black walnut genetic improvement program were numerous and substantial. First, the variation of traits in the natural population was unknown. Second, walnut occurs as a scattered tree in uneven-aged stands, and candidate-superior tree selection had not been attempted in a species of this nature. Third, walnut was known as a difficult species to vegetatively propagate by grafting or rooted cuttings. Vegetative propagation would be necessary to preserve the selection in a clone bank. In addition, techniques for controlled pollination and progeny testing were unknown. New management systems involving weed control, pruning, and fertilization were in early phases of experimentation. Cultural practices were not well developed. It was a formidable task.

One would not discredit the wonderful achievements of the breeders of hybrid seed corn to compare the two species. Corn has clearly separate male and female flower parts that are low to the ground and easily manipulated in pollination. One seed of corn can produce 1,000 new seeds in six months. By flying seeds to South America for growing during the North American winter, one corn seed can produce one million new seeds in one year. This *tremendous* yield or return on investment is the reason corn is the world's most valuable grain.

There were numerous corn plants from which to choose that offered a huge gene pool. The financial incentive was tremendous. Millions of acres of corn are planted each year, and the financial rewards from improved varieties are sudden and obvious to farmers so they can readily see the value of buying an improved variety. None of these features were found in the Eastern black walnut.

Hybrid seed corn has been used on Midwestern farms for about 60 years. Much has been learned from 60 seasons of experience with planting, tilling, observing, harvesting, evaluating quality and quantity, and planning for next year's crop. Together, farmers and plant breeders have achieved record corn yields for years in succession.

Despite this 60 years of experience, there is yet no *accepted* single *correct* way to grow corn. There are hundreds of hybrid seed corn varieties and numerous methods and machines for planting, tilling, and harvesting. There are many different insecticides, weed control chemicals, and fertilizer types and methods.

If we assume a black walnut production cycle of 50 years, 3,000 years will be required for mankind to become as expert at growing black walnut as it has become at growing corn in only 60 years. Black walnut research for both better varieties and better cultural techniques is in its infancy. It is not surprising that there are differences of opinion on varieties and cultural techniques, nor is it surprising that progress has been slow.

&.

Black walnut has very closely associated male and female flower parts. The tree can self-pollinate, producing selfed (not crossed with another tree) seedlings that grow slowly, lack vigor, and seldom survive the competitive forest environment. When one picks up a walnut nut, one cannot know if the father was the same tree or another.

Selfed seedlings probably contribute to the poor productivity sometimes found in black walnut plantations. Selecting out weak and puny black walnut seedlings at the time the seedlings are dug for transplanting will eliminate some of these selfed seedlings and improve the walnut plantations' early performance.

Walnuts are slow and erratic nut bearers. With luck, one walnut nut will produce a tree and a few nuts in eight to ten years. Nut production is not only slow and erratic but is subject to the hazards of weather, disease, insects, squirrels, and human nutmeat lovers.

The major *stated* purpose of the Purdue black walnut improvement program was to produce seed for the production of genetically improved seedlings grown by the Indiana Department of Natural Resources state tree nurseries. After 27 years, only five percent of the state nursery trees are from these superior selections. The 1967 stated objective has yet to be reached in volume.

The Purdue walnut genetic improvement program began with the selection of superior specimen trees. Traits were measured or observed and assigned points. These traits were: apical dominance, numbers of crooks, stem form, site, and habitat. Growth rate was included when possible. From the thousands of trees rated in the program, only 410 were accepted. To establish clone banks of these superior trees, grafting, rooted cuttings, and tissue culture were tried, but only grafting proved satisfactory.

Hybridization was tried. Despite the difficulties outlined above, in eight years, 4,200 black walnut flowers were cross pollinated. Only 1,000 seeds were produced (much fewer than one grain of corn could produce in *one growing season*), and 232 nuts were lost to rodents or cracked in hulling. Of 768 nuts actually planted, 299 seedlings resulted, but only 134 survived. Of these, 38 were selfs, leaving 96 outcrossed controlled pollinated seedlings. One second-generation selection has been made from the controlled pollinated material. Because the results of controlled crosses have been so discouraging, the control-pollinated progeny test approach to walnut improvement is now limited to special situations. To this time, despite great effort, hybridization of black walnuts has been a flop.

Because the father of any walnut nut is unknown, progeny testing of seeds produced from black walnut seed orchards evaluates only half the genetic mix: the mother tree. Nuts gathered beneath a single tree could be from several male parents, from one, or from the mother tree itself. Thus, progeny tests are half-sib; i.e., only the mother tree is known for sure, and the male half is random. The results of half-sib progeny tests by Professor Beineke in

Indiana indicate: 1) large tree-to-tree variation exists in black walnut, 2) hereditability of important traits is large enough to genetically improve black walnut, 3) provided good sites are planted, families that do well in one location also do well in other locations and years, 4) correlations between desirable traits are favorable, 5) by about age four, rankings in height, diameter, volume, and form have stabilized to the extent that correlation with future rankings is significant, and 6) the top 20 percent of families have shown an improvement over nursery-run checks of 6 percent, 10 percent, 25 percent, and 21 percent for height, diameter, volume, and form, respectively.

By 1982, in 11 central and southern states, 97 acres of seedling seed orchards, 127 acres of clonal seed orchards, and 143 acres of progeny tests had been established. Target dates for seed production from seed orchards varied from 1985 to the year 2000. Black walnut was the top priority species in nine of the states, second in one, and rated low priority in the other.

In 1986 and 1987, the Indiana nurseries produced 30,000 seedlings for landowners from seed orchards resulting from the Purdue program. But by 1992, Indiana state nurseries were still producing only about five percent of their seedlings from superior selections.

Because of the vexing problems of black walnut nut pollination and seed production, seedlings produced from these selected seed orchards may be superior to seedlings from wild trees, but still may be inferior to grafted clones of selected superior trees.

Grafting of black walnut provides an opportunity to produce quantities of propagules from a young tree with known genetic characteristics. Patenting of this genetic entity provides protection from indiscriminate propagation of the improved clones. In 1984, Professor Beineke explained the Purdue patents:

> The first three patents ever granted for timber trees were patented by the Purdue Research Foundation in 1980. The next six were patented in 1982. The first license to propagate was granted in 1981. The Foundation collects a royalty on each graft sold, thus obtaining a return on the

investment in research by the university. Grafts from the patented trees outperform seedlings by an average of 34 percent, 29 percent, 78 percent and 34 percent for height, diameter, volume, and form, respectively.

Despite the passing of ten years since Professor Beineke released these performance comparisons, no new performance comparisons have been revealed. Have these comparisons held up over time? Have they been verified under various conditions? I could not find out.

Beineke, Associate Professor of Forest Genetics at Purdue, wrote *Characteristics of Purdue University's Patented Black Walnut Trees,* which was published undated as Forestry and Natural Resources Bulletin 115 by the Purdue University Cooperative Extension Service. In it, he states:

> Original selections were made from wild trees found in forests, parks, yards, and plantations in the Midwest. A rigorous screening system was applied, based on form and growth observations, to determine the trees to be tested for superiority.
>
> Grafting wood was collected from the superior selections, and grafts were planted in the research clone bank at Martell Forest ten miles west of the Purdue Campus (See photo p. 207). Since all the grafts are growing in essentially the same environment, differences in growth rate, form, and disease resistance are genetic. Grafting captures and preserves the genetic identity of the superior selection and transfers its genetic advantage intact to the next cycle of grafts.
>
> We have learned that black walnut has tremendous genetic variability in growth rate, stem form, date of leafing, disease resistance, and nut production. These traits are inherited to a degree that allows for rapid genetic improvement.
>
> Landowners, reluctant to wait for improved seedlings from the state seed orchards, requested access to grafted trees. Grafted trees theoretically are exact genetic copies of the original selection and do not suffer from the inherent variability of seedlings produced through the sexual process where the pollen parent is unknown and often of inferior origin.

In 1977 (sic), a group of Indiana businessmen formed a company and negotiated a license agreement with the Purdue Research Foundation to produce the grafted cultivars. This company had exclusive propagation rights to the walnut clones. Presently grafted trees are being marketed. (p.1) [1]

Beineke discussed stem form, late leafing, anthracnose resistance, nut production, and the individual characteristics of the nine patented walnut cultivars. He concluded:

It can be assumed that the patented trees will do well on good sites in the central region of the natural range of black walnut including all or portions of the states of Indiana, Michigan, Illinois, Ohio, Missouri, and Kentucky. They will *possibly* outgrow local trees in other areas of the country. However, *this cannot be stated with certainty without testing.* Growth and form of grafted trees will vary even though they are genetically identical, because of factors such as soils, site, climate, weed control, pruning, fertilization, irrigation, and *rootstock.*

It would be highly speculative to estimate yields and economic returns from plantations of these cultivars with the limited data available at present. These black walnut cultivars have been released with less scientific performance testing than is normally expected for agronomic and horticultural varieties. But comparable testing of the species such as black walnut would require major expenditures of funds and *50 or more years in time.* Thus, we decided to release the cultivars without specific performance data or predicted gains. Regretfully, *only time can provide the data on which to base long term growth and yield predictions.* (Italics added.) (p. 3)

Was this fair warning? Should exclusive propagation rights have been granted to a group of Indiana businessmen? How are these patented black walnut cultivars being marketed? What is being written and claimed about

---

[1] *While this undated publication gives the year 1977 as the date "a group of Indiana businessmen formed a company to negotiate a license agreement with the Purdue Research Foundation," the first patents were not granted until 1980.*

these cultivars? What has Purdue done since 1981 to provide oversight to the sale of these patented cultivars? How much money has Purdue recovered of its research costs? Who owns the tree plantations whose genetic material provides the clone bank essential to producing the cultivars? Has publicity about valuable black walnut veneer logs created an extraordinary popular delusion? Has greed overcome good sense? Will private greed produce a public good? These are questions that I've tried to answer with only limited success.

Ralph L. Davis, now retired, was Director, Office of Technology Transfer, Purdue Research Foundation when the licensee was selected. Davis related the process:

> Many attempts were made to license the technology. Stark Brothers was contacted but they were not interested in a license. All potentially interested Indiana parties were contacted. We did negotiate a license agreement with a licensee in Ohio, but the party terminated the agreement in less than a year since the licensee was unable to propagate the material.
>
> You must understand that in order to retain genetic purity, the material required asexual propagation. When Mr. Norman O'Bryan showed up at the office requesting a license, we had tried for about two years to find a licensee. We ran a financial check on Mr. O'Bryan and found his assets adequate to do the things that he proposed to do to get the trees on the market. Mr. O'Bryan was able to successfully graft the material, and therefore reproduce the genotype.

Who was Norman O'Bryan? Why did O'Bryan alone have the foresight and vision to recognize the growing demand for superior black walnut cultivars when others did not? Why did he have the desire to propagate and sell the Purdue patented grafted cultivar when others did not? O'Bryan had little experience in grafting trees or running a nursery. His previous experience had been as hairdresser and the owner of a school for beauticians.

To explore this matter further, I contacted Bill Baitinger who is currently Director, Office of Technology Transfer, Purdue Research Foundation. He confirmed the informa-

tion I had received from Davis that in the early days of the
Purdue patented black walnut program it had been difficult
to find anyone interested in propagating and marketing the
Purdue patented selections. The Purdue University Agriculture Alumni Seed Association, which markets grain varieties developed at the university, was not interested. They
thought there was no market for the grafted trees and did
not have the resources to pursue it.

Baitinger described his problem. O'Bryan devoted resources and time to propagate and market the patented
trees. It was a long and difficult process, and the sales curve
grew very slowly, then leveled off and declined. Sales in
the best year were only about 20,000 trees. O'Bryan was
having difficulty marketing the trees. O'Bryan also had
problems grafting the trees successfully and obtaining viable plantations. Sales were lagging.

In 1988, with all this in mind, Baitinger reviewed the
license agreement, because he "was not satisfied that the
trees were reaching the public in the quantity desired." He
does not seem to have considered that the price asked for
the trees might exceed the value or that selling the patented
trees at the prices asked might require some exaggerated
claims of performance. What were Purdue patented black
walnut cultivars worth?

Professor Beineke had evaluated the Purdue patented
grafted cultivar's performance as 29 to 78 percent better than
seedlings. These cultivars were offered at over $20 each,
compared to $.15 for the state nursery seedlings. How do
you sell a product that *may be* 29 to 78 percent better than an
alternative for 130 *times* the price of that alternative? That
required salesmanship! Purdue patented grafted cultivars
had to do a *lot better* to justify their cost.

Baitinger acknowledged that he had received "complaints" about the licensee, which were investigated. He
would not disclose the number or exact nature of these
"complaints" but said nothing had been proven. Further, he
would not disclose either annual sales volume or royalties
received by the Purdue Research Foundation. To this date,
sales figures and revenues received by Purdue for Purdue
patented cultivars remain a secret. Learning the "facts"

about the Purdue black walnut improvement program was very difficult.

After two years of monitoring progress, Baitinger decided to withdraw the exclusive license from O'Bryan's company on the grounds of "non performance." Baitinger would not define or clarify the expression "non performance" except to indicate that it had to do with sales volume. This was done in 1990, nine years after O'Bryan had first been granted the license.

The exclusive license to market the Purdue patented trees was then granted to Gutwein Seed Company of Francesville, Indiana. Since Gutwein had no Purdue patented trees, scionwood, or experience in grafting black walnuts, O'Bryan and his company, American Forestry Technology, provided the Gutwein Seed Company with grafted trees and helped to market the product. Gutwein had over 600 seed corn salesmen in the field who could now offer Purdue patented walnuts.

In the fall of 1994, Gutwein returned its license to Purdue and withdrew completely from the black walnut business. Baitinger decided to license on a *non-exclusive* basis and began receiving new applications. O'Bryan was one of the first to apply.

Baitinger explained that Purdue does not want to be in the business of growing or marketing trees. He maintains that the role of Purdue University is to do research and make the results of that research available to private business. Baitinger does not believe he has any further responsibility in the marketing of these patented Purdue trees. It seems no one else at Purdue has either.

Purdue Research Foundation retains the patent that controls the asexual reproduction of the patented cultivars, but does not control *seedlings* from these cultivars. Seedlings from the nuts from Purdue #1 cultivars are now called Purdue "patented" seedlings or Purdue #1 seedlings. Purdue has lost control of its name. The university has no control over Purdue #1 seedling sales or the use of the university name with them. It is the name of a great university and a name that sells walnuts.

Walnuts stain many items, and the brown stain is hard to remove. Black walnuts could stain the name of a great university. Baitinger agrees that the Purdue name should not have been associated with the trees, and everyone at Purdue agrees that this was a mistake that happened through oversight. No other plant or seed selection has carried the name Purdue.

Seedlings from Purdue patented trees can be sold by anyone who has the nuts to grow them. In the nine years he was the licensee of the Purdue Research Foundation, O'Bryan accumulated many more Purdue patented trees than the Indiana state nursery and may be selling more Purdue #1 seedlings. This was not what the Indiana black walnut improvement program set out to accomplish in 1967.

The Indiana state nurseries sell their walnut seedlings (five percent from the Purdue selections) for about $.15 each and O'Bryan sells his seedlings for about $7.00 each. Some landowners do not understand the difference between Purdue #1 seedlings and Purdue #1 patented cultivars.

Purdue also issued a one-year license to an Indiana nursery for clonal reproduction of the genetic material, but the effort failed. Efforts continue at Carbondale to propagate black walnut trees clonally with some success, but volume production has not been achieved. Baitinger says he is eager to make the Purdue patented Eastern black walnuts available in quantity to the public at a reasonable cost. He offers to license anyone to reproduce the Purdue patented black walnuts by cloning them in the laboratory rather than grafting them. The trick is in the doing.

There have been some problems with establishing plantations of the Purdue patented grafted cultivars. More difficulty seems to be encountered in transplanting potted grafted trees than with bare root seedlings, which generally have a high survival rate. Unlike seedlings, which are bare root, one-year-old trees planted early in the spring before they leaf, the grafted trees are planted from May 20th to the end of July as leafed trees in cartons. A hole for the tree is dug, the cartons are slipped off, the trees are enclosed in a tree shelter until August 15th, and mulched in a six-foot circle. If it is dry, the trees must be watered. This is a labor-intensive, difficult, and expensive procedure.

Some reports from Iowa have not been encouraging when the grafted trees were planted there. In some cases, growth has been slow, and trees have died. One Ohio University official reported he was trying to keep the Purdue licensee from selling Purdue grafted trees in Ohio. As with all living nursery material, it is difficult to establish who or what killed a living plant.

⁂

Nearly all foresters believe pure stands of black walnut are less desirable than mixed hardwood plantations. Pure stands of Eastern black walnut have been planted in small quantities since the 1800s, and some did well and some did not. A vigorous stand of pure Eastern black walnut is a beautiful sight. I saw one 12-year-old plantation that Beineke had planted in the edge of West Lafayette. This plantation demonstrated the possibilities of his superior selections when planted on a good site and given careful attention. The rate of growth of these trees was impressive.

Twelve-year-old black walnut plantation in West Lafayette, Indiana, Summer 1992. (See also p. 213).

It is paradoxical that the Purdue Research Foundation on one side of the Purdue campus has licensed private companies that advocate the planting of pure stands of black walnut clones, while on the opposite side of the campus the Department of Forestry and Natural Resources— which did the research and selected the superior black walnut trees— teaches and advocates the planting of mixed stands of several species. Which approach is better?

Baitinger argues that the Purdue Research Foundation is "simply licensing a product — the land owner plants as he chooses." He maintains that the Purdue Research Foundation is not "advocating either pure or mixed stands through the licensing process." Perhaps there is no "better" way, but the differences are substantial and important when a landowner is planting trees unlikely to be mature for 40 - 80 years. Such long-term commitment makes it essential that one get it right in the beginning.

Bruce Wakeland ACF is a professional forester in Culver, Indiana. On May 25, 1992, he wrote:

> I have planted millions of hardwood trees over the last 20 years and have studied many old hardwood plantings, and the two most important lessons I have learned are to never plant just one species and to have good weed control. We plant a lot of black walnut, but it is usually one of four to six species that we mix into a planting depending on soils and owner objectives. I strongly recommend mixed plantings of at least 500 trees per acre because of soil variability, wildlife damage, for protection from insects and diseases, because of changes in markets over time, to establish early crown closure, and to reduce the need for thinning and pruning. Properly mixed plantings allow a manager to select crop trees after 15 to 30 years instead of at the time of planting. If someone thinks that he can consistently select the best tree species to plant in a given spot in a field for a future timber market, he will someday change his mind.

Calvin Gatch, Cascade Forestry Nursery, Cascade, Iowa, agrees. He wrote:

> We plant 1,000 to 1,500 acres of trees a year and believe black walnut does better in mixed plantations. We have planted some of the Purdue patented trees and they have not produced exceptional growth in Iowa. We advocate mixed plantings.

The Pike Lumber Company of Carbon, Indiana has 300 acres of hardwood tree plantations, and approximately 85 acres of that are black walnut. Philip G. Carew, Manager of Timberlands for Pike wrote March 2, 1993, as follows:

Your question concerning solid Black Walnut plantations as opposed to mixed species plantations is a valid question. There has been some evidence that mixed species plantations produce a somewhat better quality wood in the walnut trees from a color standpoint. We have found that from a production standpoint, it is better to plant mixed species plantations, because it gives you some insurance that your plantation will succeed. With a single species plantation, if it happens to be off site for the species you plant, then you have a poor-quality plantation or a failure. The mixed species gives you some insurance against that. We have planted some of the Purdue #1 Walnut seedlings and have not found them to be substantially superior in the same plantations as the State Nursery seedling stock that we buy. The State Nursery seedling stock does contain a few seedlings that are offspring of the Purdue selections and we do gather seed from some trees on our properties that we have found to be reasonably good performers.

We do have a considerable problem with deer browse and have not been successful in eliminating it entirely. We had tried the single strand electric fence on three plantation fields and found it to be helpful, although not 100 percent effective.

We have increased the number of seedlings that we plant to offset some of the loss to the deer. Where we were planting 435 seedlings to the acre, now we are planting as many as 1,244 seedlings to the acre.

Robert E. Hollowell, President of Pierson-Hollowell Company, Inc., the first Indiana veneer company to establish large black walnut plantations wrote: "We have lost much of our enthusiasm for Walnut cultivation. I favor planting Walnut mixed with other species."

I have found no professional forester who urges pure plantations of one species of hardwood. Some members of the Walnut Council have planted pure stands of Eastern black walnut, but the practice is now less common and nearly all have told me they would plant a mixed species stand if they were doing it over and would plant more trees per acre.

A clonal plantation of walnuts, such as American Forestry Technology promotes, is not only just one species, but just one individual reproduced many times. This exposes the planting to danger of pests or major miscalculation not found in natural stands. Research data suggests a safe number of *different* clones to be 10 to 27 clones to equal a natural stand. Purdue has patented only nine. Most cultivars sold are of only two of these nine. This is genetic concentration of a high order.

While Professor Beineke has been cautious in claiming that his patented trees would guarantee superior economic returns, O'Bryan has been less cautious. Professor Beineke believes his selected trees will produce timber in 30 to 50 years. American Forestry Technology has printed and distributed literature that claims, "Because of their rapid growth, Purdue Number One grafts can be harvested as early as just 25 to 30 years, seedlings in 35 to 40 years." This is pure speculation since none have been growing this long. Perhaps it is true, but at what size and should they be harvested so soon?

Quality and size of a sawlog determines veneer value. The value is in the amount and color of the darker heartwood. Most people believe it takes from 40 to 80 years to grow a quality black walnut veneer log. There is no doubt that older, slower-growing black walnut trees have more valuable *heartwood*. Walnuts do not begin to produce the darker and more valuable heartwood until they are teenagers, around 12-13 years old. From that age on, they add heartwood at about the same rate they add diameter. A 25-year-old black walnut would have only about 12-13 years of heartwood.

Initial cost is important too. A one-acre plantation of Purdue grafted patented black walnut trees planted and protected with tree shelters would cost about $4,000. This can be compared to a cost of about $3,500 for Purdue "patented" seedlings or $200 for seedlings from the state nursery. If you plant nuts that you pick up yourself, your only cost would be your own labor. If you set aside some land near mature, nut-producing black walnut trees, and let the squirrels plant nuts for you, the cost is nil. Squirrel labor comes cheap. However, you will have a challenge persuading squirrels to plant the nuts in rows.

Given the small percentage of improved performance of the Purdue patented black walnut trees over wild seedlings as observed by Professor Beineke, the price differential between grafted cultivars and wild seedlings is hard to justify. Front loading the economic equation with such a large initial investment makes the economics of grafted plantations suspect. Timber economists typically calculate that a dollar invested in trees, if invested elsewhere, could earn five to six percent real interest (after allowing for inflation) per year. As a hypothetical example provided by Weyerhaeuser Paper Company, that means $200 spent preparing and planting a forest acre today would have grown to $2,293 if invested at five percent real interest compounded for 50 years.

On this same basis, $4,000 invested in an acre of Purdue patented grafted black walnuts would grow to about $45,000 in 50 years. If state nursery seedlings are planted at a cost of $200, the amount after 50 years would compound to only about $2,300. It does not take an economic genius to determine which would offer the best opportunity for economic gain. Initial cost is important.

Aristotle is quoted as saying, "Men become wealthier, not only by adding to what they already possess, but also by cutting down expenses." Superior black walnut trees are a good investment only if they can be acquired at a competitive cost. At current costs, Purdue patented black walnut cultivars *must* survive and grow *very* fast to justify the much larger initial investment.

ঌ

Field grafting of scionwood onto growing black walnut trees might be a way that superior trees could be established at a lower cost. There are many good walnut trees from which scionwood could be selected. However, as long as the Purdue Research Foundation enforces their patents and restricts open propagation of the Purdue patented trees, it is not possible for anyone to try this on a commercial basis with the Purdue patented trees.

And, what about the original object of the research effort, which was to improve the quality of the seedlings from the Indiana state nurseries? Why are only five percent of those seedlings from the Purdue patented trees? American Forestry Technology offers Purdue "patented" seedlings at over 40 times the state nursery price while attempting to stop the Indiana state nurseries from selling black walnut seedlings. Purdue receives no share of the revenue from the sale of these Purdue #1 seedlings even though state funds were devoted to selecting and patenting the cultivar seed source and the university name adheres to them like glue. Purdue receives a royalty only from the sale of Purdue patented grafted cultivars.

Many Walnut Council members believe the Purdue program was a "good idea gone wrong." Baitinger claims he is not pleased with the royalty Purdue has received or the number of trees offered to the public. The Indiana professional foresters are not pleased that the former Purdue licensee is trying to stop the state nurseries from growing and selling low-cost black walnut seedlings. Some individuals who purchased the Purdue patented trees are not pleased with their survival or performance.

Advertising material issued by American Forestry Technology Inc. in 1994 employs the name Purdue 14 times in one small brochure. The brochure states, "However, some people mistakenly believe that buying common seedlings at a few pennies each makes good sense." The clear implication is that buying state nursery seedlings makes bad sense. This is an implication with which few people who have bought and planted state nursery seedlings would concur.

This brochure includes a table comparing costs between plantings of common seedlings, "patented" seedlings and patented grafts. Total cost is made to appear very close by including the cost of tree shelters and stakes on each tree on each planting, which would mean putting shelters costing several dollars each on common seedlings costing about 15 cents each. I've never seen this done.

Walnut Council members will be waiting and watching the Purdue black walnut genetic improvement and marketing program evolve with some concern. The Purdue genetic improvement program may evolve right out of existence. Professor Beineke has been granted early semi-retirement and will continue to teach, but do no more walnut research.

Professor Beineke has done extensive black walnut research for 27 years. He has accomplished a great deal in addressing a need that attracted much press attention in the 1960s. But times change and new priorities, fads, and job opportunities dictate Forestry School policy. Ecology, environmental quality, water quality, urban forestry, suburban landscaping, and other studies are the current "hot" topics that interest young students and which offer job opportunities. The university reacts and the walnut genetic improvement program may give way to these "higher priorities."

ॐ

Some Hoosiers believe they have been taken for a ride in a big gold bus with PURDUE #1 in big black letters on the side. (Purdue school colors are black and gold.) Indiana taxpayers and Purdue students and alumni have bought the gas (by funding Martell Forest and Professor Beineke's 27 years of research through their taxes, fees, and donations.) They don't know just how much this cost, because Purdue either doesn't know or won't say.

The bus started on a journey in 1967 to develop better black walnut trees for Hoosiers to obtain from their two state nurseries. In 1980, the bus turned down a side road when the Purdue Research Foundation patented the first of Beineke's walnut selections. Apparently, the diversion was to obtain money for more gas. Purdue won't say how much money was earned by this diversion, or if the money was used for more gas. Regardless, the research program is now out of gas (no more funding) and the bus is stalled on a dusty gravel side road.

The state nurseries are still waiting for the bus to arrive. Only five percent of their seedlings are from Beineke's selections. However, from the back of this bus with PURDUE #1 still emblazoned on it, Norman O'Bryan's company, American Forestry Technology, is selling seedlings from Beineke's trees for $7.00 each and using Martell Forest to hold seminars to "educate" his customers. In sales literature, American Forestry Technology tells Hoosiers that, "they mistakenly believe that buying common seedlings at a few pennies each makes good sense." In other words, it makes *bad* sense to buy the state nursery seedlings for $.15, but *good* sense to buy his for $7.00. Is anyone selling the patented Purdue cultivars? Baitinger is trying to decide this.

Who was driving this bus? Not surprisingly, Purdue officials are vague about this. Most point at Baitinger, but I suspect it was a committee, and while the committee dithered, the bus lost direction and stopped. This is sad because I believe it started in the right direction on a worthwhile project.

≈

Genetic improvement of black walnut may end at Purdue, but it may not end elsewhere. In 1986, with the help of U.S. Forest Service funds, the North Central Fine Hardwood Tree Improvement Cooperative was formed. The cooperative goal was to consolidate effort toward long-term, high-level genetic improvement of fine hardwoods in the North-Central United States. The first two priority species were the Eastern black walnut and red oak. The region was divided into three broad-based breeding zones for black walnut. Candidate trees were selected from plantations and natural stands using the Purdue selection and grading system.

Thus the states of Illinois, Indiana, Iowa, Michigan, Minnesota, Missouri, Ohio, and Wisconsin have begun a long-term walnut genetic improvement program that may eventually improve the walnut seedlings from state and private nurseries. It will take a long time, and it's questionable that any "cooperative" will successfully develop improved walnuts. History teaches that individuals who have a driving motivation accomplish much more than organizations.

≈

Elsewhere in the mid 1960s, at Carbondale, Illinois, the USDA Forest Service's Research Laboratory was becoming the center for hardwood research with emphasis on a strong specialization and competence in walnut research. Research had begun there after WW II on reforestation problems. By 1960, the staff at the Carbondale Center totaled 37, but *not one specialized in black walnut*. By 1968, ten scientists were devoted to silviculture of black walnut and high-value hardwoods and two more to breeding of black walnut. Black walnut was in vogue!!

At Carbondale, Research Work Units were developed to 1) provide basic knowledge on the soils and water required for the culture of black walnut and other high-value hardwoods used for timber and related products, 2) determine how to establish plantations, encourage natural regeneration, and improve growth and quality of immature black walnut, and 3) provide basic genetic knowledge required for the breeding of superior varieties of black walnut for timber products and to breed and release superior varieties.

In August of 1966, a landmark walnut workshop was held at Southern Illinois University in Carbondale. It was followed by three more symposia in 1973, 1981, and 1989. At each, discussions were held, speeches given, and learned papers presented. The sole object of these four symposia was the exchange of knowledge and experience in the search for methods of improving, propagating, growing, and using Eastern black walnut.

The published record of these four symposia consists of over 600 pages of printed matter. The efforts of 133 scientists, foresters, educators, and walnut users were reported in 119 papers. Subject areas such as recognizing quality, establishing walnut, managing established walnut, tree improvement, pest management, nut culture and agroforestry, and economic opportunities were covered.

The 1966 workshop was jointly sponsored by the USDA Forest Service, The American Walnut Manufacturers Association, and Southern Illinois University. In his keynote address, Edward P. Cliff, Chief of the Forest Service said:

> Efforts to improve supplies of quality timber in America are long overdue. The over-all quality of our hardwood timber resources has been in a long decline as

we harvested the best trees of the most desirable species and left the poorest to grow and reproduce.

Gradually, a substantial body of knowledge about Eastern black walnut was accumulated. The published results of these four symposia are interesting reading to anyone who wishes to learn more about the history of science and silviculture of Eastern black walnut. They offer a sequential history of the "Walnut Project" at the Forestry Sciences Laboratory in Carbondale, Illinois.

In 1988, members of the "Walnut Project" wrote and published the accumulated knowledge and experience of this 20-year effort. This publication, called *Walnut Notes,* is to be updated as new facts develop. To anyone interested in growing Eastern black walnut it is a good place to begin study. (See Directory)

The North Central Forest Experimentation Station defines its job in the *Walnut Notes*:

> Our job at the North Central Forest Experimentation Station is discovering and creating new knowledge and technology in the field of natural resources and conveying this information to the people who can use it—in short, "finding out and telling." As a new generation of forests emerges in our region, managers are confronted with two unique challenges; 1) Dealing with the great diversity in composition, quality, and ownership of the forests, and 2) Reconciling the conflicting demands of the people who use them. Helping the forest manager to meet these challenges while protecting the environment is what research at North Central is all about.

At the 1966 symposium, Edward P. Cliff stated clearly the problem of transmitting acquired knowledge to the end user:

> The secret lies, I think, in applying much more energy and skill in getting adequate knowledge of black walnut culture to the landowner. We are challenged to devise vigorous, almost heroic, education, extension, training and demonstration programs. And we have the big job of motivating as well as teaching landowners. The State forestry organization, Extension Directors, univer-

sities, county agents, private foresters, the timber and nut industries, the Soil Conservation Service, the Forest Service, the Tennessee Valley Authority, and associations of landowners — in fact everyone interested in the future of black walnut has a job to do!

Walnut Notes is one step in this transmission process. What may be needed is a giant leap. Perhaps this book will help.

On September 1, 1970, largely as a result of the efforts of Don Gott, then Executive Director of the American Walnut Manufacturers Association, the Walnut Council was born. The general objectives of the Council are to advance knowledge of the culture of walnut species, to encourage the planting of walnut, to encourage the management of naturally established walnut, and to perpetuate the utilization of all walnut products. It is essentially an organization of individual landowners and walnut growers with the support, encouragement and sponsorship of private industry, university forestry professors, and the U. S. Forest Service.

To achieve the above objectives, a *Walnut Council Bulletin* is published quarterly. It contains articles about black walnut, a summary of annotated walnut literature, walnut nut recipes, and general information about all aspects of Eastern black walnut. Anyone interested in black walnut who reads several issues of the *Walnut Council Bulletin* will learn a lot about black walnut. If he is a true believer in Eastern black walnut, he also will find kindred spirits among the Walnut Council membership. (See Directory.)

In addition to the National Walnut Council, state chapters have been formed in Iowa, Illinois, Kentucky, Maryland, Michigan, Missouri, Nebraska, Oregon, Indiana, and Wisconsin. More are expected. These state chapters allow members in their state to meet and discuss local problems in growing Eastern black walnut. Each August a national meeting is held at a different location. Members attending the three-day meeting have the opportunity to share experiences with other walnut growers, meet walnut scientists, hear of the latest discoveries, visit local black walnut plantations and tour the facilities of black walnut users.

Membership in the Walnut Council has grown from 441 in 1969, to over 1,000 in 1994, with members in 43 states and four foreign countries. However, membership in the Walnut Council has fallen short of expectations. At the 1981 Black Walnut Symposium, West Lafayette, Indiana, Gary Naughton, Chairman, Assistant State Forester, Kansas suggested the Walnut Council set a goal to triple membership to 2,000 by 1985, and work hard to reach 5,000 by 1990.

The 1994 membership of 1,000 was way short of the 5,000 goal. Was the goal unrealistic? Is the $20 annual membership fee too high? Are there too many competing organizations? Is there overall apathy among landowners? Has the Walnut Council failed to publicize their organization adequately? No one seems to know the answers to these questions. Efforts to increase membership continue.

Indiana has about 100,000 private landowners who hold forest land, but under 100 members in the Walnut Council. Of 31 professional foresters listed in the Indiana 1991-92 Directory of Professional Foresters, only four claim membership in the Walnut Council. Indiana had no state Walnut Council chapter until a 1992 fall meeting planned and organized one. Why this apparent apathy in the state world famous for its quality black walnut veneer logs and the acknowledged center of the veneer industry?

Indiana may be the state with the most to gain from growing more walnut trees. Individuals in other states outside the natural range of black walnut are actively planting walnut trees. Iowa residents have a particularly strong interest in black walnuts. Do Hoosiers take their walnuts for granted? Does Indiana depend too much on natural reforestation? Research indicates that black walnuts do not reproduce naturally in some circumstances.

Ivan L. Sander, Silviculturist, Northeastern Forest Experiment Station, Berea, Kentucky, reported the results of a study of three harvesting methods in southern Indiana. In his article, "Natural Reproduction" reprinted in *Black Walnut Culture,* a report of the 1966 Walnut Workshop, Sander states:

"... natural reproduction of black walnut is *not likely to be abundant anywhere* but it will generally be present, especially where mature trees have been cut. From the information at hand it appears that *clearcutting is the best method to use in reproducing black walnut naturally."* (Italics added.)

For the last 30 years, Indiana and other Midwestern states have been harvesting black walnuts that reproduced naturally after the clearcutting of the late 1800s and early 1900s. That clearcutting provided the "best method to reproduce black walnut naturally." When selective cutting was the method of harvest, Sander reported that the population count of black walnut trees five years after cutting was *only 15 percent of that found in clearcut areas.*

Clearcutting is rare in this age. Ecologists and foresters are convinced that sustained yield, selective cutting, or high grading are the most acceptable ways to harvest timber. These terms all refer to the practice of cutting certain selected trees in the forest and leaving others standing to be cut at a later date. The trees that are left provide shade that discourages both oak and black walnut from regenerating naturally.

Selective cutting may be good timber management, aesthetically pleasing and ecologically sound, but probably will result in only 15 percent as many black walnut trees regenerating in the next generation forest. Selective cutting may gradually eliminate black walnut from Indiana forests or limit their growth to forest perimeters and large open areas. They simply do not grow without adequate sunlight. Walnut will grow in fence rows, open abandoned pastures, barn lots, beside streams, and in open fields. Walnut will not grow among taller trees in dense forests.

ﻉﺀ

Some Walnut Council members hold an almost religious fervor for black walnut, which makes some foresters uncomfortable. Almost all professional foresters will recommend the planting of a mixed stand of several species when reforesting. Many Walnut Council members have planted pure stands of black walnut, but many seem less and less inclined to plant pure stands of only walnut as they learn more about the advantages of mixed stands.

The average Walnut Council member has a plantation of one to five acres, which he cares for almost as a hobby. The average age of Council members is high, and many are retired professionals who have developed an interest in forestry late in life. Many have land with walnut trees very distant from their homes.

When the land is ideal black walnut land, when acreage is small, and if one is buying relatively expensive grafted black walnut trees, a solid stand of only black walnut may be desirable. A solid stand of black walnut assures that the dominant species will be walnut. In mixed stands, other species may grow faster and shade out the black walnuts. In natural stands, wild cherry, mulberry, osage orange, hackberry, and locust all grow quickly and on occasion will top over and kill black walnut if not watched carefully and controlled.

A mix of species offers the safety of variety, less exposure to disease problems, and the opportunity to thin for sale the less desirable species as time passes. Also, a mix of species is more natural and may produce a better veneer tree than do solid stands of black walnut. But walnuts can be grown in pure stands.

Despite evidence to the contrary, many still believe black walnuts growing in pure stands are inferior trees. In the late 50s, three pure stands of black walnut in different parts of the Midwest were located that were 75 to 100 years old. Some of these trees were cut and evaluated by the Government Wood Testing Laboratory for all walnut lumber characteristics and pronounced absolutely acceptable. This test has been repeated several times with the same result. Superior quality black walnut has grown and can be grown in pure stands. It can happen naturally and can be accomplished with the help of man, but the risks remain.

Two hardwood species have been almost entirely destroyed in the United States in the past 100 years. In 1900, 40 percent of the trees in the state of Pennsylvania were American chestnuts. Nearly all were killed by *Endothia parasitica*, known more commonly as the chestnut blight. The beautiful American elm, which once graced lawns and campuses throughout much of America, was almost entirely killed by the Dutch elm disease. The Illinois campus had nearly all elm trees. They *all died*! The population of a close relative of the Eastern black walnut, *Juglans cinerea* or butternut, is currently being reduced by the spread of a canker caused by the fungus *Sirococcus clavigignenti-juglandacearum*. Some disease could attack and destroy the black walnut as well. Although the probability may be small, anyone planting a plantation of only one species runs the risk of total loss.

Much of the Eastern black walnut research effort has been directed toward the goal of producing quality timber in less time. Jonathan W. Wright, Professor of Forestry at Michigan State University, at the 1966 Symposium said, "I think a 25-year veneer log rotation is entirely possible if we start with a fast-growing variety and care for it intensively." Twenty-eight years later, few would agree with that statement. A goal of 40 or 50 years is more possible. This seems to be true for several reasons.

Fast-growing black walnuts have a larger percentage of sapwood, which is lighter and less desirable than heartwood, with its dark colors desired by the veneer user. In most cases, the veneer user cuts off and discards the lighter colored sapwood. While fast growth produces more black walnut wood, the incremental increase in heartwood is slower and smaller, and veneer companies want the heartwood color. This is why most veneer companies want natural old growth black walnut and speak with little enthusiasm about rapidly grown plantation black walnut.

Often, lumber companies will steam black walnut lumber to blend the heartwood color into the sapwood. This steaming produces a product of more uniform color that is less desirable than heartwood color alone, but there is a greater volume of lumber than if the sapwood had been cut away and discarded. When they must, the solid walnut furniture makers use both sapwood and heartwood by staining the sapwood darker in the finishing of their furniture so that the two look almost identical.

The Martell plantation at Purdue and the Pierson-Hollowell plantation in Martinsville, Indiana, are both over 25 years old but not yet of harvest size for quality veneer. By pruning lateral branches to increase length of log, the leaf area is reduced, and the total diameter growth is slowed as the tree grows higher and higher. It does not seem possible to rapidly produce both height and diameter when leaf area is reduced.

A 25-year-old black walnut grove of the Pierson-Hollowell Company in Southern Indiana.

Black walnut trees in a plantation at Martell Forest, Purdue University in West Lafayette, Indiana. This plantation is also about 25 years old.

Jim Jones' Hammons Sho-Neff black walnut plantation in Stockton, Missouri seems nearer to harvest size at about the same age as those in Indiana. But his trees are dual-purpose trees intended to produce both nuts and veneer. They are spaced farther apart, have lower branches, shorter trunks, have a larger mast, and greater diameter, but probably about the same volume of wood. Jim will get one veneer log from his trees and has fewer trees per acre in Missouri, while the two plantations in Indiana may get two logs per tree and have more trees per acre. Eventually, the Indiana trees will be more valuable, but it will take longer to produce them. There is a trade off here, and as economists say, "There is no such thing as a free lunch."

These three plantations are examples of what can be done on good walnut sites with 25 years of constant effort. They represent a very large investment of time and money and, except for some walnut nuts and crops grown between the trees in Missouri, have provided no economic returns yet.

Both Walt Beineke of Purdue and Bob Burke of Pierson-Hollowell have demonstrated that plantation trees will grow to substantial size in 25 years, but neither have trees fully mature and ready to harvest for veneer in that length of time. Both would agree that a more likely time frame to produce quality veneer timber is over 35 years. The longer the time, the bigger the tree, the more the heartwood and the more veneer value.

ఽ

The U.S. Forest Service has maintained research programs on black walnut since the 1920s. One of the first researchers was L.F. Kellogg who studied site characteristics and growth patterns for walnut in plantations in the Central States region. In 1924, U.S. Dept. of Agriculture Farmers' Bulletin No. 1392 *Black Walnut for Timber and Nuts* was published. It offered good advice and information about growing black walnut to farmers and landowners. Was the advice followed? Apparently not to any great degree.

In 1960, the forestry committee of the Indiana Hardwood Lumbermen's Association recommended that a study be made to find out what has happened to the seed and seedlings shipped from the Indiana state nurseries. The Indiana Division of Forestry had extensive nursery stock distribution records dating back to the late 1920s, when stock was first distributed. F. Bryan Clark reported the results of that study on January 26, 1992, at the Indiana

Hardwood Lumbermen's Association meeting. Clark reported:

> The average survival in all plantations visited was about 40 percent. This average includes many complete failures and a few highly successful plantings. In a similar survey of plantings made in Missouri in 1948, black walnut survival averaged 31 percent. In Indiana nearly half the plantings have 30 percent or less survival. The fieldmen making the survey judged that only one out of three plantings was successful. Records for plantations established from seed and seedlings were kept separate. Survival was 25 percent where seed were used and 44 percent where seedlings were used. Rodent pilferage was a common cause of failure in the direct seedings.
>
> Growth varied widely from poor to good. At 20 years the 'average' stand was only 25 feet tall and diameter at breast height was four to five inches. Two-thirds of the plantings were pure walnut, consequently bole form and clear length were poor. Survival was affected by many factors, but several reasons for failure showed up regularly. Lack of early plantation care accounts for much of the poor survival. More than half of the plantings received no care at all, yet dense weeds were commonly listed as a cause of failure. In a third of the plantations visited, 50 percent or more of the walnuts were overtopped by weeds, vines, shrubs, or trees.
>
> A common cause of poor survival and the major cause for poor growth and form was planting on the wrong site. Site selection is unquestionably the weak link in black walnut establishment. Grazing remains a deterrent to forestry efforts in Indiana. About 13 percent of the plantings were grazed when visited, but many more had been in previous years. Survival, growth, and form are all adversely affected by grazing.

It seems evident that merely planting black walnuts is not enough. Considerable care and effort must be expended over a long period of time to achieve success. Just what had to be done to establish and produce quality black walnut trees?

Much of the 1960s research effort at Carbondale was directed toward learning how to establish and manage black walnut plantations. They verified much that was known in the 1920s, and learned even more.

Procedures for handling, storing, planting, and germinating walnuts were verified. The problem of squirrel theft of planted nuts was reexamined, and it was learned that *fresh* cow manure placed over the planted nuts would reduce squirrel theft. It did not specify just how *fresh* was required or the method of placement. I assume real *fresh* is best. Supposedly, you plant the nut and then back your cow up to the spot where you buried the nut and wait. Some will argue that this is too time consuming, but time means nothing to a cow.

Richard Shultz at Iowa State University learned that the big tap roots of walnuts make the transplanting of seedlings difficult and sometimes unsuccessful. He learned that undercutting walnut roots by pulling a blade under the seedlings several times when the trees were still in the seedling beds encouraged the growth of lateral roots and reduced the shock and loss upon transplanting. It was learned that the larger the seedling and the greater the number and the larger the size of the stem and the lateral feeder roots, the better chance the seedling has of surviving the shock of transplanting. Undercutting the roots of black walnut seedlings has become common practice at better nurseries.

They learned that correct planting is essential to starting the black walnut seedlings. The hole must be large enough to accommodate the full root growth and the seedling must be vertical in the hole. Walnuts have a tremendous tap root that can be nine feet long in nine years. This large, deep growing tap root is supplemented by equally long and more numerous large lateral feeder roots that grow horizontally from the tap root to feed near the surface of the soil. The root system must get the right start.

In evaluating black walnut seedlings, it has been determined that larger diameter stems and larger diameter and more numerous lateral feeder roots are essential to mortality, health, and rapidly growing trees. If a seedling does not develop these vital roots when young, it will not develop them later, and if they are once lost, they are lost forever.

More research needs to be done on the roots of black walnut. Scionwood from a superior selection grafted onto the root of a inferior seedling is unlikely to produce a superior tree. The roots are as important to the success of the tree as the top. But roots are harder to see and evaluate and cannot be cloned. Purdue #1 scionwood grafted onto an *inferior seedling* is unlikely to produce a superior tree, because the limiting factor would be the inferior roots.

It is accepted that even a superior tree will not do well in a poor site. The *soil is the single most important factor in producing quality black walnut trees.* It was verified that fertile, well-drained, deep, sandy loam soils are best suited for growing black walnuts. Poor soil is the major factor in failure of walnuts.

Al Huff, Atlantic Veneer Company, had told me that the best black walnut veneer logs came from Indiana, and parts of Ohio and Iowa. In the spring of 1993, I decided to visit these areas to see what they had in common. I found in each area numerous outcroppings of limestone. It has been noted that the pH of soils under black walnuts is higher than surrounding areas. I believe black walnuts feed on subsoil limestone and bring it to the surface in the form of leaves and surface roots. Limestone is one of the keys to good black walnut. Subsoil pH and subsoil texture should be a good measure of how well walnut will do on a site.

It was learned that subsoil obstructions, such as fragipans, high water tables, rocks, and gravel, are barriers that restrict root growth and walnut growth. However, I believe walnut will grow in wet soil if the water contains oxygen, the soil is rich, and there is no subsoil obstruction. I saw a beautiful stand of black walnuts not ten feet from, and not over two feet above, the water level of Northern Indiana lake. Walnuts grow along and quite near streams in all parts of their natural range.

Soils were classified by type and index curves developed for each type that could be used to estimate the tree height that trees should achieve in a given period of years. Walnut trees planted on poor soil produce poor trees. Unless the soil is right, one should plant something else.

Various fertilizer programs were compared to determine the best method to fertilize black walnut plantations.

They learned that fertilization does little to help young trees. However, later field tests have shown that high levels of nitrogen will increase black walnut growth rates and extend the growing season. In some cases, very rapid growth rates have been obtained with high levels of nitrogen. However, these rapid, nitrogen-stimulated growth rates have been associated with increased risk of tree damage from wind or ice storms. The optimum level of fertilization and the maximum rate of growth obtainable with acceptable levels of risk of tree damage have yet to be determined.

It was verified that early control of grass and perhaps weeds was essential to establishing the young walnut trees. Grass is encouraged by mowing and seems to cause more problems to young walnuts than weeds. In earlier days, cultivation controlled this competition, but modern herbicides have been developed that can be used to spray upon the ground and vegetation to control the undesirable competitive growth of weeds and grass. Various herbicides were compared with each other and with cultivation to determine which was most cost effective. Failure to control plant competition is second only to poor site selection as the cause of plantation failure with black walnut.

It was verified that spacing young walnut seedlings is important, and various spacings were compared to determine which was most desirable. On this issue, O'Bryan and foresters are in direct disagreement. O'Bryan believes you should plant fewer trees to avoid thinning and to lower the cost per acre, so you can afford his expensive trees. Carbondale researchers and professional foresters believe you should plant more trees and thin out the excess and the culls and retain those that demonstrate superior form and rate of growth. Who is right? This question remains open to debate.

Various interplantings were compared and analyzed to determine if and when agroforestry was desirable and if the returns of other crops would raise the return of the plantation. Agroforestry offers an earlier cash return than solid plantation planting but requires more work, more management, and more care in tilling to avoid damage to the growing trees. Perhaps the final timber crop will be reduced, but the intermediate nut yield should be higher.

It was verified that pruning lateral branches was essential to the production of veneer-quality logs and various pruning methods were compared and analyzed. It was discovered that more frequent pruning of smaller branches was preferable to infrequent pruning. The pruning of branches over two inches in diameter and removal of branches from over half the tree height were found to be harmful to log quality and tree growth. It was learned that pruning at the outer edge of the collar was preferable to pruning closer to the trunk. The best season to prune is late winter, late in the dormant period, and before the sap begins to rise in the spring. I prune in late February now.

A 12-year-old Eastern black walnut plantation in West Lafayette, Indiana, showing need for thinning and pruning.

Another view of the same West Lafayette black walnut plantation in June 1993, after pruning and thinning had been done.

In 1984, Professor Beineke submitted a paper titled "Corrective Pruning in Black Walnut: Does It Pay?" to the 15th Annual Meeting of the Walnut Council. (Beineke uses the term "corrective pruning" to include lateral branch pruning. To some, corrective pruning means cutting, taping, etc., which is the hardest part of pruning.) In this paper, Beineke argued convincingly that corrective pruning over the first 14 years of the walnut tree's life would result in future increased value far in excess of the original cost. He argued that corrective pruning would increase profit by $9,110.55 per acre at a 40-year harvest age.

Ed Workman, U.S. Forest Service, Carbondale, Illinois, believes a few minutes each year with each black walnut devoted to lateral branch pruning, weed control, fertilization, or thinning is worth $100 per hour in increased timber value. Both men offer convincing arguments for more pruning of black walnuts in plantations and in natural stands. Why don't more landowners prune their young trees? Where else can the average landowner earn $100 per hour for pleasant work on a sunny day in February or March? Most farmers are inactive during this period of the year unless they are in Florida playing golf. It is one of the most pleasant and surest ways of building wealth. It requires only a few pruning tools or a small chainsaw.

The University of Nebraska, Lincoln, Nebraska has produced and sells a 40-minute videotape titled: *Pruning Black Walnut Trees for Profit.* This television tape covers all the essential steps toward corrective pruning for better walnut trees and toward earning $100 per hour. Of course you must wait about 30 years for the financial return on your effort in the form of a more valuable walnut tree. The psychic reward comes sooner. Foresight and patience are required; both are uncommon traits. Both are worth developing for this and other reasons. (See Appendix III)

The difficult and painful process of thinning was analyzed, and a scientific formula developed to help encourage the walnut grower to sacrifice some young trees so that other potentially valuable trees would have space to grow and thrive. *Thinning Black Walnut* is a quick reference booklet published by the North Central Forest Experiment Station. Everyone who loves trees hates to cut a young tree, but black walnuts require space and must have sun and moisture. Only a limited number of mature black walnut trees can be produced per acre, and some must be sacrificed so that others can do well. It is difficult work but it is financially rewarding. It's a bit like thinning carrots, which most people don't enjoy either.

Various damaging agents were analyzed, such as walnut anthracnose, mycosphaerella leaf spot, canker disease, walnut caterpillars, and other defoliators, twig and stem borers, deer, squirrels, other rodents and birds. It is a jungle out there, and only the fit, the lucky, or the protected survive. Of these damaging agents, only the deer are extremely serious, and then only when trees are young.

Deer are increasing in number and range. During the winter, hungry deer will eat buds and branches from young walnut trees resulting in deformed and stunted trees. Building a very high fence around a tree plantation will fence deer out, but fences are expensive and unattractive. Electric fences are being developed that offer promise at lower cost. Repellants such as rotten egg emulsions, deodorant soaps, lion feces, and commercial products have been tried with only limited success. They wash off in the rain, lose their power, and very hungry deer will eat the trees anyway. Anyone who develops an effective and economical system to keep deer from eating young trees can help the timber industry while becoming a wealthy person.

Treeshelters are a comparatively new and expensive system that is being heavily promoted. There are several types offered for sale that have been tried with mixed results and in considerable controversy. The leader in tree shelters seems to be Tubex of Saint Paul, Minnesota, which publishes a 16-page booklet titled *Tubex Planting Success*.

This booklet explains that the first treeshelters were tested in 1979, at Alice Holt Lodge Research Forest in England, in an attempt to solve the problem of deer predation on newly planted seedlings. Several systems were tried, but the best seemed to be solid sheets of translucent polyethylene wrapped around nylon mesh tubes. The results of these published tests encouraged a number of companies to begin mass-producing treeshelters.

Tom Mills, West Lafayette, Indiana, has developed TREE PRO tree protectors and has come up with the idea of offering a package that includes a TREE PRO tree protector, an oak stake, a bluebird net, a five-year NUTRI PAK fertilizer system, and a black walnut nut. Tom hopes his packages will provide individuals with a method for starting black walnut plantations. (See Directory.)

A demonstration of treeshelters at Amana, Iowa in 1992, revealed that deer will eat tree branches emerging from a four-foot tall treeshelter. Thus, a shelter of at least five feet or higher is required if deer are plentiful. Treeshelters add a considerable cost to establishing a tree plantation and require careful management. Problems of thin trunk growth, poor form, dieback inside the shelter, rodent invasion, and bluebird deaths when trapped inside the shelters are common. Efforts to overcome these problems and to develop better treeshelters continue.

Lastly, the research at Carbondale offered suggestions on record keeping and harvesting. It was suggested that veneer-quality trees be identified early, numbered and mapped and that periodic measurements of girth be made to evaluate health and growth rates. When a tree stops increasing in girth and the mast or top shows signs of dieback, it probably is time to harvest the tree.

Carbondale had verified much of what was known about the growing of black walnut, much more had been learned, and much had been published and offered to the growers of black walnuts. Now, it would be up to landowners to take this knowledge and act. Would they?

&

During the Reagan years, the budget of the Forest Service was reduced and the staff at the Forestry Sciences Laboratory at Carbondale gradually declined from 12 to four. Research continues but on a greatly reduced scale. Ed Workman, Physical Sciences Technician at the laboratory, is working with David R. Webb Co., Inc., a large veneer company, to determine what soil characteristics are responsible for the more valuable color and luminescence found in certain Eastern black walnuts. Logs are tagged and followed by computer through the entire veneer process until sold and their fair market value determined. The stump is also tagged and soil samples are taken and analyzed so that veneer value and soil characteristics can be matched. Workman obtains sample sheets of veneer from the veneer flitch that he analyzes chemically and with a spectrometer to determine what properties and elements in each veneer sample are associated with greater value in the marketplace. The effort continues to determine why certain soils produce higher value black walnut veneer logs.

John E. Preece, Professor of Wood Plant Biotechnology at Southern Illinois University at Carbondale is cloning black walnut tissues in laboratory cultures. He hopes to replicate superior black walnut trees in greater quantity, more efficiently and at lower cost than is done by grafting. His work offers great promise that superior black walnut individuals can be mass produced and offered for lower cost at some time in the future. But the time is not yet here.

Much has been done, but much remains to do. The link from research to field application by the landowner remains the weak link. This book offers some general information about black walnuts and can be used as a reference source. I hope it will encourage more woodland owners to obtain and study *Walnut Notes,* join the Walnut Council and other black walnut grower groups, plant more black walnuts, encourage the natural regeneration of black walnuts, correctly prune young walnut trees, and thin trees where necessary.

Only God can make a tree,
but he needs help
from tools
or fools
like you and me.

7

BLACK WALNUT
FARMERS

ૐ

Give fools their gold and knaves their power,
Let fortune's bubble rise and fall;
Who sows a field or trains a flower,
Or plants a tree is more than all.

—Whittier

The Man Who Planted Trees by Jean Giono, is the story of Elzéard Bouffier, a man of great simplicity and determination. Bouffier lost his wife and children and traveled to a remote and desolate part of Provence, in southeastern France. There, alone with his sheep and dog, he built a stone house and began his work — the steadfast daily planting of 100 acorns. This was the work of a lifetime. This is a story of a titanic enterprise that takes a reader and lifts him majestically above the confines of his own life.

The Man Who Planted Trees follows Bouffier's life for 40 years. First, a reader sees Bouffier before the outbreak of WW I, then shortly after the war, then again before the outbreak of WW II, and finally, at the end of that war. Bouffier has labored continuously, in peace, without interruption, and in complete anonymity. Bouffier's Godlike transformation of the region, once desiccated and ravaged

by relentless winds, brings life—nurtured human life—
back to it. Like a jubilant stream, young people return to the
ancient land to live again, in a landscape reforested by the
hand of one old man.

Giono opens his story in this way:

> For a human character to reveal truly exceptional
> qualities, one must have the good fortune to be able to
> observe its performance over many years. If this perfor-
> mance is devoid of all egoism, if its guiding motive is
> unparalleled generosity, if it is absolutely certain that
> there is no thought of recompense and that, in addition, it
> has left its visible mark upon the earth, then there can be
> no mistake. (p. 7)

Giono's story is a work of fiction. Nevertheless, it has
swept around the world and been translated into at least a
dozen languages. It appeared in illustrated form on Public
Television. It was first accepted by *Vogue* in 1954, and has
long since inspired reforestation efforts worldwide. Giono
later wrote to an American admirer of the tale that his
purpose in creating Bouffier "was to make people love the
tree, or more precisely, to make them *love planting trees*.
There are times in life when a person has to rush off in
pursuit of hopefulness." Many readers wish the story was
true.

છ

The story of John Chapman, however, is true. Known
as Johnny Appleseed, John Chapman began collecting apple
seeds from cider presses in western Pennsylvania around
1800. Soon he began his trek westward, planting a series of
apple nurseries from the Alleghenies to central Ohio and
beyond. He sold or gave away thousands of apple seedlings
to pioneers whose acres of productive orchards became a
memorial to Chapman. Johnny Appleseed was real, although many thought his story was myth.

છ

The story of the Honorable A.N. Abbott is true as well. In the early 1900s, Abbott farmed land overlooking the Mississippi River in northwest Illinois near Fulton. Part of his land was composed of huge sand dunes much like those found today at Indiana Dunes on the south edge of Lake Michigan. Nearly 1/2 million acres of these sand dunes, referred to as Bull Sand Hills, stretch across northern Illinois. Abbott had 55 acres of sand dunes, and the sand blew and drifted across his good farmland. He proposed to plant trees to stop the sand from blowing. But could you grow trees in sand?

Beginning in 1903, Abbott planted black locust, osage orange, cottonwood, catalpa, white ash, mulberry, elm, Carolina poplar, hard maple, spruce, hackberry, cedar, white pine, apple, pear, and black walnuts in his huge sand pile. He planted trees every year for nearly ten years. He planted seedlings in furrows plowed with a team of horses. He planted buckets of black walnut nuts.

Abbott persisted despite the damage rabbits did eating his young trees. He persisted despite the frequent fires started by trains passing beside his land. He persisted despite blowing sand and drought. He planted over 50,000 trees on his 55 acres of sand.

Gradually he began to turn the sand dunes into a forest of young trees. Those who scoffed came to see the miracle. Abbott wrote articles for publications describing his method of turning sand dunes into woodland. Foresters who had been skeptical came to see and believe.

Abbott gave a great deal of credit for this restoration to the black locust trees, which are legumes that fix nitrogen from the air. He was convinced these trees provided nitrogen in the poor soil for the other trees. He learned that planting only one species is not wise. Some species did well and some did not survive at all. On his lower ground, the walnuts did very well.

They did so well that in 1984, nearly 80 years after he began planting these trees, his heirs sold 68 black walnut trees for $33,850. These trees were grown on what had been worthless sand. Many very nice black walnuts up to 24 inches DBH remain.

In November 1994, I visited Walt Fields and his wife, Dorothy Abbott Fields, who live now in the house built by R.N. Abbott. Mrs. Fields is the granddaughter of Abbott, and along with her sister owns this lovely forest. Mr. Fields works in the forest doing timber stand improvement and maintenance. It is a task he enjoys immensely, but the Fields both wonder who will care for the forest when they are gone.

Walt Fields and 24" DBH black walnut in forest established almost 100 years earlier by A.N. Abbott.

છે.

The story of Robert Daubendiek, known as Johnny Walnutseed, is also true. He probably planted more black walnut trees than any man who ever lived. From 1960 to 1974, Daubendiek and his family worked from his Decorah Nursery, in northeastern Iowa, to plant seven million black walnuts on approximately 7,000 acres in Iowa and surrounding states. In addition to planting seedlings, Daubendiek bought walnut nuts, stratified them, and sold stratified nuts and seedlings all over the United States and to several foreign countries.

Mrs. Mae Daubendiek developed the idea of buying land, planting it to black walnuts, and then selling five- and 10- acre plots of black walnut trees as "Walnut Gems." The Daubendieks found ready buyers for these plots located in northeastern Iowa. Buyers came from as far away as Texas to buy their "Walnut Gems."

Daubendiek offered a service contract to buyers of these gems that would provide for periodic visits by him to

inspect the plantations and recommend care and maintenance. Mrs. Daubendiek, who still lives in Decorah, Iowa,
told me that of all the gems sold, only one customer took the
service contract. Many bought the walnut gems on time and
paid a few dollars each month for them. While buyers were
willing to buy the walnut plantations, most were unwilling
to invest in care and maintenance. Most walnut gems were
allowed to fend for themselves with poor results. We have
since learned that a walnut plantation requires much care in
its early years.

For many years, Daubendiek was the only commercial
black walnut tree planter. Johnny Walnutseed was a nature
lover and an idealist as well. He had a small sign on his desk
that said, "What we have done for ourselves alone dies
with us, and what we have done for others in the world
remains and is immortal. Tomorrow's America will be
what we make it today."

Daubendiek died of cancer on October 30, 1975. His
monument, in the cemetery at West Bend, Iowa, reads:

Robert Willard Daubendiek
1918-1975
Iowa's Johnny Walnutseed
"He who plants a tree, plants hope."

His widow, Mae Daubendiek, who had worked beside
him since they were married on Christmas Day 1938, wrote
a book to record his life and story. Five thousand copies of
the book, *Johnny Walnutseed & Growing Black Walnut,* were
published by Vantage Press. Mrs. Daubendiek used her
maiden name, J. M. Sloan, as author.

This book carries a speech that Johnny Walnutseed
gave at the Northern Nut Growers Association annual meeting in Columbia, Missouri, on August 24, 1965, just ten
years before he died. Excerpts from that speech as quoted in
Sloan's book follow:

> With a background of some forestry training, wild-
> life interest, and time on my hands, I started about 15
> years ago custom planting trees for various landowner
> friends, doing reforestation work in Iowa with small,
> cheap seedlings in quantity.

Now Iowa is just like the home territory each of you comes from in this great United States. It has many small areas on practically every land holding, as well as rough timbered areas in many locations that are presently or a short time ago were growing brush, scrub, or low-value timber which should be improved, by paying its way or producing a fortune in valuable wood for its owners. Land which time actually means nothing to, in the respect that these lands for a long time to come will be just as they are, scrub and brush and low-value producing areas unless someone takes the time, effort, and a bit of money to establish a stand of well-doing and valuable trees there.

Being unable to find quantities (of black walnut seedlings) anywhere, I set up my own nursery where, since 1960, we have produced about one and a half million black walnut seedlings and stratified seed nuts for planting throughout Iowa and shipments of small quantities to practically every state. Mainly I plant what I sell, moving in my own private C.C.C. gang working under my direct on-the-job supervision.

My operation is not a desk-to-desk one or a big government bureau. It means traveling about 40,000 miles a year, all winter going over the grounds, walking the areas, and making up planting plans, tree orders, and planting contracts. Then moving in with stock, men, and equipment in the spring, following up in summer on management.

I have lined up, sold, and planted with my crews in 58 of Iowa's counties, a bit over four million trees with over one million of these Black Walnut. Also about 200,000 in surrounding states of Minnesota, Wisconsin, and Illinois. Plus shipping stock I did not plant to many states and several foreign countries.

I plant mainly for doctors, attorneys, and other professional people who own land. Perhaps five percent are working farmers who pause briefly while trying to out-produce one another on one dollar per bushel corn.

I am a firm believer in planting dense stands. I plant at least 1,000 walnuts per acre, often 2,000 per acre. My own pleasurable show-off planting has a bit more than 4,000 trees per acre. Trees will grow tall and straight if planted thick, and with proper pruning and other management will produce a fantastic per-acre crop.

Among my successful and interesting plantings has been a two-acre forest beside the gravesite of our beloved President, Herbert Hoover. To, as he himself said, "Re-establish a walnut woods there" to replace those he recalled to make a corn field.

My three millionth tree, a walnut, planted at a large tree planting at a housing project near Cedar Rapids, dedicated by the United States Steel President "to future enjoyment of our citizens."

I have planted walnut for an insurance executive who declares his insurance is not good enough for his children as compared with the 320-acre walnut area we are establishing for his estate.

The greatest enjoyment I get from my work with walnut, aside from the tremendous amount of money I make at it, I usually jokingly say, is the genuine pleasure and sense of accomplishment those I work for get from their trees once they get above the grass and weeds and can be viewed.

When a naturalist "discovers" a fact, and knows it, he will fight for it. He deems it a sin not to preach "what is so." Daubendiek had walked the woods and streams of Iowa and observed nature closely for years. He found three old stands of black walnut, planted over 75 years earlier by farmers, in a spacing of five feet by six feet. These stands had succeeded in producing long, straight logs supporting good crowns. He concluded that black walnut could be grown in thickly planted plantations and worked hard to convince anyone who would listen to plant the Eastern black walnut.

Daubendiek was an extraordinary man who truly deserved the title Johnny Walnutseed. However, he was human, and humans make mistakes. His biggest mistake was planting walnuts on poor sites. It is the most common mistake made in planting black walnuts. Buyers of his seedlings and Walnut Gems made mistakes too. They did not give the trees the care they require. That is the second most common mistake made in growing black walnuts.

In June 1993, I visited some of his walnut gems near Jericho, Iowa. One 20-year old stand of walnuts was stunted, deformed, and would never amount to anything. It had been planted on poorly drained soil and the subsoil must have had some obstruction that was preventing the walnuts from rooting deeply as they must. Some recent efforts at pruning these trees had been made. However, the pruning was obviously belated, amateurish, and incomplete.

Nearby, Mae Daubendiek had directed Neal Flatjard, who has farmed her land since 1983, to plow under about 80 acres of black walnut trees. She told me she had them plowed under because the government would not compensate her for pruning them and they were not doing well. Even Johnny Walnutseed could not get black walnuts to do well on a poor site.

Anyone who has strong opinions and works hard to accomplish a goal will expose himself to criticism. Some say Daubendiek was a "promoter," meaning one who sells more or harder than he can deliver. Some say Daubendiek was in favor of high populations of black walnut trees because thick plantings enabled him to sell more walnut seedlings from his nursery. Over 20 years have passed since most of Daubendiek's work was done, and it should be possible now to evaluate his black walnut plantations.

Is this being done? I wrote the Iowa Department of Natural Resources to learn. Jerry Kemperman, Forestry Supervisor, Iowa Department of Natural Resources replied:

> There is no research effort of which I am aware to locate and study Daubendiek's plantings. Although he had many plantings, they generally were not successful. As you found, most are not growing well due to many reasons including off site and lack of follow-up management. Some were planted in high graded timbers and could not compete. I am not aware of any real successes.

Even if Daubendiek failed to establish viable and valuable walnut plantations, something positive might yet come from his tremendous effort if a study is made of why he failed. And some of his walnuts will do well even if the number is small. Unfortunately, truth is often not as good as fiction.

❧

On New Years Eve 1994, Robert A. Green of Nashville, Tennessee showed me his 100-acre black walnut plantation situated on a second bottom of the Cumberland River near The Hermitage, President Andrew Jackson's plantation home. Before he planted walnuts, Green consulted with many professionals and after weighing their conflicting advice decided to plant walnut nuts. In November 1977, at the age of 66, Green purchased 3,000 pounds of walnuts in the hulls for $.64 per pound.

Thirty-five acres were planted that fall with four unhulled nuts planted every 10 feet. Nuts were covered with dirt pulled over them by a garden hoe. The remaining 65 acres were planted in March in the same manner with nuts kept through the winter in cold storage.

Heavy woods are located on two sides of this planting and Green's walnuts attracted squirrels. He used traps and caught 200 squirrels in three weeks and had little further problem. Both spring and fall plantings germinated and grew well. In fact, Green had too many trees in each location and thinning was a job. He sprayed with simazine solution to control weeds.

During the fall of 1980, Green planted rows of Emerald crown vetch between the rows of trees. This legume reseeded and quickly spread to cover the ground by the spring of 1982. It would fix nitrogen for the young trees. Green recommends vetch.

Robert A. Green, December 31, 1994, in his 16-year-old black walnut plantation near Nashville, Tennessee.

About 40 acres of his planting did not do well because the soil was too wet. Initially many of his trees looked bad, displayed poor form and forestry experts advised him to destroy the entire plantation and begin again. He did not take this advice and by 1994, at age 16, the largest of his walnut trees were 11 inches DBH. On the well-drained 60 acres of his land, the walnuts I saw were straight and impressive. The average DBH was about seven inches.

Green's plantation proves that a good stand of quality trees can be produced from ordinary walnut nuts—on well-drained land. It also proves that poorly drained land will not grow black walnuts.

ೞ

In March 1984, the *South China Morning Post* carried a story titled "Madman Honored for Tree Planting," which related the story of a Chinese clothing merchant who abandoned his wife of more than 40 years and the rest of his family and, at the age of 66, moved to a mountain cave and planted trees. He lived on yams and wild herbs with a little bean, corn, and millet and for more than 10 years did not buy himself new clothes or new shoes. Working with a hoe for 18 years, Zhang Houla had planted more than one million trees in a remote valley and hill slope in north-central China. At 84, the "madman" was honored by the People's Republic of China. This story may be truth or fiction. However, perhaps China and the world could use more "madmen" such as Zhang Houla. Is it madness to plant large numbers of trees?

Thomas Paine, writer, political pamphleteer, and spokesman for independence during the American revolution wrote in *Crisis*:

> I am enough of an existentialist to believe that each member of a community recreates society each day for himself and his neighbors through the scores of separate, often seemingly inconsequential decisions that they make. The cumulative effects of the daily decisions of a people tend to determine the quality of life that they and their progeny enjoy or suffer. All men of intellect are largely self-educated after they leave school. What we obtain too

cheap we esteem too lightly, 'tis dearness only that gives every thing its value.

ॐ

Each summer about 250 Walnut Council members attend a meeting to compare experiences in growing black walnuts, learn from each other, and hear from experts. The cost for a couple to attend such a meeting is about $500, including both registration and room, but not transportation. Some drive or fly over 1,000 miles to attend, but most live within 500 miles of the annual meeting site, which is in a different state each year.

The ages of those present range from four to 84, but the average age of members is not low, and gray hair is prominent. Most qualify for senior discounts. Several members have attended over 20 of the 25 meetings held including 1994, when the Walnut Council marked its 25th Anniversary at the Lied Conference Center, Arbor Day Farm, Nebraska City, Nebraska. The Lied Conference Center is a new, attractive facility boasting a lounge paneled in black walnut.

Nearly all Walnut Council members own some natural or planted black walnut trees growing on land they inherited or purchased. Most have planted only a few acres, but several have planted much more. Some have planted nuts, some seedlings, and some have planted grafted cultivars at great expense. Many members are retired or semi-retired, some are professional people or farmers, and many own land and walnut trees far from their current residence.

One of the most popular and interesting annual events is the landowner show-and-tell in which landowners explain their experiences and problems growing black walnut trees. These stories clearly reveal that growing black walnuts is an art and not a science. They also reveal the amount of time, effort, and money some landowners are expending to reach an objective that shimmers in the far distant future that they have little hope of ever reaching. Even at an advanced age when some people want only to sit by the fire, Walnut Council members are planting trees.

The show-and-tell sessions reveal common problems in getting a stand of walnut trees established. Squirrels dig up the nuts, drought kills young trees, weeds and grass are serious competition, deer, mice and other varmints are a constant threat, and the art of pruning and thinning is always a new learning experience. Cultural methods that work for one will, on occasion, not work for another. The common bond is the universal effort to grow black walnuts and to share ideas and experience with others. Sessions are friendly and jovial but devoted to serious business without frivolity. Growing young walnuts—like young children—is both frustrating and rewarding.

Larry Krotz of Washington, Iowa, explained what could be called the U.S. Grant approach to tree farming. He drilled walnut nuts and acorns by the thousands until he had a complete thick stand of young seedlings. Then he let the trees struggle and compete to let the fittest survive. Not unlike the way General Grant fought the Civil War.

Another member expressed problems he had experienced with insects, squirrels, and deer. However, he concluded, he had the solutions down by the numbers now. "It's Sevin for the bugs, a twenty-two for the squirrels and a thirty-0-six for the deer." That got a laugh from the members present.

Hugh and Judith Pence showed color slides and explained their experience with their 124-acre plantation of corn and walnut trees planted near Lafayette, Indiana. In March 1989, they planted 44,000 black walnut seedlings, purchased from the Indiana State Nursery at Vallonia, in rows 22 1/2 feet apart with a tree every five feet in the rows. Since then, six rows of corn have been planted between the tree rows each year, in what is called agroforestry. The soil was rated as capable of producing 125 bushels of corn per acre and also as a good black walnut site. Hugh emphasized the importance of site selection, site selection, and site selection before planting black walnut trees.

Hugh explained that the chemicals used to control weeds in the corn were also excellent in controlling weeds among the walnuts. Moreover, a total corn fertility program, particularly nitrogen, was very beneficial to these young trees as they got their start. He was pleasantly surprised that the "hot house" effect of the tall corn benefited the walnut growth during the first three years.

Another plus with the corn/walnut arrangement pertains to higher corn yield on the outside corn rows. Each six rows of corn planted in this way had two outside rows producing 1/3 more than inside rows. With 1/3 of the land allocated to trees, only 2/3 of the land was actually planted to corn. For the 2/3 of the farm actually planted to corn, the yields have been 165 bushels per acre in 1989, 180 bushels per acre in 1990, 40 bushels per acre in 1991, and 100 bushels per acre in 1992. Both 1989 and 1990 were excellent growing seasons, but 1991 was the worst year of drought since 1936. The young trees survived the drought but set on terminal buds earlier than normal. The 1992 crop was a high amylose corn with the yield equivalent to 165 bushels per acre of regular field corn.

Hugh and Judith have devoted many hours to hand spraying to control weeds and to hand pruning to develop good form. They had 15,000 trees grazed by deer the second year and all had to be hand pruned. They realize corn will thrive only until the trees intrude and shade forces them to switch to soybeans and eventually to forage crops. This switch to another crop may be required soon, as the trees were averaging ten feet or more in height and towering over the corn at the end of the fourth growing season. They realize it takes 40 to 60 years to produce a mature black walnut tree but are willing to make this investment of time and money for their children and grandchildren. They hope these young people like trees; I would bet money they will.

Judith Pence, center, shows Jim and Ruth White their young black walnut plantation in July 1989. Photo by Hugh Pence.

Hugh and Judith Pence's black walnut plantation in July 1990. Photo by Hugh Pence.

Hugh and Judith Pence's black walnut plantation in June 1992. Photo by Hugh Pence.

Workers in the Pence walnut plantation shred branches from newly pruned black walnuts in March of 1994.

ઈ‌‍

"Things are different in the West," writes Dr. Gary Goby, M.D. who is the Oregon State Walnut Council Chapter President and owner of Goby Walnut Products. He continues:

> The Oregon Walnut Chapter members have planted about 5,000 walnuts in the last two years and are pushing for more in 1995. We plant a cross between *Juglans nigra* and *Juglans hindsii*, which can produce a four-foot diameter tree in 60 years. Walnut trees in the temperate climate of the Willamette Valley grow large and healthy. Walnut trees attaining five feet in diameter that yield wide, high-quality lumber are not unusual. Our iron-rich soils and plentiful rain result in lumber of exceptional color with frequent black and orange contrasts in the normal walnut tones.
>
> While our walnuts grow quickly, they have a lot of sapwood and do not begin to form colorful heartwood until they are 18-20 years old. Normally, Eastern black walnuts begin to form heartwood at 8-9 years of age. Our company has one of the largest inventories of Western black walnut wood in the United States. We inventory dimensional lumber and about 3,000 gunstock blanks. We do not steam to darken sapwood but allow our bright colors to show by natural drying.

The crosses of *Juglans nigra*, *Juglans hindsii*, and *Jugla regia* that grow and thrive in California and Oregon produce some magnificent trees and wood of exceptional color. While the blood lines or saplines of these crosses are hard to identify, there is no question that some spectacular wood is produced by walnuts in the West. (See Directory.)

Dr. Gary Goby of Albany, Oregon stands beside an Oregon walnut that is 103 feet tall, five feet DBH, and estimated to be 110 years old. This is not Juglans nigra, *but a cross.*

આ

Another member, Bill Slagle of West Virginia, explained how he was growing black walnuts in rows and ginsing under his young walnuts. The ginsing root is highly valued in many Asian cultures for its reported therapeutic and restorative effects. Ginsing is consumed as tea or powder, and can sell for $50 per pound of root. It takes several years to produce a sizable root. Slagle's walnuts and ginsing were growing well together and neither seemed to harm the other. The gypsy moth has reached West Virginia, and Slagle had been spraying every few days in an effort to reduce their damage to his young trees.

આ

Leo C. Bird, Walnut Council member, of Stockton, Kansas, described his thoughts in "Why Grow Trees" in the *Walnut Council Bulletin*, summer 1991. Bird wrote:

The joy of planting and caring for trees is not to be found in the anticipation of that moment in time when they are mature and ready for harvest a half century from now. Rather, it is in the pleasure which comes to us each day, each month, and each year that we are privileged to devote ourselves to the endeavor. Our reward comes in the knowledge that our efforts are the foundation of a legacy to future generations, not only in tangible terms, but, more significantly, in terms of the intangible. While this alone is sufficient reason to like tree farming, I like it for many other reasons.

I like tree farming because trees are like people. They are all different. There are some good and some bad, some straight and some crooked, some tall and some short, some bullies and some cowards, some responsive and some not. Some mature at an early age and some never do.

I like tree farming because it is anxiety and uncertainty. It is not knowing what we may or may not be doing that is in our best interest as a tree farmer. It is not knowing whether technology will produce a product which will replace the quality saw log we are attempting to grow. It is not knowing if someone else will devote time and effort to the care of our trees when we are no longer able to do so. It is not knowing if our pruning technique is as good as it should be.

I like tree farming because it is patience. In the course of a single summer we can grow tomatoes or onions or flowers. Nut crops, firewood and saw log production takes years.

I like tree farming because it is private enterprise. It can be practiced on thousands of acres or on less than one. Size is limited only by the capacity of the individual. Tree farming requires capital and labor. It requires management. It requires planning and foresight. Hopefully, it will prove to be profitable.

I like tree farming because it is work. Work is that form of human activity which generates a feeling of accomplishment resulting from creative and productive pursuits. Most certainly, the effort required to manage and tend a tree farm is no less than work. Work is good for the body. It is good for the soul.

I like tree farming because it is satisfaction. If your tree farm consists of a hundred trees or of thousands, you take pleasure in the knowledge that they would not exist were it not for your efforts in their planting and their care.

And, though you may be disappointed in the growth or performance of some of your trees, those which are beautiful, healthy and sturdy are the ones which make your efforts all worthwhile.

I like tree farming because it benefits wildlife. One cannot be a tree farmer without being friend and benefactor of wildlife. Habitat creation and improvement is a natural by-product of tree farming. Without fanfare, and perhaps even without intent, we become a provider of food and shelter to a variety of creatures which occupy the outdoors. We focus on wildlife in the management of our own acreage, not for the singular purpose of being able to harvest the surplus production, but because birds and animals make our lives more enjoyable. Creating a home for forest and woodlot inhabitants is one of the benefits which accrue from planting trees in an on-going partnership with Mother Nature. If we do our part, she will do hers.

I like tree farming because it is solitude. We all, from time to time, are faced with a variety of personal pressures. One can find no better place for quiet retreat than in the company of trees. Just being there is good therapy. Our conflicts won't be automatically resolved, but they usually seem a bit more manageable in such an environment.

I like tree farming because it gives me reason to feel needed and responsible. It adds meaning to my life and satisfies a desire to serve a worthwhile purpose.

Bird then quoted the following poem, titled "The Tree Planter" by an anonymous poet.[1]

"Old man," cried the fellow passing near,
"You are wasting your strength with planting here.
Your journey will end with the ending day
And you never again will pass this way."

"You have crossed the chasm deep and wide.
Why plant a tree at eventide?"

---

[1]This poem is very similar to and almost surely derived from "The Bridge Builder" by Will Allen Dromgoole.

The planter raised his old grey head.
"Good friend, on the path I have come," he said,
"There followeth after me today
A youth whose feet will pass this way."

"He has not come to the twilight dim.
Good friend, I am planting a tree for him."

Bird continued with his own thoughts:

I frequently take a walk after the evening meal. In the place I walk there are no traffic lights or busy thoroughfares. Instead, there are winding trails, only faintly visible, not made by the feet of man. There are no screaming tires or automobile horns. Instead, there are the sounds of rustling leaves, both overhead and under foot, new ones from this year and old ones from last. There are no beer cans or plastic cups. Instead there are tiny wildflowers and other fragile, growing things.

There are no bricks precisely stacked one upon the other, no great pieces of steel or concrete, monuments to man shaped in harsh designs of rectangles and triangles. Rather, there are a multitude of exquisite little patterns, each unique and different, each begging to be examined. There are no foul odors, only the pleasant scents of the season.

I encounter no hostilities on these leisurely journeys, nor do I find myself absorbed in the pursuit of negative thoughts or engaged in sorting priorities. To do so would be to focus on the ugly in the midst of the beautiful. This place to which I refer is not where I go to escape reality, I go there to sense and to feel reality. It is there, in the woods, in solitude, that I find it.

I could express reasons for planting trees no better. Bird has also produced and acted in a videotape that shows his method of gathering, cleaning, and stratifying nuts, and offers hints on planting, cultivating, selecting, and pruning black walnuts. (See Directory.)

❧

Bird and other Walnut Council members are not a young group of tree farmers. Why does man come so late in life to the planting of trees? Surely a young man planting a tree at 15 or 20 years of age has a better chance to see it mature and to realize the economic rewards of his efforts. Old men have so little time left.

I believe the planting of trees by older men is greatly influenced by relativity. Time, as we perceive it, is relative to our experience of it. Children have little experience with time. Two hours riding to grandma's house seems like an eternity. "Are we there yet? How much longer will it be?"

Two hours is a long time to a five-year-old. He compares two hours to the experiences of his one year of remembered life. Two hours relative to one year is a long time. Fifty years to him is a length of time he cannot judge. He believes 50 years is an eternity. There is so much time for him, and hours, days, and years pass and each seems to pass more quickly than earlier periods. Each time period is relative to a longer *remembered* past and *seems* shorter. He does not realize that minutes go by . . . you turn around, and years have passed. Time gone.

After one passes his 50th birthday, he perceives that 50 years has passed so quickly it seems like it took only a moment. Two hours is such a short time it hardly allows for a good nap. He then notes that trees that were small when he was small are now grown or gone. He realizes that if he had planted a tree 30 years ago, it would be a large and nearly mature tree now. How did he fail to understand that? Why did he not plant then? It is not too late. After all, 50 years is such a short time.

Some plant trees for children or grandchildren, in search of immortality, or to pass on a legacy. Some may be motivated by greed. The concept of future value is not an easy one to grasp.

Why do some plan for the future and others ignore it? Why do some worry about the future while others worry only about the present?

Thomas Hine, in his book *Facing Tomorrow*, gives his thoughts on the future:

Economic orthodoxy tells us that the value of the future to people today declines so rapidly that it is hardly worth including when calculating the choices we make. During the last two decades, altruistic ideas about the future have fallen into disrepute. A sense of the future implies that there are some things worth making sacrifices for, even if all of those making the sacrifice won't necessarily be present for the pay off.

The future is a generous concept, with an eye toward the well-being of generations yet unborn. And, it is also a conservative idea, a belief that actions will communicate lasting values through time. In having a sense of the future, we place ourselves in the role of loving parents, rather than clamorous children who know only their immediate desires.

Today, people become angry at the future because it is not going to provide what was once expected. We need a clearer idea of what we can anticipate, what we can create, so that we can once again feel the exaltation of moving toward something we want rather than the bitterness of settling for less. Finding that guide, that sense of the future, is the goal of all that follow . . . It begins with a postulate. The future is a matter of life and death . . . Human progress does not consist of a few people having control of immense power, but in all people having access to great opportunity to live satisfying lives. We can look in the mirror and see evidence of our own mortality. We look to the future for its promise of a kind of immortality. We look to the future to celebrate life. (p. 18)

Without exception, the walnut growers I have met are looking to the future with eagerness. Each spring, they are eager to see how their trees will leaf and grow. Each summer, they look to see how much the young trees will grow and shape themselves and how many nuts will form. Each fall, they look to see how many nuts will drop and what the quality will be. Some even anticipate the game of trying to beat the squirrels. Most walnut growers I met are of advanced age, but filled with life and a desire to live. None reflected the anomie that is reported to be so common in modern society.

Man's Search for Meaning by Viktor E. Frankl, has been published in 21 languages. English editions alone have sold more than three million copies. It was judged one of the ten most influential books in America in 1991. In this book, Frankl explains his concept of psychology, called logotherapy, which focuses on the future, and the meanings to be fulfilled by each of us. According to Frankl, striving to find meaning in one's life is the primary motivational force in man. To live is to suffer, to survive is to find meaning in the suffering.

Frankl knows of suffering, for he survived terrible years in various Nazi concentration camps. If there is a purpose in life at all, there must be a purpose in suffering and in dying. But no man can tell another what that purpose is. Without purpose, there is a vacuum. Frankl points out that the existential vacuum is a widespread phenomenon of the 20th century and that it manifests itself mainly in a state of boredom.

The avoidance of boredom may be another reason why older men turn to planting trees after they have retired from a career. Many have time and money and seek to add meaning to a life which no longer is filled with the work of their earlier days. Frankl maintains that each situation in life represents a challenge to man and presents a problem for him to solve. He says:

> In a word, each man is questioned by life; and he can only answer to life by *answering for* his own life; to life he can only respond by being responsible. Thus, logotherapy sees in responsibleness the very essence of human existence. (p. 113)

Fortunately, some see responsibleness as concern for the land they own and express it by planting and caring for trees.

ঽ

The rapid rise in value of standing black walnut in the past three decades and the publicity given these price increases as noted in Chapter 1, Sylvania, have led many to look upon black walnut as a sure source of future wealth. Substantial effort has been made by some to calculate the investment value of black walnut and to prove that the probable return will approximate or exceed the return from common stocks. This book will not do that.

Any long-term investment carries hazards. The longer the term, the greater the risk of obsolescence or failure to anticipate future events of importance. Any drive through the Midwest will reveal numerous examples of abandoned barns, grain cribs, and other structures that became obsolete long before they wore out.

The time, material, and money invested in these structures was viewed as "wise" by someone in the past, and are now viewed as "unwise" with our benefit of hindsight. This could be true of investments in trees if some major changes occur in the future.

Nevertheless, calculations are made of costs and future market values to determine expected rates of return from planting black walnut plantations. These calculations contain so many assumptions over such a long period of time that they are not fully persuasive. Because the time to harvest is so long (40 - 80 years); the initial investment so substantial ($300-$4,000 per acre plus land value); and the effort and expense each year for weed control, pruning, and thinning so great, few foresters or economists would consider a black walnut plantation of great size a "wise" investment. Most Walnut Council members limit their commitment to a small investment in a few acres.

Corporations that have indefinite life expectancy could be expected to invest in black walnut plantations for timber if they offered reasonably sure prospects of a high rate of return. But I have found only three corporations that have made a large commitment. Hammons Products Company, Pierson-Hollowell, and Pike Lumber Company, Inc. are the only three I've found that have planted and cared for black walnut plantations of any size. (See photo pp. 153 and 207.)

The retirement funds of pension plans would seem like a good source of investment funds to plant black walnut trees, but I have found none so committed. Fund managers are more comfortable with intangible assets whose value can be measured each day in the financial pages of the *Wall Street Journal*. It seems odd to some that they are more comfortable with intangible paper assets than with tangible and growing trees.

Timberland investments by corporations, institutions, fund managers, and individuals may be in the early stages of a substantial increase. *Timberland Investments, A Portfolio Perspective,* written by Zinkhan, Sizemore, Mason and Ebner, Timber Press, 1992, expresses their opinion that interest in timberland investments is increasing. They argue:

> As a portfolio asset, timberland is in an early phase of its product life cycle. Pension fund holdings through timberland investment management firms totalled approximately $1.39 billion in early 1991. Although minuscule by institutional standards, this amount represents 5,460 percent of what such funds had invested in timberland in 1981. (p. 161)

Although *Timberland Investments* mentions black walnut only once in general terms and is more oriented toward conifer forests for lumber and pulp, anyone interested in timberland investment will find this book the first and only book covering a wide spectrum of forest-related financial considerations. After explaining some aspects of timberland's investment characteristics, forest management concepts, capital asset pricing, timber markets, taxes and investment strategies, the authors conclude:

> During the next 50 years, we will observe substantial changes in timberland as an investment vehicle. Despite the risks, its flexibility and variety of potential benefits will likely encourage additional portfolio managers and curious individual investors to test our green seas of trees with small exposures. (p. 178)

State and federal government agencies have provided assistance funds, technical assistance, and financial incentives for long-range reforestation under various programs for almost 100 years. Most states offer reduced tax rates on forested land compared to other land uses. Technical assistance is offered by state and federally paid foresters as well as private foresters.

Since 1900, the Division of Forestry has offered advice and assistance, but too few trees have resulted. In 1924, the U.S. Department of Agriculture published the excellent bulletin *Black Walnut for Timber and Nuts*, for five cents, but few trees have resulted. This was only one of a long series of booklets advocating the planting of black walnut trees. *Planting Black Walnut for Timber*, Leaflet No. 487, U.S. Department of Agriculture Forest Service, revised January 1976, for 35 cents, is the current offering. It is 10 pages long, versus 30 in the 1924 version and is far inferior. It offers one-third the pages for seven times the money. (See Directory.)

In the 1930s, the Civilian Conservation Corps planted many walnuts, but apparently the squirrels and other rodents followed and dug many up. Much of the CCC reforestation effort was on eroded, nutrient-depleted land unsuited to growing walnuts. Most of the trees that grew were neglected. A recent survey of CCC-planted acres found few black walnut trees.

In the last 30 years, more trees have been planted than in the preceding 50. Federal and state assistance under various programs has been extensive. It remains to be seen how many trees will result. There is more to reforestation than just planting trees. Seedling trees require extensive care and management over several years until they reach sufficient size to fend for themselves. Even then, they benefit from pruning and thinning.

It is very difficult to estimate the impact of man's efforts to grow black walnuts. If we assume all growing walnuts are represented by the water in a five gallon bucket, do those walnuts planted by man represent a cup, teaspoonful, or only an eyedrop? No one knows, but some foresters believe not as much as a tablespoonful. There is no reason for concern about oversupply.

Although it is difficult to prove by financial calculation that the investment in black walnut tree culture is a wise financial endeavor, logic tells us it is. Worldwide, hardwood timber is being cut and consumed at a rate far in excess of regrowth. The rapid and unsustainable harvest of tropical rainforests in South America, Africa, and Asia is attracting worldwide attention and concern. Efforts are increasing to reduce the cutting of tropical rainforests. If successful, the flow of hardwoods into world markets will decline.

In *The Final Forest, The Battle for the Last Great Trees of the Pacific Northwest* (1992), William Dietrich described one view of the world forest scene. He wrote:

> In the summer of 1990, I had the opportunity while on assignment for the *Seattle Times* newspaper to look at trees around the world. I saw the tightly managed, heavily pressured forests of Japan, still recovering from disastrous overharvesting in the years during and after World War II. I saw the eucalyptus plantations in Thailand that are replacing the logged-off teak jungles: bleak new fields where pole-like saplings about 30 feet high, planted in monotonous rows, are cut after only three to five years to keep pace with the nation's pressing demand for lumber and firewood. I saw shaven Himalayan foothills in India, the oak replaced with seedlings of faster-growing pine and the weakened hillsides sheering off in monsoon rains to fill valleys with glacial rock. I saw parched plains in Pakistan, where pathetic seedlings planted in a brown pan of land are hand-watered with five-gallon cans, a tree-by-tree attempt to slow growing desertification. I saw the scrubby maquis of the Mediterranean, the product of thousands of years of overgrazing and resulting erosion, with grand acacia trees preserved for centuries in a Turkish village giving some notion of what the forests there must once have been like. I saw the forests of Germany, so weakened by acid rain that heavy winds toppled in one month what normally would have been harvested in five years. (p. 289)

Preservation efforts and environmental restrictions in the United States annually remove substantial hardwood acreage from current and future harvest. The gypsy moth caterpillar is killing large acreage of oak and other hardwood species in larger and larger areas of the Northeast. The gypsy moth spreads further west and south each year from its origins in Massachusetts. Population growth places increased demands on the supply of hardwoods. Residential and urban development consumes forested lands.

Planting black walnut and other hardwood species makes good economic sense for the nation. We are plagued by large and chronic deficits in the federal budget and our national balance of payments. In just a few years, the United States has become a debtor nation of historic size. Only a few years earlier, we were the world's largest creditor nation. We've gone from being a cash rich nation to a nation deeply in debt in just 30 years.

The United States owes money to other nations in larger and larger amounts. Interest and principal on these debts must be paid with United States products, services, raw materials, assets, or labor. Our hardwoods are in great demand worldwide. They are a unique renewable resource, but renewal is not automatic and cannot be taken for granted.

Throughout the Midwest, throughout the natural range of the Eastern black walnut, vast amounts of land are abandoned, untilled, or marginal as farmland. The U. S. Department of Agriculture's Consolidated Farm Service Agency classifies 279 million acres of 20 states in the northeastern-midwestern area as marginal farmland. Many tracts of land are small parcels but many are large. They are former cultivated fields, pastures, streambeds, abandoned fence rows, former building sites and vacant lots.

President Eisenhower's experience in leading a convoy from coast to coast before the Second World War, combined with his observations of Germany's autobahns, is credited with his leadership to promote the United States' interstate highway system. Now, as that highway system nears completion, it is possible for one to cruise comfortably at 70 m.p.h. in an imported car, consuming imported fuel, through the Midwest. If you do, you should observe the eroded grain fields, the abandoned homesites, and the depleted and neglected woodlots.

These magnificent highways enable one to avoid the small rural towns that are declining and decaying, in part, because the highways enable rural residents to send their children farther afield to consolidated schools, and for them to go farther to larger cities to shop. The small rural communities die, rural populations shrink, more people end up in cities, and the rural land is abandoned and neglected.

Tourists often comment that driving through the Midwest is dull and uninteresting because there is nothing to see but corn and soybeans. It is true that the Midwest has become more and more devoted to these two crops and exposed to the risks of such two-crop specialization. It is also true that excess production of these two crops has led to the abandonment and withdrawal from production of more and more land. Despite huge government subsidies, the farm population declines and the appearance of the countryside deteriorates as more land is farmed by fewer farmers with larger machines. Land that was cleared of magnificent timber at such great effort only a little over a century before is idled and abandoned to its fate.

Some of this idle land reverts slowly to natural forest, but to less desirable species and lower quality individuals than the black walnut, which is the most valuable. Natural forests can be improved in quality by planting more desirable species, pruning and selective thinning. Many chainsaws are sold each year, but few are used for pruning or upgrading the natural stands that develop. Many more chainsaws are sold each year than dibble bars, which are a common and economical tree planting tool. Sears carries at least a dozen varieties of chain saws but not dibble bars. Sears employees at the King of Prussia, Pennsylvania Sears store had never heard of dibble bars when I inquired about them.

Unfortunately, the natural regeneration of Eastern black walnut is often thwarted throughout the Midwest. It has become the fashion to mow vast areas of lawn and roadside with riding mowers. Many acres of former pasture are mowed to control weeds or for neat appearance alone. The expense of these mowers and the cost of fuel, repairs, and time represent a huge expenditure for fleeting beauty. A lawn may represent affluence, riding the mower may give a pleasurable high, a mowed pasture may look better than an unmowed pasture filled with weeds and young trees, but this fetish for neat and tidy mowed areas destroys young black walnut seedlings by the millions. A double waste.

After 40 years of mowing, after several new mowing machines have been purchased and discarded, after countless hours of riding in circles, there will be nothing to show for that huge expenditure. The valuable energy from the sun, the rain, and the rich soil have produced only grass clippings. There will be no beautiful, stately, valuable walnut trees where there could be. There will only be the lawn or pasture yet in need of mowing again each week. How blind we often are to that which is all around us. We are remembered by our acts, those we touch, and what we leave behind. A mowed lawn or pasture will not be long remembered.

F. Herbert Bormann, emeritus professor of forest ecology at Yale University School of Forestry and Environmental Studies co-authored a book published by Yale University Press called *Redesigning the American Lawn: A Search for Environmental Harmony* (1993). Some facts disclosed in this book are thought provoking. Bormann concludes:

> In area, grass is the largest single crop in the United States. If aggregated, American lawns would cover 25 million acres, an area equivalent to that occupied by the state of Pennsylvania. Grass uses as much as 10 times more chemical pesticides per acre than does an equivalent area of cropland. U.S. lawns absorb more synthetic fertilizers than India applies to all of its food crops. In the mindless hours of back-and-forth traversals, the power mower spews pollutants equivalent to a car driving 350 miles. (p.167)

Planting hardwood trees, particularly Eastern black walnut *where the site is suitable,* is good management of our land. The chronic excess production of most agriculture products is in sharp contrast to the shortage, now and projected, of hardwoods. The rain falls on the rich soil. The sun shines and brings free energy to the Earth. We can dictate what will grow. Will it be grass, which has no long-term value, crops, or trees? Why continue to till land, encourage erosion of topsoil, and produce excess milk or grain when we can plant trees and produce valuable and badly needed hardwood timber?

Ecologists argue convincingly that trees are good for our environment. Trees produce essential oxygen, tie up undesirable carbon from carbon dioxide for long periods of time, hold the soil against erosion, retain and release moisture into the atmosphere, and improve the quality of groundwater. Trees shelter wildlife and provide recreational opportunities.

Ecologists as preservationists miss the fact that forests cannot be preserved. Living things die and are replaced by other living things. Mature trees should be harvested, making way for new, young trees. Ecologists who really want to help the environment should be more active in encouraging reforestation efforts and not just in preserving already-growing trees and obstructing logging. Why is there so much concern for the tropical rainforests and so little for our own forests? Why is there so much concern about what we can't influence and so little action on what we can?

Environmental organizations are large, powerful, and popular with the press. The 12 largest environmental organizations boast a total membership of nearly seven million, a total annual budget of nearly $600 million, and total staff of over 4,000. Greenpeace USA has a membership of 1.6 million, a budget of $40 million, and a staff of 400. The Nature Conservancy has a membership of 724,000, a budget of $21.6 million, and a staff of 1,500. The Sierra Club has a membership of 650,000, an annual budget over $50 million and a staff of 380.

By comparison, the Walnut Council struggles to maintain a membership of 1,000 and operates on a budget of $30,000 with a staff of two. It is tiny by comparison, but it is accomplishing small wonders that could be much larger wonders with more members and a larger budget.

These large environmental organizations are exercising substantial economic and political power. Their influence has been felt in land grant colleges that have acknowledged our times by changing the title of their former Departments of Forestry to Departments of Forestry and Natural Resources. At many, the enrollment in what had been forestry is now running over 50 percent in environmental studies related to air, water, and wildlife. Students see job opportunities working for environmental organizations and for companies and governments dealing with new legislation on environmental quality generated by the environmental lobby. Why study forestry and tree care when more jobs are available elsewhere?

Many of those who do study forestry and tree care are expecting to obtain jobs caring for suburban and city trees and as landscape specialists. While landscaped lawns and suburban and corporate plantings are lovely to look at and are good for morale, they do nothing to help the productive hardwood forests of America. We are spending fortunes for cosmetic benefits while the hardwood forests upon which our veneer and hardwood timber industry is based are neglected.

Many landowners who own woodlands spend more on landscaping for their homes and on their lawns than they do on their woodlands. Active reforestation and woodland management need to receive much more attention and active participation by landowners than they currently receive.

Surveys of those owning the hardwood timberlands reveal most place very low emphasis on growing timber and own the land primarily for recreation, personal enjoyment, investment, etc. Most make little or no effort to establish hardwoods or improve naturally regenerated forests. What can be done to change these attitudes? What can be done to convince over seven million private landowners that they have a responsibility to future generations as well as to current citizens? What are the environmental organizations doing in this cause?

What legacy will we leave for our grandchildren? Will it be hardwood forests of low quality and quantity? Will it be abandoned and eroded pastures and fields? Will it be photos of extensively mowed fields, lawns and roadsides when it could be young and growing trees? Will it be a huge national debt and no growing assets to repay it? Will we be remembered as only another of the many "civilizations" that consumed natural resources without taking enough steps to replace them? Have we learned nothing from the past?

᠔

Near the end of his life, in 1930 (an age when old men could say or write what they believed without fear,) Luther Burbank commented upon his 40 years in California in *The Harvest of the Years*:

> Traveling about the countryside of Sonoma and neighboring counties today, I am amazed myself to come on old friends standing in groups or lining entrance roads or following fences — old, old trees that I planted with my own hands for my friends or customers, or raised and sold to them for their own planting. I had not realized how much time I spent in those earlier years on the growing of trees nor how much success I had, in this new country, in inducing others to grow them. You will notice that the substantial, the thrifty, the worthy, and the likable classes of people plant trees, no matter whether they are in a new and treeless country or in one already well-planted, and that the shiftless, the transient, the careless, and the self-ish are as little likely to set out sheltering trees as they are to be neat, thrifty, or good neighbors. Show me a devel-oped town with no trees and I will show you a town to avoid as a home for your families. Go through districts where want and squalor and crime and filth are the rule and you will be lucky to find even a gaunt specimen of a tree anywhere about. This is not by chance; the planted and tended tree is as sure a sign of civilization as a revered flag or a church spire or a schoolhouse belfry, and the English, who have carried civilization to every part of their dominions scattered far and wide about the earth, plant shade trees almost before they finish their houses or start their towns! (p. 284)
>
> I was never able to do nearly as much as I always wanted to with trees. A hardwood tree that will grow rapidly and in temperate climates would in time revolu-tionize the lumber industry. (p. 285)

We are now only beginning to realize that living stan-dards are no longer increasing steadily and constantly. We are only now becoming aware that resources are finite. We have yet to learn that the future *must* depend upon renew-able resources, and that renewal is not automatic. We have yet to learn that greater investments in renewable resources will be required if future generations are to enjoy decent living standards.

The Eastern black walnut is a unique renewable American resource whose potential has not been realized. It has been used without sufficient regard to renewal. Natural regeneration under current forestry techniques is unlikely to produce as many black walnut trees as have been produced under early harvesting techniques. Because of man and without the help of man, the Eastern black walnut will continue to have potential that is unrealized.

ða

The Amish live close to their soil and their God. An Amish man wrote the following in one of their Amish periodicals:

> [Tourists] take a special interest in the countryside, giving the Amish a lot of credit for its beauty. However, they don't realize that the Lord made the rolling hills and gave the fertile soil, the sunshine, and the rain. He gave us the seed to plant that is germinated. No person in the world is able to germinate a grain of seed. Neither can they make a blade of grass grow and reproduce. We can cultivate the soil, plant and harvest, but we have no power to make a plant grow. So there is no honor to the human race for this beautiful countryside. We live on the land like renters. After this generation passes on, the land is left behind for another generation to live on.

Lancaster County, which is the home of many Amish, is one of the major tourist attractions of Pennsylvania, and it is beautiful. Under the intensive cultivation and husbandry of these plain and gentle people, who live close to their soil and their God, a tremendous volume of fruit, vegetables, feed grains, and livestock is produced each year.

Some black walnuts survive on their land from the time when the area was heavily forested. But these surviving black walnuts are a sad and scruffy lot now outside their natural forest environment and isolated in pastures, roadsides and barnlots where they are subjected to numerous indignities. They appear totally unrelated to the magnificent specimens in Cox Woods, Paoli, Indiana, but they are. Commercial and housing development threatens this rich farmland just as intensive farming has threatened these forlorn surviving black walnuts.

ﻬ

Most scientists now believe the Universe began about 18 billion years ago with the "Big Bang," and that the Earth coalesced from cosmic dust about 4.55 billion years ago. They believe life began about 3.5 billion years ago and geological evidence indicates that *Juglans nigra* has been present on Earth for 100 million years. The earliest evidence of manlike creatures on earth was about 4 million years ago, but our early ancestors, *homo sapiens,* appeared only a mere 40,000 years ago.

Ancestors of native Americans are believed to have crossed the land bridge from Asia and began spreading across the continent near the end of the last Ice Age, about 14,000 years ago. Europeans "discovered" America 500 years ago and began "developing" it by exploiting it and spreading themselves and their works across the continent. The magnificent hardwood forests of Indiana, but for Cox Woods, were first "harvested" about 100 years ago. Now, the second-growth "harvest" is nearly complete. Walnut trees of size are rare and walnut reforestation is uncertain.

In 1980, Carl Sagan observed:

> Part of the resistance to Darwin and Wallace derives from our difficulty in imagining the passage of millennia, much less the aeons. What does 70 million years mean to beings who live only one-millionth as long? We are like butterflies who flutter for a day and think it is forever.

Yes, like butterflies. But butterflies with an extraordinary ability to exploit and consume the natural resources of the Earth. We are like the grasshopper who played and danced as winter approached without regard to the future. Despite our vaunted "intelligence," we have demonstrated remarkably little wisdom or willingness to invest in renewable resources for the future. Native Americans had a saying, "We did not inherit the earth from our parents. We are borrowing it from our children."

We have become more and more selfish. Hedonism has replaced Calvinism as our predominant value system. Denial and deferral are considered foolish traits. We save a smaller share of our higher incomes than earlier generations. However, we humans have clearly demonstrated a remarkable ability to reproduce ourselves.

Experts believe that 10,000 years ago there were probably several million humans alive on Earth. By A.D. 1, nearly 2,000 years ago, the world population was estimated to be about 200 million. Today the world population is estimated to be about 5.3 billion, which totals more people than *altogether* have lived before. There has been a 1,000-fold increase in the living human population in the last 10,000 years. Some 250,000 more people are born than die every day! If the world population continues to grow at its current rate, by the year 2029 our present population will double, and by the year 2050 our present population will triple.

Man devotes great effort and expense to education and immodestly believes himself to be the most intelligent of all Earth's creatures. An objective outside opinion might conclude otherwise. We believe we are smart, but we may not be wise. The history, use, and unrealized potential of our unique American renewable natural resource, the Eastern black walnut, reflects upon us all.

If you would not be forgotten
as soon as you are dead and rotten,
either write things worth reading
or do things worth writing.

—*Benjamin Franklin*

Shoe

8

SOME ILLINOIS HISTORY

1828—1995

ैॐ

"A man almost always knows about his ancestors and respects them; his imagination extends to his great-grandchildren, and he loves them. He freely does his duty by both ancestors and descendants and often sacrifices personal pleasures for the sake of beings who are no longer alive or not born yet."

—Alexis de Tocqueville

In 1828, 25 years after Lewis and Clark explored the way west to the Pacific and 13 years after the Chicago Massacre, Elizabeth Davison, age 12, moved with her parents, two brothers and three sisters from Ohio to Vermilion County, Illinois. The first Europeans to settle in Vermilion county had arrived only nine years earlier in 1819. The Davison family settled on land 12 miles north of Danville on the west bank of the North Fork, Vermilion River. The North Fork flows south and joins the Vermilion, which flows southeast into Indiana where it joins the Wabash, which flows south between the two states until it joins the Ohio.

Illinois had been part of the Northwest Territory and, in his first five years of office, Governor William Henry

Harrison had acquired, from the bewildered and divided chiefs, the southern half of Indiana, southern Wisconsin, and all of Illinois. Vermilion County had been acquired in 1803, as part of this land reaching from the Ohio River to Lake Michigan. This vast, fertile area was bought for $400 from native Americans reduced by disease and whiskey. This land was surveyed by the government, awarded to army veterans as land grants, and offered for sale from government land offices for $.62 to $1.25 per acre.

European immigrants were pouring into the heartland of America. In 1810, the combined population of Kentucky, Ohio, Indiana, and Illinois was 674,073; in 1830 it was 2,131,296. Illinois had been declared a territory on February 9, 1809 and a state on December 3, 1818. The Illinois population in 1818 was about 34,620. This was less than required by law to form a state, but the population count had been fudged. In the 1830 census, the population was 157,445.

Only fringes of Illinois, which was then second in size only to Georgia and half the size of Great Britain, had been settled by 1828. Abraham Lincoln was 19 years old that year and still living at Little Pigeon Creek south of Paoli, Indiana. He would help his father move to New Salem, Illinois, on the Sangamon River in 1831.

The Davison family chose bench woodland on the edge of the Grand Prairie, which was unsettled and stretched from Chicago into midstate Illinois. At that time, settlements at the Kinzie trading post, at the Chicago portage, had almost no connection to the two main areas of settlement radiating from Kaskaskia, with its tradition of comparative wealth and culture, and Shawneetown, the fairly new port of entry on the Ohio River. Most settlements were along waterways that were the superhighways of the period.

The land the Davisons chose was close to Hubbard's Trace, which was a route Gurdon Saltonstall Hubbard blazed south from Chicago in the late 1820s. Hubbard traveled south from Chicago with pack ponies through Watseka and Danville toward the Wabash River country. Hubbard's trail was then the only clearly marked trail and later became the State Road, Illinois Route #1, The Dixie Highway.

The area had been opened by fur traders, and although Canada produced better pelts, chiefly because of climatic differences, the Illinois and Wabash river valleys and the Mississippi between St. Louis and Prairie du Chien were major fur-bearing areas. From the Illinois valley in 1816, traders shipped the hides of 10,000 deer, 300 bears, 10,000 raccoons, 400 otter, beaver, cat, fox, and mink for a total value of $23,700.

In 1828, bones of buffalo and elk could still be found bleaching on the prairie, but both species had been hunted to extinction east of the Mississippi. There were still some deer and native Americans living in the area around Danville, but most of both were gone. The last armed conflict with native Americans east of the Mississippi was the brief and tragic Black Hawk War of 1831, fought for control of Northern Illinois and Wisconsin. For his service in this war, Abraham Lincoln received 200 acres of land.

In the summer of 1828, Elizabeth Davison lived with her family in a covered wagon until a cabin was built near a spring close to the river in deep woods. On October 14, 1841, she married John Johnston Chenoweth, and they lived on the land and were the parents of 11 children. Only five lived to adulthood. Pioneer mothers buried many children. Illinois was considered unhealthy, and ague and fever were common.

The next to own the land was Elizabeth's oldest son, Henry Wilson Chenoweth, born July 9, 1843. During the Civil War, Henry served four years in Company F, Fourth Illinois Cavalry, which was attached to Sherman's Army in its march to the sea. After the war, on February 26, 1868, Henry married Catharine Butt. They had four children, but only two sons lived to adulthood. Their oldest son, Frank Morton Chenoweth, was born July 10, 1877, and a second son, Evard Leroy Chenoweth, was born September 19, 1879.

These two men lived on the land, and eventually shared ownership and farmed it. The two brothers looked so much alike that they were often mistaken for each other. They were both general farmers and raised chickens, hogs, cattle, and horses. They both had a small orchard, grew a vegetable garden called a "truck patch," and lived only a mile apart so they could work together at some tasks and share some machinery, such as a grain binder and cider press.

Each man married, lost his first wife to death and remarried. Evard's second wife died also, and he had no children. Frank had only one son, E. Thomas Chenoweth born August 2, 1904, who eventually became my father. Frank was my grandfather, and Evard my granduncle.

Both Frank and Evard were slight, wiry, pious, and frugal. They were men with common tastes who found comfort in simple pleasures. Frank's farm was 1.5 miles northwest of the original homestead on the Grand Prairie, and he took pride in having "Prairie View Farm" lettered on his big red barn. He enjoyed gazing west across the prairie less than a mile to the Dixie Highway, Route # 1, which was a main road from Chicago to Florida in mid-century.

A little over a mile southeast and closer to the original homestead, Evard's farm was on the edge of the woodland where the cabin had been built in 1828. The two brothers shared the land along the North Fork and a pasture referred to as "the woods pasture," because it had never been completely cleared of native timber. They both grazed cattle there during part of the year. Evard owned woodland south of the woods pasture that was referred to as "the big woods," since it had tall trees and was not grazed. Evard owned a cleared field of nine acres south and west of the woods pasture and Frank owned a cleared field of 13 acres north of the woods pasture. The woods pasture contained the original cabin site.

While the two brothers looked much alike and shared common habits and mannerisms, they had different personalities and opinions. Frank placed great stress on neatness and tidiness and worked long hours in the hot, humid summers digging weeds and mowing fence rows. Evard laughed at this and napped. Frank spent long hours trimming his orchard, stacking branches, saving each twig and working up the trimmings for firewood. Evard went into the big woods, dropped a tree or two, sawed it, split it, and burned sizable chunks of good firewood. Evard split oak for fence posts and had lovely fence posts, but they did not last as long as the smaller, crooked osage orange posts that Frank used.

Frank was very allergic to poison ivy, while Evard had a natural immunity that allowed him to pull the vines bare handed from fence rows without getting a rash. Frank treated his inevitable summer poison ivy rash with water from the tank where Mr. Beck cooled plow shares. The theory was that the iron in the water reduced the rash. Beck, who never lost his heavy German accent, was the short, stout blacksmith in Henning, Illinois who re-shaped and sharpened plow shares that broke the heavy black soil of the Grand Prairie. Unsharpened and sharp-ened shares filled the street outside the blacksmith's shop with the chalked names of the owners on each share. Status was associated with the number of shares awaiting each owner with his name on them. Frank and Evard had few.

When the two brothers spoke to discuss work to be done together or a common project, they seldom spoke directly to each other or looked at each other. Facing oppo-site directions, they would eventually reach some agree-ment on procedure. Frank was a social person and enjoyed people and their company. Evard enjoyed solitude and, after his second wife died, lived alone many years in a house not without clutter. Evard's lifestyle supported the contention that, "Men without women often live like bears with furniture." When working the field on a summer day and sighting a well-dressed visitor walking toward them, Frank could be expected to react enthusiastically: "Oh, good, here comes someone!" Evard might react: "Oh dear, I wonder what the devil he wants?"

The land along the North Fork River had some black walnut trees both in the big woods and in the woods pas-ture. Every few years a buyer would contact one brother or the other seeking to buy the trees. During WW II, Evard responded to a government plea for black walnut timber to produce gunstocks. In 1945, he sold some black walnut trees that were cut and transported to Danville, Illinois, where the logs were allowed to remain and rot. It was too late in the war.

Frank was an air raid warden during the war. I vividly recall riding with him in his gray Ford, lights out, along the dark country roads of Illinois to visit neighbors' homes to advise them that they were supposed to have window blinds pulled and be practicing blackout conditions during the drill. He had a metal hat and a badge and took his job very seriously. Fortunately, neither Germany nor Japan managed to bomb central Illinois. I was about ten and found it all rather strange, even then.

Evard managed the big woods by harvesting larger trees for posts and lumber. He cut trees that died from natural causes or were of no other use, for firewood. Evard's sharp eyes enabled him to find many arrowheads and stone tools left on this land by native Americans who had hunted or camped there. Had they in any way been responsible for the oak and walnut trees Evard cut?

No one knows how long native Americans walked this land, but evidence suggests it may have been for over 10,000 years. If so, some 500 generations of native Americans may have walked and hunted here before Europeans arrived. I am only the sixth generation of European origin to "own" this land. How new we are.

The woods pasture, except for a rare walnut tree harvest, was not managed, but kept as a pasture. Frank would mow the grass between the trees with a horsedrawn mower. The fence row around the pasture was mowed to keep weeds and young trees off the wire. When I was 19 and very tough, I mowed nearly a mile of fence row with a scythe one very hot, humid day in August. I thought I was pretty good with a scythe, but Frank was a master and proud of it.

Frank had a cradle scythe that had belonged to his grandfather and that he had used in his youth to harvest some wheat. He often spoke of using the cradle to cut wheat, and I believe it was one of his most valued possessions. For many years the cradle lay unused in the dusty loft above his garage. He gave it to me before he died.

The woods pasture contained a few older black walnut, red cedar, shingle oak, red oak, white oak, burr oak and hickory. Under light grazing, young trees of many species such as hickory, red oak, burr oak, white oak, red cedar, maple, catalpa, osage orange, black cherry and black or honey locust, which had long sharp thorns, began to grow.

Multiflora rose, gooseberry, blackberry, poison ivy, and grape vines began to intrude when Frank quit mowing after he grew old and his last team of horses was sold in the mid '60s.

To the best of my knowledge, neither Frank or Evard planted or pruned trees or practiced what is commonly referred to as timber stand improvement. Now, it seems odd to me that neither ever did any of this. I'm not sure why they did not, but I would guess it was because they accepted the woods as a part of nature. It was a given, and it never occurred to them to intervene to improve it or to manage it in any way. To this day, many land-owners leave their forests unmanaged and practice no timber stand improvement.

Tom Chenoweth, Frank's son (my father), attended Centennial School, a one-room grade school, and then Bismarck High School. He rode a horse, buggy, or bicycle past Evard's home, through the woods pasture and the big woods, across the North Fork River at a ford and on to Bismarck. In the '20s, Tom enrolled at the University of Illinois in the School of Agriculture. While there, he heard of the increasing shortage of good quality black walnut and obtained U.S. Department of Agriculture Farmer's Bulletin No. 1392 titled "Black Walnut for Timber and Nuts," dated August 1924, for five cents, which I still have.

One fall day in 1928, he took a bucket filled with walnut nuts and a spade and planted walnut nuts along the Prairie View Farm pasture roadside fence in one long row with a nut planted about every 20 feet. He did the same along the north fence of the woods pasture near the North Fork River. At each location he planted about 30 nuts which, in 66 years, have grown into fairly large walnut trees.

These trees were never pruned with the intent of producing veneer timber but were allowed to grow and mature on their own. Frank did remove bag worms each summer from those growing along his pasture fence and did prune branches that obstructed him when he mowed his pasture. Now, 67 years later, the trees on the prairie are 11

A row of black walnuts now 67 years old that were planted as nuts in 1928 by my father, E. Thomas Chenoweth. The largest is 23 inches in diameter. Growing on the prairie in heavy, wet soil and unpruned, they are of little value.

to 23 inches in diameter, poorly shaped and near timber size, but they are not veneer quality. Those nearest the river are 24 to 35 inches in diameter, twice as large, and could be harvested, but their branches are low to the ground and they would not make good veneer logs. If these trees had been pruned in the 1930s and 1940s, their value could have been greatly enhanced. I believe it just did not occur to Tom, Frank, or Evard to do it. Or to me, either.

On June 13, 1928, Tom graduated from the University of Illinois with a Bachelor of Science degree in Agriculture. In 1930, he bought a 121-acre farm in Prairie Township, Warren County, Indiana, 22 miles northeast of his boyhood home. On February 24, 1931, he married Vera Alece Roberts, an Illinois neighbor, who had lived on the farm just north of the cabin site land. On November 27, 1933, in Frank's home on Prairie View Farm, she gave birth to Robert Thomas Chenoweth. I was named Robert after Frank's uncle, and Thomas after my father.

Tom and Vera visited often with Frank and Evard. Tom worked with his father and uncle at many tasks. Often

I visited my grandfather during school vacations, week-
ends and summers. Prairie View Farm became a second
home to me. For five summers, 1951-1955, while on summer
vacation from Purdue University, I worked on the farm for
my grandfather. There was no written record of the family
in the 1800s, and the cabin site was the earliest record of the
family history. Visiting the woods brought us close to the
past and our pioneer heritage, and I always enjoyed a walk
in the woods.

In 1974, through the generosity of Vera and Tom
Chenoweth, I gained title to 60 acres along the North Fork
River including the cabin site, what had been Frank's 13-
acre cleared field, the woods pasture, the big woods, and
Evard's nine-acre cleared field. On December 7, 1973, my
father wrote me, explaining this gift:

> This 60 acres, I am sure, has a sentimental value to
> you and it is best you should own it before you are too old
> for it to mean anything to you. I was in possession in 1971,
> and then over 66 years old. It did not mean anything to me
> then. At one time, I was all wrapped up in that. You
> seemed to wish the walnut trees to stay and if you own
> them they can stay if someone doesn't steal them. They
> are not too easy to reach.

The two cleared fields continued to be farmed by a
neighbor. The big woods and the woods pasture, which
was last grazed in 1976, were untouched and grew undisturbed. The woods pasture rapidly began to look like a
Midwestern jungle with a heavy growth of poison ivy,
multiflora rose, blackberry bushes, weeds, and a variety of
native trees replacing bluegrass sod.

At that time I was in the Army, stationed in the East
and seldom able to visit the land, but I did manage to see
it every two or three years. In summer it was not a hospi-
table place. Waist-high poison ivy, brambles, vines, and
ferocious mosquitoes made a summer walk in the woods an
uncomfortable and chilling experience. In spring, fall, and
winter it was quite lovely and a pleasure to visit. I decided
to let the big woods and woods pasture revert to nature
undisturbed and let Mother Nature do what she wanted.

I'm not sure why I had this idea, but at the time it seemed like a good one. Back to nature it was.

In the spring of 1987, I visited the land and walked the woods. I noticed several large, mature trees had fallen and were decaying on the forest floor. Several others had died standing and would eventually fall.

The last timber harvest had been in 1964, when Frank sold some black walnuts from the woods pasture to a buyer from Potomac, Illinois. The buyer cut and removed several trees, but Frank was never paid. He went to collect but was told the buyer's capital was tied up in logs and he had no money. The loggers were not experienced, and they left tall stumps. My father and I spent a few hours one hot, humid summer day attempting to remove a cross section of a walnut stump with a crosscut saw because mother wanted a walnut coffee table. The stump was over four feet in diameter and we were unequal to the task and gave up.

In 1970, a timber buyer had offered my father $15,000 for the walnut trees, including $2,400 for the largest tree. The trees were to be shipped to Schlobach Gebr in Germany. My father wrote, "I haven't been in those woods much since 1955 when I helped Uncle Eb. Seems like a fantastic sum - $15,000. Wonder what the Germans do with that? I believe the back 64 acres woods, pasture, and fields were appraised at about $9,000." My father decided not to sell the trees then, and they were still there in 1987.

In 1987, it was obvious that the timber had many mature trees, and that trees were very close and struggling for light. It seemed a waste to let such lovely trees die and decay, so I decided to seek professional advice. I wrote to the Department of Forestry, University of Illinois and requested advice or their recommendation on a professional forester who could help me. Gary Rolfe, Head, Department of Forestry, replied with the names and addresses of several professional foresters who could survey the timber and advise me on what to do.

In October 1987, two foresters from a firm in Terre Haute, Indiana met with me and together we spent two days surveying the timber, marking mature trees, identifying species, judging size and quality, and making decisions on which trees to save and which could be harvested. They debated whether it would be best to hold two separate sales, one as veneer and another as standard timber, or just one that would include all the timber.

Eventually, they decided to include all the timber in one sale and prepared an invitation to bid on timber that included a detailed timber sale summary, a set of bidding instructions, a map of the 60 acres and a copy of the Vermilion County plat book showing the location of the property. Individual trees to be sold were marked with orange paint and those deemed of veneer quality were numbered and listed individually on a supplemental sheet. Only black walnut and white oak were numbered and designated for veneer.

We selected and marked for sale 33 Eastern black walnuts that had an average diameter at breast height (DBH) of 23 inches. These trees were estimated to contain an average of 300 board feet of veneer, of which 270 was prime and 30 select, plus 104 board feet of lumber. The largest tree of this group was 34 inches in diameter and contained 450 board feet of prime veneer. We selected for sale no trees less than 18 inches DBH.

Before the auction, I received a letter from the forester advising me as follows:

> Appraising trees of this caliber is difficult because accurate market prices are not commonly reported. We have used the Purdue University current timber price report to arrive at an appraisal that should be considered as an absolute minimum acceptable value. This value is $61,564.56. We then added $2.00/board foot to the walnut veneer to arrive at what we consider to be the value in the true "competitive" market. This is based on comparables to other sales which we have had with similar quality trees. Taking this into account, the appraisal increases to $81,329.51. Of this total, $64,000 was attributable to the 33 black walnut, $6,800 to the 21 white oak and the remainder to the other trees.

On the day of the scheduled auction, November 23, 1987, I received an unsolicited phone call from someone I did not know and had never met. He offered me $50,000 for the walnut trees. I said, "No thank you."

and referred the caller to my professional forester. I explained that the auction was to be held at the Beefhouse Restaurant near Covington, Indiana later that day.

We received ten bids at the auction, and the highest was from the Hoosier Veneer Corporation, Trafalger, Indiana for $112,200. I accepted this bid, and we entered into a contract in which the buyer paid me $107,712 and paid the Illinois Department of Conservation $4,488. Under the Illinois Forestry Development Act, Illinois collects four percent of timber sales for the purpose of encouraging further timber improvement. In addition, I paid my professional foresters an eight percent commission on the total ($8,976) for their services, which included making the survey, marking the trees, preparing the bid proposal, advertising the auction, supervising the timber harvest and preparing a Forest Management Plan. The Hoosier Veneer Corporation had until December 1, 1989, to cut and remove the trees. They completed their harvest before the spring of 1989.

After these expenses, I netted $98,736. Of course there were state and federal income taxes due. After paying these there was enough cash left to purchase 62 acres of excellent farmland 18 miles northeast on the Indiana side of the state

A cutter for the Hoosier Veneer Company prepares to harvest an Eastern black walnut in the winter of 1989. Photo courtesy of Hoosier Veneer Company.

line in Prairie Township, Warren County. Those mature trees, only a few of the total on only a small portion of the 60 acres, had provided money to the Illinois Forestry Department, jobs and money to the foresters, jobs for timber harvesters, truckers and veneer slicers, jobs and raw material to cover walls and furniture, money through taxes for federal and state governments, and yet enough money to purchase an additional 62 acres of very good farmland.

While the bigger trees were gone, many large and many more young trees remained. Over 30 large walnuts remained that could have been harvested but were left to grow larger. It was still a beautiful wooded area and a pleasure to visit. Preservationists might argue that the trees should not have been cut but should have been placed into a nature preserve. Had this been done, it would have been at the cost of all the jobs and the income to many individuals, and the state and federal government. And the trees would have eventually died and rotted into the forest floor to be lost forever. Preservation is not without considerable cost to many people.

In addition, there was enough money to finance the reforestation of the two fields, cleared by my ancestors in the 1800s, and farmed for over 100 years. While conducting the survey in October 1987, I decided to reforest the two cleared fields of nine and 13 acres and thus make the entire 60 acres woodland. When Frank and Evard farmed these fields they had grown corn, oats, and clover. This was a less severe rotation than is now commonly practiced throughout the Midwest. A rotation of corn and soybeans is now common. The two fields are subject to mild erosion, are wet in places, contain some rocks, and because of size are inconvenient for large modern farm equipment. Since both corn and soybeans were abundant and prices weak, planting trees on these two fields seemed like the good and wise thing to do. It would be an act of conservation.

My father, Tom Chenoweth, was a devoted conservationist. He read and studied nature all his life and admired the books of Louis Bromfield. Bromfield was a prolific writer and wrote such popular novels as *The Rains Came, Mrs. Parkington, Pleasant Valley,* and *The Man Who Had Everything.* Many of his novels were made into motion pictures. With his substantial income from writing, Bromfield purchased three poor, eroded farms in Ohio, and devoted himself and a good amount of his money to this land. Then he wrote about that.

In *Malabar Farm* and *Out of the Earth*, Bromfield described his successful efforts to restore the soil of his poor, run-down land to return it to a productive and fruitful dairy farm. Bromfield was an enthusiastic advocate of conservation and good husbandry of the soil. He was a true believer. I read some of Bromfield's books and learned from them, but I learned more listening to my father talk soils and conservation with anyone who would listen.

One who listened most was Joe Lesny, a family friend who often spent long winter days talking soils and conservation with my father. While I listened and absorbed some, Joe absorbed more and became an even more devoted conservationist than my father. While my father had an agriculture degree from the University of Illinois, Joe Lesny had only a fourth grade education.

Joe had come out of Chicago during the Depression and taken a job with an elderly lawyer in the small town of Ambia, Indiana, which was two miles north of my father's farm. When the lawyer died, Joe managed his affairs, sold insurance, and gradually began to manage farmland for absentee owners. Joe loved to hunt and fish and could tell stories like no one I've ever known. Joe served in the army in WW I, returned and married, but when his wife died shortly after they were married, enlisted to fight again in WW II and saw service in the Pacific. While he was away, my father handled his farm management work and returned the business to Joe when he returned from the war.

Shortly after Joe returned from the Pacific, he bought 80 acres on the south slope of a moraine a mile south of my father's farm. "Joe's Eighty," as it became known by all, was a poor, eroded piece of land that had been farmed and abused for about 75 years when Joe bought it. Joe applied large quantities of limestone, potash, nitrogen, and phosphate. First he grew wheat and sweet clover, which he plowed under as a green manure crop. He tiled the land, filled two deep gullies, and installed two beautiful grass waterways to channel runoff water. He picked up rocks and walked the land nearly every day. Joe loved that Eighty like he would have loved the child he never had.

My father and Joe Lesny influenced me in many ways. Listening to them talk about soils, waterways, erosion, tilth, organic matter, clover, alfalfa, limestone, phosphates, potash, and all the subjects related to agriculture, I became convinced too, of the importance of conservation. They decried the practice of fall plowing and the trend to a rotation of corn and soybeans, which they saw as the major cause of massive sheet erosion that was taking topsoil from the land at an unsustainable rate. My father often said, "Mankind owed his survival to six inches of topsoil and the fact that it rained." Like Bromfield, their goal was to leave their land better than when they got it, and they did.

Such a philosophy was not common. Both men could have made more money farming the land heavily and abusing it, but they did not. Both could have bought more land and exploited it for more money, but they did not. Both held the view that ownership of land was a sacred trust and that their stewardship was a responsibility that they did not take lightly. The long conversations between these two men and my close association with them strongly influenced me and my decision to reforest these two fields.

Robert Bly, poet, public speaker, and author of *Iron John*, in seminar speeches and in his writings, argues that a young man who is not being praised and encouraged by an older man is being hurt. He argues that young men need older men after whom they mold their own lives. Bly is right! When I was young, I was blessed by knowing well and working closely with several older men. I wish all young men could have such an opportunity. A farm life offers that opportunity to young men, but fewer and fewer young men now live on farms. Fewer have close work-related experiences with older men. Working together on any common project bonds men.

After deciding to reforest these 22 acres, I learned from my professional foresters that it was not only a good thing to do, but that it was timely and good economics as well. If I applied for assistance from the State of Illinois, I could expect to receive financial help to recover part of the $4,488 paid to them under the Forestry Development Act. I needed to have a Forest Management Plan, and I had one prepared by my professional foresters.

In the plan, my professional foresters recommended planting seven tree species: white pine, black walnut, white oak, red oak, white ash, tulip poplar, and black alder. The black alder were to be half the total and were intended to produce nitrogen to feed the other trees. They were also to provide rapid growth and competition so the other trees would grow taller with fewer side branches, thus requiring less pruning to produce desirable veneer trees. The white pine were intended to provide a wind break on the west of each field since part of each field was exposed to the prevailing west and northwesterly winter winds blowing across the Grand Prairie. The plan also stated, "All trees except the black alder will be sprayed with the chemical 'Oust' (Alder can be sprayed after the first year). Spraying will retard the growth of unwanted grasses and weeds and will enable the trees to become established." I decided to follow their advice completely.

On June 12, 1988, I signed a contract with my professional foresters in which they agreed to plant the trees, and I agreed to pay them $5,244. We worked out details for the planting during the winter and spring of 88/89. On February 10, 1989, I received a pleasant letter from one of the professional foresters explaining the tree harvest that had been completed and firming details for planting. He said:

> It is nice to work for you Bob, because you actually show interest in good land stewardship. This is contrary to most of our clients, where we have to do a lot of educating. We ask you to understand that nothing in the field of Forestry is exact . . . we must contend with Mother Nature, changing markets and government programs, and of course people (perhaps the most unpredictable!)

This letter proved to be prophetic. In May 1989, we met to plant 15,000 trees on the 22 acres. The land was wet, but had been in clover and grass the preceding year, and we were able to work. My professional foresters had acquired a new tractor with a mounted hydraulically lifted planter, and a liquid tank mounted on the front with a hose leading to a sprayer nozzle at the rear.

The foresters brought the trees from the Indiana state nursery at Vallonia. They were one-year-old seedlings, wrapped in sisal craft paper and packed with sphagnum moss soaked in water to keep roots moist and alive. One forester drove the tractor, another rode the planter and planted the trees, and two men trimmed roots and tops of the seedlings so they would fit the planter channel and clear the planter as it passed over the trees. As time permitted, we all walked the area, inspecting the planting and stepping on soil around the trees to improve their soil contact.

Trees were planted six feet apart in rows 12 feet apart with the rows running north and south. We began with two rows of white pine along the west and then alternated a row of black alder with the other species so that half the planting was black alder.

Despite the plan statement that the black alder would not be sprayed with Oust, the professional foresters decided to spray all the rows and did so. This would later prove to be a mistake, as we lost half the black alder, which were half the planting. This loss was probably caused by the Oust spray, which was not recommended for alder by DuPont, manufacturers of Oust.

One-year-old seedlings from the Indiana Division of Forestry, DNR ready for planting.

In two days, we completed the planting of 500 white pine, 1,600 black walnut, 1,400 white oak, 1,400 red oak, 1,400 white ash, 1,400 yellow poplar and 7,300 black alder. Using dibble bars, which are hand tools similar to spades, we planted the smaller, rejected seedlings in the woods pasture and big woods.

The tractor-mounted planter consisted of a three-foot disk, two plow shares to open the soil after the disk had cut it, two spreaders to hold the soil apart for the planter to insert a tree, a seat for the planter, two boxes to hold trees, two rubber wheels to press the soil back around the planted tree, and then at the end, a spray nozzle spraying a two-foot band of Oust onto the tree and soil. A man walked each row putting in marker flags and stomping on the soil to set the tree.

The walnut were planted primarily on the east side of each field nearer the North Fork River in a soil type more suitable to black walnut. The other species were intermixed throughout the plantation in groups of 10 or 12 together in a row. If I were doing it over, I would intermix them even more, because tulip poplar, in Vermilion County, are at the extreme northwest of their natural range and survival seems to be low. As the population grows and matures, I believe it will be better if the trees are more evenly mixed so that better choices will be offered when it is necessary to thin trees. In addition, when mowing in heavy weed growth, it is easier to see the trees if there is more variety evenly mixed.

The start of planting 15,000 trees in May 1989 on 22 acres.

Of the $5,244 cost for reforestation, I recovered $2,686.20 from the State of Illinois (60 percent of $4,488 I had paid into the fund) and an additional $777 cost sharing from the Vermilion County ASCS office of the U.S. Department of Agriculture. I placed the 22 acres into the conservation reserve program (CRP) with the U.S. Department of Agriculture, thus taking it out of grain production and would receive $1,887 per year for 10 years. After 10 years, there will be no further subsidy, and it would be a long, long time before any of the trees were large enough to harvest. Also, property taxes were lowered in recognition of the change from crop land to timber land.

But it was soon evident we were not finished. During the summer of 1989, it rained heavily and conditions seemed to be ideal for establishing a new forest. However, there was a tremendous explosion of rodents, which were probably field mice or voles. They seemed to find the channel provided by the planter a great place to meet, reproduce, nest, and move undetected by predators. They probably killed some of the trees by eating around them and girdling them during the winter of 89-90.

More serious was the loss during the first summer of about half the black alder, which died without sprouting. I believe the Oust killed them, but it was impossible to prove, and my professional foresters maintained it was because of excessive rain. They said that the decision to spray the black alder with Oust was based on a single study that had proved alder were not harmed by Oust. So, based on this single field test that had been conducted in a dry year, and contrary to their own forest management plan and the recommendations of DuPont, they had sprayed with Oust, and the tree population consisted of only 75 percent of the plan. I was deeply disappointed and upset.

I went to Terre Haute in the fall of 1989, and argued with one of the two foresters about the damage done by the Oust. He would not admit it was the Oust and would not admit any mistake or accept any responsibility. I realized I was stuck. What choices did I have? I could forget it and accept a 75 percent stand, go to another forester for help, get a lawyer and sue, or try to cut a deal. I decided to compromise and offered to pay for replacement trees and the hired labor to plant them by hand if the two foresters would supervise the work, arrange the planting and not charge for their own work or charge an additional fee. The professional foresters agreed to this proposal, and we entered into another contract to replant trees by hand in the spring of 1990. But, upon the recommendation of Gary Rolfe, head of the Department of Forestry at the University of Illinois, we would replant with white oak and black walnut, and not replant with black alder.

In March 1990, we met again, and with a crew of nine men using dibble bars, replanted by hand 4,400 white oak and black walnut seedlings. We placed these new trees in the rows beside their dead companions planted by machine the spring before. This cost $898, and there was no financial help from anyone.

Having done all I could for the moment for the new planting, and since I was there already, I turned my attention to the woods pasture, which had been growing unmanaged and was ungrazed by cattle for 14 years. Louis Bromfield had a woodland situation on his Malabar Farm, and in *Out of the Earth* (1948), he wrote about it:

> There are about 160 acres of wooded land, most of which was pastured by sheep and cattle a couple of generations before we took over the land. The practice was poor management and the results in some parts of the woodland disastrous, for the animals found in the woodland very little to eat and what they did find had little more nutritive value than so much old wheat straw. Forced to eat anything at hand, they had largely destroyed all the protective covering of forest floor vegetation—the ferns, the wildflowers, and, worst of all, the forest seedlings. Some parts of the woodland were little more than a handful of big trees of doubtful value with low-quality weeds and sickly grass growing underneath.
>
> Our predecessors at Malabar were getting from that woodland neither any decent forage nor any succession of good timber. Much of the land covered by trees is rocky and rough and of little value if cleared even as pasture land, so the trees were left undisturbed, but the woodlands were fenced to keep cattle out.

In the period of ten years since the cattle were first kept out of the woodland, a miraculous and beautiful change has taken place. The forest cover has returned with its carpet of ferns and wildflowers as well as thousands of seedlings of beech, maple, white ash, black walnut, hickory, tulip poplar and many kinds of oak. Some of these seedlings have already attained a height of 25 or 30 feet, according to the species, and all are straight-growing and smooth. The whole crop may not be harvested during my lifetime, but in the meanwhile we have back the singular, almost tropical beauty of the Ohio hardwood forests, an increase in game even to deer and grouse, and no water any longer runs off the forest floor. Even the old gullies have healed over as the run-off water from the fields above has been totally checked. (p.127)

My experience was very similar. When we surveyed the land in October 1987, we found approximately 300-350 young black walnut trees had come about naturally in what had been the woods pasture. Young walnut trees need sun and a clear space to grow. These had both. However, in open space, young walnuts branch low to the ground and seldom have good form, and form determines their ultimate value. Teenagers now, these walnuts were just entering their vital formative years. The next few years would determine their value 30 to 40 years hence.

These young walnut trees were two to 15 feet tall and would benefit from lateral branch pruning, removal of vines, removal of competition, and eventually some thinning. I set to work with a chain saw and spent 13 days working six to seven hours a day doing what is referred to as timber stand improvement (TSI). The two professional foresters had recommended this TSI and estimated the cost at $1,280 for them to do it. Based on the time I spent, I believe that was a low estimate. Also, I am convinced they would not have done the work I did.

The district forester of Illinois refused compensation for the cost of TSI at this time. But as I got into the work, I realized it was needed and the time was right. There were a large number of honey locust throughout the area that had long, vicious thorns and other young locusts were springing

1974 air view of woods pasture in Vermilion County, Illinois.

1989 air view of the same land in Vermilion County, Illinois. Note that natural reforestation has filled the pasture area with young trees and the field has been planted to young trees.

up at an alarming rate. When I worked there in the 1950s, there had been only a few locust trees and they had not seemed to be a threat. Now there were hundreds, and seed pods in profusion promised more. I have since noticed honey locust with long, vicious thorns spreading into much abandoned land throughout the Midwest. Landowners who neglect these invasive trees will have many more. While the seeds furnish food for wildlife, the trees crowd out other species and are of questionable commercial value.

I cut locust, wild cherry, osage orange, hackberry, mulberry, and vines to give space to the young black walnut. I pruned black walnut, oak, and black cherry. As I did this, I learned more about the 20 acres of former woods pasture than ever before. I saw signs of beaver and fox. I was amazed at the variety of birds, and in particular the woodpeckers. We had left standing many dead trees that provided excellent woodpecker habitat. The 60 acres provided water and a diversity of habitat for nearly every Midwestern species of wildlife. Harvesting the trees had not disturbed this habitat.

Operating a chain saw, to me, was exhilarating and satisfying. To have the choice of life or death over young trees gave me a tremendous sense of power. I have had positions of leadership, executive positions, teaching positions, and desk jobs, but none offered the satisfaction of operating a chain saw in my own woods with the power to influence the growth of a young forest for what I believed was the better. There was no committee to approve my choices. I had no need to delegate. I stood alone with power and death in my own hands, surveyed the young living trees and immediately decided which would live and which would die.

It was hard and satisfying, though dangerous, work. Someone once commented that starting a chain saw lowers the I.Q. of the operator 30 points or 30 percent, whichever is greater. It may very well be true. I had used a chain saw before and knew they were dangerous, but this was made clearer one afternoon. I had cut the branch from a cherry and, as I swung the saw around to cut another, the blade passed near my left leg and I felt a strange sensation. I looked down and saw a three-inch jagged hole in my denim trousers. Under that hole was a two-inch hole in my long underwear and under that a 1 1/2-inch skin abrasion about 1/8 inch deep. I was bleeding just a little. Another inch, and I would have bled a lot. Two inches and I would have cut a muscle, and five inches and I could have lost a leg. I sat down to think a few minutes about safety.

I was about 1/4 mile from the nearest dwelling and working alone deep in the woods. No one knew I was there, and I was staying alone in the summer home of Joe Lesny's nephew in Ambia, Indiana, which was over 20 miles away. No one would miss me for several days if I did not return to Ambia. It was dangerous, but I enjoy solitude, and I decided not to trade it for insurance. Life offers no guarantees. I would just be more careful.

In June 1990, unable to get a local farmer to mow between the new trees, I bought a previously owned 1950 International Harvester M tractor and a Woods 72-inch rotary mower for $1,800. After removing the corn picker mounted on the tractor and overcoming several obstacles, I had a working tractor and mower. Despite the fact it was 40 years old, the tractor ran beautifully.

The growth of grass and weeds was truly tremendous. I mowed wild parsnips six feet high and could hardly see the little trees among the weeds and grass. Although I dreaded doing it because of my Oust experience, I decided it was necessary to spray again with herbicide to control weeds and grass.

In the spring of 1990, after returning to Pennsylvania, I wrote to the professional foresters in Terre Haute, Indiana seeking their bid to spray the trees as called for in the forest management plan they had developed for me. On June 22 1990, one of the foresters wrote, "We will not be able to assist you with your forest management in the future. To date we have not been able to please you, and probably never will."

So after developing a plan for me and accepting $14,220 in commission and service fees they dropped me and have not answered questions or provided any further assistance despite several written requests for advice and help. Was I difficult? Yes, because I wanted the job done right. Was I not pleased? I was not pleased with a 75 percent stand or their failure to accept any responsibility for the loss of half the alder.

Since this land is on the far north edge of the southern Indiana/Illinois timber area and near the Grand Prairie, it was difficult to obtain another forester to assist me. I was unable to get anyone to spray in 1990 or 1991, and grass and weeds were serious competition to the young trees. Mowing a 72-inch path between the rows may be helpful, but there was direct competition in the rows with the trees. Some argue mowing only increases grasses that compete more severely with young trees than weeds. This surely seemed to be the case, because with each mowing there was more brome grass and alfalfa and fewer weeds.

On Labor Day 1990, after mowing between the trees a second time that summer, I drove around the north field of 13 acres with my wife, and it looked good. We saw a doe with two fawns come out of the woods pasture and begin to graze between the rows of trees, and it was lovely. Nature in harmony. The deer were graceful and beautiful. As we came near them, they bounded back into the woods with their white tails flying high.

Frank had often told the story of his grandfather shooting a deer from the front step of the cabin along the creek; the cabin I never had seen and which was long gone. This seemed like ancient history to me as a boy. There had been no deer in the 1950s when I was a young man working with Frank and Evard in the woods. Now the deer had come back, and I was delighted. There had been no beaver or coyote, but now the beaver and coyote were back also. It was very encouraging that despite all the publicity about environmental decay, here was a place where nature was thriving, and the present seemed to be better than the past.

I returned in January 1991, to walk through the woods to see how the new trees were doing. I discovered that deer, those cute little creatures Walt Disney had led us to love in "Bambi" ate trees! The lovely young walnut trees that had been five to six feet tall in August and covered with leaves were now two-to-three-feet-tall stubs with buds all gone, and rough ends where fat buds had been and should be. It was very discouraging. No one had told me about deer. My two professional foresters had not mentioned deer as a problem in the plan.

When I mowed again in the spring of 1991, the trees were still alive and growing but were stunted, deformed, shortened, and weakened. It was obvious that unless something was done, the trees were in danger. I did not know how serious the danger was or if the trees could be saved, but I vowed to see what could be done about the deer problem. It was obvious that growing trees led one further and further into new and uncharted territory. What was the history of deer in America?

It has been estimated that before Europeans came to America, the deer population was about 30 million. In two stages of hunting, first by native Americans and second by European immigrants, the white-tail population was reduced to only about two million by 1900. Deer were scarce in Illinois in 1901. That year, the general assembly of the state passed a bill calling for a five-year total ban on deer hunting. It came 11 years after Illinois' herd was listed as being "near zero." The moratorium was extended again and again.

The Illinois Fish and Game Conservation Commission's 1913-1914 Annual Report stated: "We may never expect to see deer plentiful in the State of Illinois." As Lord Salisbury said, "No fact of life seems so obvious as, one should never trust the word of experts."

Beginning in the late 1930s, the Department of Conservation began restocking the state of Illinois with deer received from other states. Hunting resumed in 1957, and hunters took 1,735 deer that year. In 1994, 96,230 deer were harvested in Illinois during the firearm season, but deer numbers still grow. Conservation efforts have done much to bring back the white-tail deer. Now, the national deer population is estimated by some at 25 million and rising very rapidly. Some claim it is higher now than when Columbus arrived.

No one knows how many deer there are, but deer/vehicle accidents are also rising. According to the Illinois Department of Transportation, the number of accidents involving deer statewide was 2,345 in 1981, 14,000 in 1990, and 16,504 in 1993. In 1993, there were three human fatalities in Illinois attributed to deer.

The Indiana Farm Bureau Insurance Company paid $4.5 million in 1993 for deer damage claims to automobiles. This figure represents about 35 percent of the total claim dollars paid under the comprehensive coverage. Wabash County had 110 claims for a cost of $184,000. Eighteen counties had $70,000 or more in claims. Deer are seen everywhere in increasing numbers.

Illinois has taken some tentative steps to respond to the complaints of citizens about damage caused by the increasing deer population. Illinois has raised the number of deer harvested by hunters. In response to the complaints of farmers, a law was passed in 1990 permitting a landowner to "remove" up to 10 deer if the Illinois Wildlife Biologist of his region determines that injury is resulting. The law was new and subject to interpretation and enforcement varied with the biologists. Nevertheless, I decided to pursue it, and in August 1991, called upon John Cole, my local wildlife biologist in Gibson City, Illinois.

John listened to my story of the eaten trees and agreed to meet me at the site and inspect the trees. We met, he looked at the trees and admitted that they had been eaten and stunted by deer. But, he maintained that the eating had occurred "last winter." "Of course," I said, "in summer they have corn, wheat, soybeans and fresh grass, so they eat those. They eat trees in winter." He suggested I call him in the winter when the deer are eating the trees and he would take another look.

When I explained that I lived in Pennsylvania, 700 miles east, he suggested I build an electric fence around the trees. When I asked how I'd keep it electrified and who would pay for it, he was rather vague, but gave me an approved plan for building a fence. The drawings of the fence reminded me of pictures I'd seen of Soviet prison camps and I decided to seek other solutions rather than construct a gulag in Illinois.

Illinois also offers owners of 40 acres or more two permits to take deer during the regular hunting season. Seeking relief for the trees and revenge, I applied for permits and received two. One was for an antlerless deer only, and one for a deer of either sex. I had never shot at anything larger than a woodchuck and had not hunted in 30 years. Again, I decided I needed professional help, and since Pennsylvania is a big deer hunting state, I went to a gunshop near my home to see what they would suggest.

Illinois hunters can use a bow, muzzleloader, shotgun, or handgun during various authorized hunting periods. Reviewing the options, I decided that my best chance would be with a muzzleloader and asked the gunshop folks what they recommended. They suggested a Lyman .50 caliber Great Plains muzzleloader with a percussion cap. I ordered one for $327.54. It was a beautiful weapon made in Italy. I was told the walnut stock was from Turkey. I am very fond of the rifle, but I wish it had been made in the United States and the stock was made from American black walnut.

I practiced with this rifle at 25, 50 and 100 yards. It makes a terrific noise, fills the air with smoke and dust but has less kick than a 12-gauge shotgun. I loved it! I fired it about 100 times and finally was able to consistently hit a six-inch target at 100 yards. I did not know the maximum effective range of the weapon or where one should aim to kill a deer. I decided I needed to know more about deer and hunting them.

I had found no book on black walnut, but found a great one on deer. *The Deer of North America*, by Leonard Lee Rue III was updated, expanded, and published by Outdoor Life Books in 1989. It is a fascinating and extremely well-written book explaining the life and habits of deer in 544 detailed pages with many fine photographs taken by the author. In this work, Rue says, "... Illinois has fine habitat and big white-tails." He was right. I was providing the habitat!

Rue explains the history of deer hunting in the United States and relates:

> The white-tail was as important to the eastern wood-land Indians as bison was to the Indians of the plains. Venison was a dietary staple, their "bread of life." Deer hides were made into clothing, sinew was used to sew the skins, the bones were fashioned into splinter awls to make the holes in the leather so that the sinew could be used, and the hoofs provided glue, ornaments, and rattles. The bones and antlers were made into tools, weapons, decorations, and religious implements. The mound build-ing Indians of Ohio deified the deer and made sacred headdresses adorned with antlers. (p. 14)

Deer were equally important to the early European settlers and soon became a major item of trade with Europe — and led to professional hunters. Rue wrote:

> The records of His Majesty's Custom Service show that 2,601,152 pounds of deerskins from 600,000 white-

tails were shipped to England from Savannah, Georgia, in the years 1755 to 1773. (p. 15)

Daniel Boone was one of those early European settlers who hunted widely throughout the Ohio Valley. In 1769-70, Boone and his party hunted seven months in the Bluegrass country of Kentucky only to have their horses and deerskins stolen by native Americans. Another party had 2,300 deerskins stolen in similar manner. Boone carried a "Kentucky" rifle with a walnut stock. In 1820, just five weeks shy of his 86th birthday, Boone died in a room with a walnut fireplace mantel in a home that still stands near Defiance, Missouri. He had helped his son, Nathan, build the large stone home, and some say Daniel Boone carved the walnut fireplace mantels. He was buried in a black walnut coffin.

Rue continues:

Thomas Meacham of Hopkinton, in St. Lawrence County, New York, kept an exact record of the game he killed as a professional hunter. When he died in 1850, he had killed 214 wolves, 77 cougars, 219 bears, and 2,550 deer. Nathaniel Foster of Herkimer, New York, killed 76 deer in a single season. Meshach Browning, who died in 1859, was a professional hunter from Garrett County, Maryland. In 44 years he killed between 1,800 and 2,000 white-tails. There were many such hunters. (p. 15)

In this way, by 1900, the white-tail deer population had dropped to only about two million from 30 million in 1500. Now, deer numbers are back to nearly 30 million and rising rapidly.

Rue comments on deer habitat:

Most of my home state of New Jersey was originally covered with mature forests, and we know that deer are not creatures of the mature forests. Most of the eastern half of the United States was also covered with such forests and undoubtedly those woods did not have high deer populations. (p. 16)

But native Americans knew that deer preferred open areas to graze and burned forests to provide deer habitat as well as to drive deer into killing fields. This provided suitable open space for black walnut to grow in full sun. Thus, native Americans provided habitat for both deer and the Eastern black walnut with fire.

Rue confirms this:

> The early Indians were efficient hunters, and they were the first to practice game management in this country. The colonists found extensive burned-over areas in the midst of the virgin forests. Some of these fires had been set by the Indians. The Indians knew that the number of deer and other animals in an area increased in direct proportion to the food available. Deer might run through the mature forests and would go there in the autumn to feed on the mast crops, but they didn't live there. They were and are creatures of the *edge*. *Edge* is a word that describes excellent wildlife habitat. Edge is where grassland or an open area meets or abuts a forested area. Edge usually means both food and shelter, and that is what habitat is all about. (p. 448)

It is also where young Eastern black walnuts grow. Rue says of the white-tail deer:

> The white-tail, in particular, has the widest range and is found in the greatest variety of habitats. It is primarily a deer of the woodlands, frequenting the edges and openings that have been created by natural conditions, fire, or humans. It cannot be stressed too often that deer are what they eat. Illinois has no overbrowsing. There is a superabundance of food from some of the richest soil in our nation, and the results show. (p. 149)

No wonder the deer were coming back in such numbers. There were many examples given of deer populations increasing to the level that overbrowsing occurred, food became less and less plentiful, and eventually the deer population crashed. The natural predators of deer—cougars and wolves—have been eliminated, and hunting restricted so that deer numbers are increasing. Some coyotes are coming back, but the main predators of deer remain hunters and Buicks. Deer reproduce at a very rapid rate, much like rabbits.

Some areas already have deer in excess, and this excess is causing alarm. In areas of excess deer, young trees will not grow, the forest shows a browse line several feet from the ground where lower limbs have been eaten away, and common plants of the forest floor are totally consumed. The habitat of other wildlife is destroyed.

Brown County State Park in Southern Indiana has such an excess of deer. Park officials have fenced off 40-by-40-foot areas for four years to show how the forest grows when deer can't eat leaves and bark. In one barren area swept by fire four years ago, no saplings grow, but in the fenced-off area, fed by the sun, a jungle of vegetation has arisen. Bird nests can be seen deep in the green. Nibbled areas just inside the fence show where deer have stretched for food through the wire. Deer foraging is so heavy it has diminished the food supply, and the animals are becoming undernourished. Reforestation is not possible with such a deer population. Other species suffer from the reduced habitat as well. Clearly, excess deer throw off the ecological balance of both flora and fauna.

Some suburban areas of Philadelphia now have excess deer and environmentalists are divided between animal lovers and plant lovers. Ridley Creek Park, near Philadelphia, held a hunt to reduce the excess population but faced the hatred and scorn of deer lovers who picketed the scene and derided hunters. Such scenes are more and more common throughout the country.

Deer have become so numerous and such a problem in urban areas of North America that an urban deer symposium was held in St. Louis, Missouri on December 12-14, 1993. Problems discussed included deer browsing on landscaping plants and gardens and deer serving as a reservoir for Lyme disease. According to U.S. Public Heath Service records, there were over 9,000 human cases of this disease in 1991. Nationwide, deer also are involved in over 200,000 automobile collisions yearly, resulting in an estimated loss of $1.3 billion dollars, 16,000 human injuries, and 114 deaths.

Despite all this damage and danger, deer have the highest preference rating of any mammal species. When respondents were asked how they wanted to see deer managed in their neighborhoods, 26 percent wanted more deer, 66 percent preferred no change, and eight percent wanted fewer deer. Count me in the latter group.

Those who understand the price we are paying and will pay for unrestricted deer reproduction have a tremendous problem. How do you educate those who love deer and enjoy seeing them run free? Officials of Valley Forge National Historical Park, 20 miles west of Philadelphia, have conducted a survey of deer inside the park. The numbers rise every year and some park officials know the day is not far away when they must do something about the excess deer.

In the summer of 1993, the deer ate all my tomatoes. On one winter night after a light snow in March 1993, I saw seven deer in my front yard a block from Valley Forge Park. During that winter, they ate all the English ivy leaves from my house up to a height of five feet, and in the spring they ate all the tulips. In 1994, for the first time, we began seeing a herd of deer in our yard during mid-day. The number of deer sightings has been rising steadily for over ten years.

When I called Valley Forge Park rangers to learn when they would do something about the deer, they said the deer are not their problem. They suggested I build a fence. They argued that the deer were here first, and perhaps they were, but they were not eating in my yard 17 years ago when we moved here.

Public anger at deer is rising. If I were to pick flowers or plants in the park, I could get arrested. The deer have more rights and freedom than I have. When the killing begins, as I believe it must, Valley Forge park officials fear public display at the Birthplace of American Independence.

&

Deer graze on a wide variety of plants, trees and scrubs and usually graze moving into the wind. Rue continues:

> Deer take a bite of food and then take a couple of steps and nibble again. This prevents overutilization of the food plant while also keeping deer moving away from

any stalking predator. Deer are primarily browsers, feeding on the tips of twigs, branches, shoots, and leaves. When a deer is feeding on browse, it prefers the tenderest, newest shoots and tips. Such tips are more palatable, more flavorful, easier to bite off, and most nutritious. Tips of twigs up to about the size of a wooden kitchen match are nipped off by the deer's front l o w e r incisors against the pad on the front of the top of the mouth. Lacking upper front teeth, the deer has to tear the twigs loose, always leaving a ragged edge. When deer are feeding on larger twigs, those up to the size of a pencil—which they do only in times of food shortage—they take the twigs in the side of their mouths and bite them off, using the third premolars and first molars. (p. 164)

From this account and my observations of the damage to the trees, I suspect deer "yarded up" (congregated) in substantial numbers in the newly planted fields in the winter of 1990-91, and fed on the twigs, branches, and buds of the young trees planted in the spring of 1989. A neighbor said he had seen a herd of 39 deer at one time that winter, a mile west of these two fields.

White-Tailed Deer: Ecology and Management, an extensive book on deer states:

Browsing is most detrimental to trees less than three years old, when the terminal buds of major branches are within reach of deer. Browsing can kill trees and reduce their vitality and growth. Perhaps more importantly, browsing on young trees removes the terminal buds of leader branches, altering growth patterns and interfering with pruning and training systems aimed at developing well-formed scaffold branches. Thus, even though young trees often survive heavy browsing pressure, they are apt to be bushy, misshapen, and of little value.

Bark removal by antler-rubbing occurs far less frequently than terminal browsing, but the effects usually are more detrimental. Antler-rubbing damages trees by breaking small branches and removing bark and cambium along the vertical axis. Rubbing normally occurs in late autumn and early winter, thereby exposing xylem four to six months before the wound has a chance to heal. Nearly all small trees died, regardless of species when bark was rubbed from more than 50 percent of the circumference. Deer may cause serious damage to young forests by browsing seedling and small trees. Repeated browsing of terminal buds can kill seedlings or suppress their vertical growth. Browsing damage usually is more severe in late winter and early spring. It is governed to some extent by the relative abundance of other more-preferred browse species. (p. 114)

I had a big problem! On November 3, 1991, I headed for Illinois with the new muzzleloading rifle, two chain saws, a car load of gear and high hopes to reduce the deer threat and continue TSI. I walked the woods and saw deer sign in great quantity and some deer at a distance. Evidence of antler rub was everywhere. In one row of young walnuts, eight trees in a row had been almost completely destroyed by a buck rubbing his antlers. The trees looked like they had been inserted into a shredder and fresh white sapwood showed where bark had been stripped away. Branches were broken completely off, central leaders broken off, and only short stubs remained standing where young trees had been.

After the buck's antlers have grown, he removes the velvet by stripping it off against the branches of trees. Rue describes the process:

The velvet is usually [though not always] stripped from the antlers within a 24-hour period. A buck is very thorough in removing the velvet. Picking a resilient sapling, he rubs his antlers lengthwise along the trunk. He does this in between the tines, on the inside of the antler's curve, and on the outside. He even turns his head sideways, parallel to the ground, to try to get the velvet completely off the antler bases. Frequently, bucks become very excited during this process. The more they rub, the more it stimulates them. The rubbing becomes faster, and the pushing harder, and the bucks really start to "work out" on the bush. (p. 290)

Antler rubbing does not end when the velvet has been removed. Rue continues:

Like a boxer in training, the bucks begin to spar with "punching bags" — saplings and small trees. Rubbing starts with the shedding of antler velvet, but continues as a form of rutting behavior. Most bucks peel the velvet from their antlers between September 7 and September 15, give or take a few days, according to the weather, food, and the physical condition of the deer. Some bucks seem to have a favorite rubbing tree, and most seem to have a favorite area. This rubbing and fighting with the bushes is done far more often than most people suspect. In a short time, many saplings and bushes in many areas will bear the bright white scars of buck rubs. People who think that bucks rub trees only to get the velvet off may get the impression that there are far more bucks in the area than there really are, not realizing the role of the rubs in depositing of scent from the forehead glands. Most bucks will scar many saplings in the process of getting ready for the rutting season. (pp. 291-293)

Since the muzzleloader deer hunting season did not begin until November 15, I began with the chain saw again to prune, cut, and work on the woods pasture trees. I started down an old abandoned fence row and had gone about 70 yards when I ran out of fuel. I refueled, and just as I was turning to start the saw, I looked up and saw a lovely buck standing near where I had parked my car. He looked at the car, turned to look at me, leaped the fence, and bounded into the woods. He was a beautiful deer with what looked to be about eight points. I assumed that this was his area and he was the one who had scraped his antlers on many of the young, severely damaged trees. This must be the culprit who stripped young trees of bark, broke them, and reduced them to stubs. I resumed work but saw no more deer for the next several days.

On November 15, the first day of muzzleloader season, I began before daylight, walking back to be on site before the sun rose just as the hunting magazines had suggested. I heard a "huff huff" and heard running animals, but it was dark, and I could not see the deer and I never did see a deer all day. I decided deer could see better, hear better, smell better, and so far had proven to be smarter. It was a frustrating experience.

The second day, discouraged but not beaten, I headed back to the woods pasture with a can of fuel for the chain saws and the loaded rifle. It was about half an hour after dawn, and as I came over a rise I saw the large buck and a doe standing in the south field of the tree plantation gazing at me. I set the fuel can down, cocked the rifle, and aimed just below the white ruff under the chin of the buck as he stood facing right with his head turned to look at me and fired. I saw him rise up and flip over backward and could see him no longer as he was obscured by the grass and small trees.

I reloaded, which takes about 30 seconds with a muzzleloader, and longer when you are shaking. First, 90 grains of black powder must be carefully poured down the muzzle. Black powder looks like black granulated sugar and 90 grains is equal to about one thimble full. Second, a circular cloth patch one inch in diameter is fitted over the .50 cal muzzle and a .49 caliber lead ball is placed over the patch. The ball is forced into the muzzle with a special hand tool and then driven home with the rammer, which is returned to the bracket under the barrel. Then, a very small percussion cap is fitted over the firing nipple and the weapon is cocked and ready to fire again.

Weapons of this type were developed in the 1830s, and gradually replaced the flash pan muzzleloaders. Many were used in the Civil War. I could only imagine the stress of reloading when faced with a charging line of Confederate Infantry giving full throat to the famous Rebel yell and carrying weapons mounted with two feet of cold steel bayonet. No wonder many weapons were found unfired on the field of battle with several balls forced down the muzzle.

With the rifle reloaded, I walked down to see if the deer was where he fell. I later paced the distance at almost 100 yards. The lead rifle ball had entered his neck just below the white ruff and passed through the chest and exited the left rib cage where it left a hole the size of a tennis ball. The buck struggled to rise but could not, and quickly died.

I was sad, but elated too. When young, I had enjoyed hunting. Old men take no joy in killing. I had killed my first deer within 200 yards of the cabin site from which my great

great grandfather had shot a deer about 150 years before. Probably, the weapon I used was very similar to the one he must have used. I was glad it was a clean kill, and the deer was not injured and had not escaped wounded.

Wildlife biology students, engaged to record deer kills at the Kickapoo State Park in Illinois, looked carefully into the dead deer's mouth and estimated the buck was 2 1/2 years old. He had seven points and weighed 175 pounds field dressed. He was fat, sleek, and had been eating corn. The next day at about 50 yards I shot a 69-pound doe that was also fat on corn and judged to be 2 1/2 years old. The students gave me a pin that said, "I got a doe so the herd won't grow." I had been tested in combat and decorated in just two days.

Both deer were processed by D & F Quality Meats, Inc., Danville, Illinois. The meat was packaged and frozen and has proven to be very tender and delicious. Through gifts of meat and dinner parties at our home, over 50 people have tasted Illinois venison, many for the first time. Revenge may not be sweet, but it can be very tasty.

It seems quite evident that the deer are back in substantial number and increasing. It is not yet evident that one can establish a hardwood forest with so many deer feeding and rubbing antlers on the young trees. But I will not give up. "There must be a beginning of any great matter, but the continuing unto the end until it be thoroughly finished yields the glory," said Sir Francis Drake in 1587. Growing hardwood trees has some of the aspects of a poker game. "In for a dime, in for a dollar." The deer had "raised" me. I either had to fold or match their bet. I decided to stay and play out the hand.

Before I headed back to Pennsylvania, I attached 300 small bars of Dial soap to 300 young walnut trees hoping the soap would deter the deer. It was recommended as a method of reducing deer browse. Upon later inspection in June 1992, it seemed to have helped some. After seven months, many of the bars of soap were still hanging on the trees. On others, the browse continued.

In 1991, in addition to the deer hunting, I worked again for 13 days at TSI. I learned that cut honey locust sprout again and, where there was one large trunk two years before, I now had two to 10 sprouts. These sprouts were growing at a rapid rate and like the tree before were covered with thorns. I cut the sprouts off again and sprayed the stumps with Tordon RTU (Ready to Use). I found many more honey locust missed two years earlier and cut and sprayed those also. I now had a two-front war going —deer and honey locust.

In March 1992, I saw four deer in the south tree plantation at some distance. If those four were three doe and one buck, and if the three doe give birth to the average number of fawn, the four would have been ten total by fall 1992, and possibly 19 by spring 1993. As mentioned, deer have a strong sex drive and reproduce rapidly. A doe fawn, born in the spring, can be bred in the fall and give birth the following spring to two more fawn. Without predators, more hunters or more Buicks, the number of deer will continue to increase at a rapid rate.

On April 1, 1992, Harold Bruner, Consulting Forester from Walton, Indiana sprayed the 22 acres of young, struggling trees with one ounce of Oust and five pints of Princep per acre. Oust should kill anything but woody plants; it works by being absorbed by the roots. Princep is a pre-emergent herbicide that kills weeds and grasses as they germinate. Bruner said the goal with these herbicides at these rates is to control at least 75 percent of the weeds for at least 60 days. Higher rates that would give longer control would risk damage to the trees.

The cost of Bruner's spraying service was $1,200. Illinois Forestry paid me $550 to help defray this cost. This spraying plus five mowings at $100 each, brought the total cost to establish the 22 acres of hardwood trees to $7,842, or $346.99 per acre. I had received $4,013 cost sharing from Illinois and the U.S. Dept. of Agriculture. This brought my cost down to $3,829, or $170 per acre. We were in the fourth growing season, and it was not yet an established hardwood forest.

Mowing for the sixth time in June 1992, I noticed a good stand of alfalfa and brome grass with fewer and smaller weeds. The three-foot spray band down each row of trees was clearly defined and had substantially reduced the weed population and grass content in the rows. The spray had not affected the alfalfa.

The damage done by the deer in the winter of 1990/91 and since was quite obvious and severe. Nearly every tree had lost the central leader. As a result, the trees had many side branches and were stunted, deformed, and dwarfed. Looking across the field it was obvious that the trees closer to the woods pasture were shorter and that those farther from the woods were taller and more dense. Recent deer browse was evident on many of the young trees. While mowing, I saw four deer. Had I known about deer and how much damage they do to young trees, I would have built a fence, but it was too late now. The job of restoring shape and form to the stunted trees would continue to be a formidable one.

I wrote to John Cole, my local biologist, in September 1992, seeking a nuisance permit to remove deer that were now browsing on the trees in summer and winter. He met with me at the site on October 1, and gave me a permit to remove four deer, but specified that I could use *only* a shotgun. This made no sense to me, but I complied, borrowed a shotgun, and on October 5, I shot a young five-point buck. Since I had to return to Pennsylvania, I left the permit with a friend to attempt to "remove" the other three deer allowed by the permit, which would expire on October 31. He failed.

Again, Cole urged me to build a fence around the trees and to drive steel concrete reinforcing rods down beside the trees to discourage antler rub. "Fourteen thousand steel rods?" I asked. "Surely, you are kidding." He wasn't.

While I was finding it very difficult because of weeds and deer to establish a new forest on the 22 acres that had been farmed, the trees in what had been the woods pasture were growing very well. The 1992 growing season was a wet one, and the black walnuts there have shown very good growth.

In late January 1993, I pruned many of these young black walnut trees for the third or fourth time. Many were now nearly six inches in diameter, up to 30 feet tall and without side branches on the lower ten to 17 feet of trunk. I used a Power Pruner manufactured by Technic Tool Corporation, Lewiston, Idaho. It has a 10-inch chain saw powered by a small air-cooled engine. The tool extends to 11 feet in length and allows a *strong* person to trim branches up to 17 feet from the ground. It eliminates the need for a ladder or platform when pruning trees.

Pruning teenage black walnut with Power Pruner.

These walnut trees were from nuts planted by squirrels before the deer had become so plentiful and were growing rapidly into a very nice young black walnut forest. It was obvious that my seven weeks of work at timber stand improvement had helped a great deal to improve the shape of these young trees and to reduce competition from less desirable species. It would soon be necessary to begin thinning to allow the better trees to have adequate growing space. It would be almost 40 more years before these trees were large enough for quality veneer, but there was joy in watching them grow.

In November 1993 and 1994, I returned to hunt again and harvested four more deer, raising the number I had killed in 37 months to seven. Of six deer shot with the Lyman Great Plains rifle, five dropped where they were hit. Only one walked away to die 100 yards from where he was hit. It has proven to be a good deer rifle.

Others hunting on the 60-acre property had taken eight deer. Thus, 15 deer had been harvested from the 60 acres in 37 months. At least six deer remained in permanent residence in the woods. We were getting a high body count, but saw no end to the war. Unlike General Westmoreland, I could see no light at the end of this tunnel. In the winter of 1993/94, a friend counted 43 deer in the corn stubble just north of my land.

In 1993, I decided to survey the walnut trees in the big woods and former woods pasture. I measured and recorded the diameter in inches on white aluminum metal tags attached to wire pressed into the soil at the base of each tree on the north side. In this way, I identified 30 large walnut trees in the big woods that could be harvested at any time, and 375 young walnuts that were 3 to 8.5 inches in diameter in the woods pasture. These smaller trees had all begun to grow after the pasture was last grazed in 1976, and thus were 17 years old or younger. Many smaller than three inches were not measured or tagged. All were planted by squirrels and most had gotten a start before the deer returned.

I plan to remeasure these trees at two-year intervals to identify their rate of growth. This information will be recorded on a computer and updated after each measurement. This may help in deciding which trees to thin and will give me some idea of how close together they can grow.

In 1998, the Walnut Council summer conference is scheduled for Danville, Illinois. Members who attend will have an opportunity to visit this walnut project. They should bring mosquito repellant.

Should I live 30 more years, when I am 90 years old in 2023, I may levitate in my zero-gravity wheelchair through this walnut grove of over 400 walnuts. They will then be 47 years old and should be 18 to 25 inches in diameter and free of limbs for the lower nine to 20 feet. It promises to be quite a ride.

I have heard a story of a wealthy Asian man who, while traveling, saw and admired a large, beautiful tree. When he returned home, he called his gardener, described the tree, and told his gardener that he wanted such a tree in his garden. The gardener explained that it took 200 years to grow such a tree. "Well," said the Asian gentleman, "you must plant it today!"

Postscript

I began work on this book in January 1992 with the hope of having it finished in time for my father to hold before he died.

When I visited my father, Tom Chenoweth, in Florida in February 1992, he gave me the January 31, 1942 issue of The *Saturday Evening Post* containing the article "Joe Cox's Trees Live On," which he kept for 50 years. It is reproduced in Appendix I.

I knew my father was very ill with cancer and hurried to complete this work. He did read the early drafts of several chapters and was pleased with the project. However, he died on September 21, 1992, before the book was completed.

I believe he would like this book and I have dedicated it to him. I wish every man could have a father who was as kind, generous, and supportive as my father was to me.

He will be missed. But through this book, his memory, his love of trees, and his belief in conservation will live.

Bob Chenoweth

E. Thomas Chenoweth in 1974 contemplating nature near the original cabin built in 1828.

Appendix I

ಕಾ

Joe Cox's Trees Live On
by
Andrew H. Hepburn

(Reprinted from the Saturday Evening Post © January 31, 1942).

Blanketing a ridge two miles south of Paoli, Indiana, is a patch of woodland that is unlike any other. For more than 100 years the people of Paoli have known it as the Cox Woods. Soon it is to be renamed the Indiana Pioneer Mothers' Memorial Forest and become a forest museum.

Cox Woods is unique for a simple but miraculous reason. It has been let alone. No tree has been cut. No roadway leads through it. Fire has never touched these hardwood trees.

That trees of great value for commercial purposes should still exist today in a region studded with wood-using industries approaches the miraculous. Forest experts who have explored the Cox Woods with awe are at a loss to understand—until they learn about Joseph Cox, who died in December, 1940, at 83.

Cox Woods stands today in its virgin majesty because the Cox family, and particularly Joseph Cox, for more than 70 years resisted very tempting opportunities to sell these trees. There was one exception. A few years ago, Joseph, in desperate need, sold two trees on the fringe of the main tract. He paid urgent debts with the proceeds—and was troubled to the end of his days by a sense of guilt at having betrayed a trust.

The story begins 130 years ago. Another Joseph Cox, living in the forests of Eastern Tennessee, heard reports that there was soon to be a new state north of the Ohio River, that new land was to be had there almost for the asking—land sheathed in a great forest of useful hardwood trees, land where streams were clear, where game was abundant, where cleared ground would grow fabulous crops.

So Joseph Cox joined a group of Quakers going to the new land of Indiana. No descendant of Joseph Cox knows just when he actually arrived, but there is evidence that it was in 1811. Joseph Cox chose a tract of 253 acres, just outside a new Quaker village called Paoli. In 1816, the year Indiana became a state, he received title to it.

The story might have ended last year with the liquidation of the Cox estate following the death of Joseph, and the sale and cutting of the timber of the Cox Woods. But it didn't. Joseph's jealously guarded trees were not sold and cut up into peach baskets and veneer and counter tops and gunstocks and tool handles—as has been the fate of practically all the rest of Indiana's once magnificent forest. Instead, a combination of events led to an unprecedented national campaign to preserve the trees. The campaign, curiously spontaneous, produced money from various unexpected quarters. The trees were saved.

The upshot has been that within less than a year of the burial of Joseph Cox, who died sorrowing that the trees he had guarded with such devotion would be sold and cut, the tract was firmly anchored in the public domain as crown jewel of the United States Forest Service.

The story is an epic cycle. It begins with a wilderness, a great uninhabited forest. At the end of the first period of the cycle, the hills of Indiana remained wooded; the land continued a promised land of abundance. The second period saw the high point of economic and agricultural balance. There were settled towns, ringed by cleared fields, scattered arms, with local wood-working industries springing up.

The third period of the cycle is the tragic period—a toboggan of destruction, whole counties denuded of their timber to provide for the needs of factories growing bigger year by year, leaving bare hills, fields washed out by floods, a declining agriculture. The fourth phase is just beginning—a new program of reforestation, aimed at restoring a new era of economic and agricultural balance.

Three generations of the Cox family lived through the first three phases of the cycle. Their forest stood like a boulder in the stream of waste. They refused to conform.

When the family migrated from Tennessee, the Ohio Valley was a land clothed in a mature forest—not a forest of conifers common to mountain slopes and uplands all over the world, but oak, walnut, maple, poplar, ash, beech, hickory, locust and dozens of other species. It was a forest peculiar to the Ohio Valley. Nowhere else were there hardwood trees in such a variety of species, and nowhere else did they grow to such great size.

It has been described as the finest hardwood forest ever known, trees growing so densely that, as one observer has said, "a squirrel might travel all the way from the crest of the Alleghenies to the Mississippi without putting foot to the ground." Below them all was a green forest floor matted with vines, and the profusion of delicate flowers that thrive in the half-light of dense woods.

The streams are numerous and clear, the hills rolling, the soil, enriched by centuries of accumulating humus, incredibly fertile. It is not surprising that the voyagers who first explored this land by canoe, or the scouts and traders who followed the silent forest trails, should carry home fantastic tales of its wealth.

There is only one place in the United States where this forest land can actually be seen today. That place is Cox Woods. It is the last authentic fragment of the wilderness.

Joseph Cox had the pick of the land and he chose a forest ridge, running north and south. It boasted a dense stand of towering trees. He selected a valley beside the ridge, with a clear small stream running through it. It would be fine land to clear, and a sheltered spot for a cabin.

The Coxes were well established in their forest when Indiana became a state in 1816. The trickle of settlers had swelled to a river. Among the thousands who entered Indiana that year was a family by the name of Lincoln. The father, Thomas Lincoln, was a restless fellow. He had a son named Abraham, who was to live for fourteen years in the Indiana forest, a neighbor of the Cox family. But in the end, Thomas Lincoln, who had buried his wife in the forest some 30 miles from the Cox place, could not clear the forest from his land fast enough to suit him and moved farther west to the prairie lands of Illinois, where one did not need to chop down trees.

The difference between Thomas Lincoln, who was typical of thousands who settled in Indiana and then moved farther west, and Joseph Cox is important. Thomas Lincoln wanted land he could plow and plant, the more the better. To him, the forest was an annoyance. Joseph Cox, on the other hand, wanted to keep his forest. He wanted to clear only as little land as might be necessary for the crops needed to provide for a growing family. And the family was growing fast. In the end there were 11 children.

Joseph Cox not only loved his forest land, but he had a practical appreciation of its proper use. From trees cut along the valley floor he made things. There was a workshop lean-to on the log barn and in it a lathe and woodworking tools. On a certain porch in Paoli today you can see a black walnut rocking cradle which Grandfather Joseph made especially for the twins, Joseph and Jesse. In a dining room in Paoli you can find an imposing cherry wood highboy, product of Joseph's craftsmanship.

The forest was a fine place, too, for the fattening of hogs. They grew sleek on the fallen acorns, on beech and hickory nuts.

Joseph died in 1838, his second log house a bit overcrowded with those of the children who remained at home, his cleared land sufficiently extensive for all garden and cropgrowing purposes, and his hill land still covered with its original forest.

William Cox succeeded to the guardianship of the Cox forest. He was 25. He died in comparative youth, at the age of 44. He had added some land for farming purposes, but kept the forest tract intact. For a time he operated a small sawmill to cut the logs of his neighbors, not his own.

Paoli had grown somewhat and there were some local woodworking industries, but they were small and consumed only a few trees. Most of the forest reduction of that time was for the purpose of clearing additional land for crops. Since there was still bottom land uncleared, the hills remained inviolate.

Elizabeth Cox, the wife of William, was 42 years old when her husband died. She was to see all of her 11 children grow to maturity. Seven became school teachers.

For the forest that reared its leafy heights before her door, she had a real reverence. For more than 20 years, this guided her children. In one of them—her last born, Joseph—the mother's love of trees flowered into a passionate devotion verging on fanaticism. Joseph was to see all the forests about him except his own destroyed to satisfy the demands of an expanding industry. And Joseph was to resist, with a hostility that many of his neighbors called queer.

Elizabeth Cox guided her brood of fatherless children through the hard days of the Civil War. In fact, the war came to her trees. John Morgan, the Confederate cavalry leader then ravaging Kentucky, sent a detachment north across the Ohio to seize horses. Word of the raid preceded the rebel cavalry and volunteers swarmed in from the hills to repel the raiders. They gathered in Paoli. Capt. Thomas H. Hines, the Confederate leader, sitting on his horse within the Cox Woods, looking north to the courthouse square of Paoli with his glasses, saw the militiamen and turned back. In the Cox Woods he exchanged a horse. Swinging down from the ridge toward the valley home, from which Elizabeth Cox and her children had fled, he found one of the Cox horses hidden in a thicket. He took it and left the one he had been riding. It is said around Paoli that half the horses of the county were subsequently sired by that rebel stallion.

It was Elizabeth Cox's second son, Joel, who helped her for a few years carry on the traditions of the family place. Joel, in 1871, built a new home for the Cox family, a wide-eaved farmhouse set up the slope of the hill at such an angle that it faced both the open fields stretching away to the north and the wall of sacred forest rising to the west.

By this time there was no question among any of the Coxes on the home place that the forest was to keep sacred. There had already been some tempting offers from local lumberyards, all refused.

Joseph Cox, the younger, whom Paoli was to know in a succeeding generation as Uncle Joseph, was two months old when his father died. He was about five years old when his mother fled with him to seek sanctuary in the forest from the Confederate raiders. It was a conditioning experience to be repeated many times in the long years ahead. Whenever trouble threatened, Joseph was to seek escape and sanctuary in his forest. At 14, he was old enough to help his brother Joel with the construction of the new house. When Joel left later for wider opportunities in Kansas, Joseph was man enough to take over the homestead.

To Joseph, the forest before his door was life itself. As a boy, his playtime was spent in it. He knew every tree, every squirrel nest.

When Joseph took over the family land, around 1880, the cycle of forest destruction was approaching its peak. Farmers found that they could make a great deal more money selling timber from their hills than by growing corn in the valleys. A farmer would sell his entire woodland to a mill agent, and see the slow perfection of hundreds of years of growth cut off in a few weeks. When their streams began to run yellow with the wash from the hills, they moved west to Illinois, to Iowa and Kansas.

Joseph's mother died in 1890, at 75. Thereafter Joseph was alone, because the other children all had married or moved along. By the turn of the century the pattern of Joseph's life had set. He called himself a farmer, but actually his farm along the valley floor was but a means of existence. He was really a forester. The spell of the forest had captured his heart. He spent long hours wandering through it. He had favorite places where he would sit by the day, bemused by the magic of it.

People began to think him a little odd. He was a quiet man, gentle, softspoken. He attended the Methodist Church regularly, but his truest religion was his devotion to his trees. He would sometimes drive his battered wagon into town, hitch his team to the iron rail by the courthouse, buy a few groceries and then trudge home afoot forgetting about his horses until some neighbor prodded his memory. He was a great reader. In books, as in the forest, he found escape and sanctuary. The forest absorbed his capacity for affection. He never married.

Southern Indiana timber eventually was exhausted. By the turn of the century the best was gone. Some of the factories moved away. Those that stayed bought what little they could locally and imported the rest. In almost exactly 100 years, a region of magnificent forest land had passed through the complete cycle. Joseph got along as best he could. But times were none too easy and he was worried with small debts.

Then came the World War. Timber prices all over the land began to soar. Some types of timber were of a special value. Among these was black walnut. Timber scouts in remote cities heard that there was a great stand of black walnut untouched on a tract in Indiana. They came to Cox Woods. It was unbelievable—tremendous walnuts towering to 130 feet, huge of bole, straight as giant lances, the first limbs 70 feet above the ground.

That was not all. There were other trees, equally large, equally fine and almost as valuable. Hundreds of them. Joseph began to get offers the likes of which he had never heard before. This only made him angry. The timber scouts persisted. If he wouldn't sell the whole tract, would he sell the walnuts? He would not!

The walnuts were his particular love. There was a special grove of them where he liked to sit and ponder by the hour. If he wouldn't sell all his walnuts, would he sell a few of them? Would he sell only one, just one of the giant, perfect black walnuts? No, he would not sell the lowliest sapling.

There were no other offers for some years after that which amounted to anything. Uncle Joseph was getting old. It was hard to keep up the home place. He wandered in his forest, sitting long hours there in its shifting shadows.

As he needed more money than he could eke from the tiny farm, he borrowed. Presently his creditors began to be persistent. They were his neighbors and they understood him, but after all, money was scarce, and it wasn't as though Uncle Joseph couldn't get it. Look at his trees. This led to the most bitter decision Uncle Joseph ever made. He hated to be in debt. He had to have money. He would sell some trees. He sold two, not in the main forest but on the fringe of it, and not the best trees. He paid his small debts. What was left gave him cash enough for three years.

About 14 years ago, Uncle Joseph's friends in Paoli, realizing the old man's growing difficulties, conceived the idea that the forest might be sold and preserved as some sort of sanctuary. Thus the trees would be saved and Uncle Joseph would gain the means to live out his declining years in comfort. Uncle Joseph was willing, provided that the trees would never be cut. The Meridian Club of Paoli, undertook the project. The state was approached.

But the state had no money for forests. Private citizens weren't interested either.

An old man, Uncle Joseph had to find refuge with nieces and nephews in Paoli. But he kept his forest. It was understood that no one could trespass without his permission. Eventually Uncle Joseph would go and when he did the forest would go too. The old man, the last of his kind, and the venerable trees.

Uncle Joseph died on December 19, 1940. He was 83. In due course, a nephew, Arthur Farlow, was named administrator of the Cox estate. Mr. Farlow knew that there was no reasonable way in which Uncle Joseph's hope might be fulfilled. There were numerous heirs, widely scattered. The trees would have to be sold. The Meridian Club members talked among themselves about the matter. Mr. Raymond Stout was named chairman of a committee to see what, if anything, might be done. But it appeared that nothing could.

In April, Clyde A. Taylor, Paoli correspondent for Indianapolis and Louisville papers, went out to the tract with Mr. Farlow and timber buyers who planned to bid on it. Taylor took pictures and they were published in the papers he represented.

A week later, a delegation of forestry experts, making a tour of the proposed Benjamin Harrison National Forest Project, which is to range over 700,000 acres of Southern Indiana, made a side trip to look over Cox Woods. With them were newspapermen from Indianapolis, including Maurice Early, whose daily front-page-editorial column is a widely read Indiana feature, and Forest Service experts, including R.H. Grabow, supervisor of all National Forest projects in Indiana.

The experts beheld with amazement. They saw something unique, a mature and perfect forest. They transmitted their enthusiasm to the newspapermen present. The next day Maurice Early wrote an editorial about the tract. Then the impossible began to happen. Mail poured into Paoli. Letters demanded that a campaign be launched to save the trees. Most of the letters contained money. From all over the state people began to flock to the forest.

Paoli people were astonished. The forest had always been on their doorstep; no one had ever thought of it as being specially remarkable. Yet here were experts claiming that Cox Woods was peerless.

Members of the Meridian Club went back into action again behind the leadership of Raymond Stout. They prepared illustrated literature, assembled lists of prospects and sent out bushels of mail. Everyone who had ever lived in or near Paoli was asked to rally to the cause.

But time was against the campaign. The court order requiring the sale of the tract had long since been issued. A date for a public sale had been set.

Most voluntary subscriptions had been small. It took a lot of time to raise contributions. Some had to be refused, since they were accompanied by conditions that could not be considered. One wealthy Indianapolis man, for example, offered a fair-sized sum provided one of the great groves of the forest was named in his honor, and so posted.

By the date of the sale only a fraction of the amount considered necessary had actually been raised. So the trees were sold for lumber. It must have been a tragic day for the spirit of Uncle Joseph.

Then three things happened to permit Uncle Joseph to sleep in peace. First, the company that had bought the tract, proposing to use it in the manufacture of fine furniture agreed to leave it intact, and to sell it back untouched if the money for its purchase could be raised by a designated date months away.

The Meridian Club renewed its efforts. They bore fruit in the second event. In Indiana, the Pioneer Mothers' Memorial Association is made up of descendants of those who, like the original Joseph and Mary Cox, came into Indiana during the pioneer days. The Pioneer Mothers voted to donate the entire sum in their treasury, $5,900, to the forest fund, on condition that it would be officially known as the Indiana Pioneer Mothers' Memorial Forest. The Meridian Club promptly accepted the gift, with its condition. The forest would need a name, and what could be a better one than the Indiana Pioneer Mothers' Memorial Forest?

Then came the decisive event. Dr. J. Alfred Hall, of the United States Forest Service, one of the first experts to discover the unique character of the tract, had gone to Washington enormously impressed with Cox Woods. He appealed to the National Forest Reservation Commission for funds to preserve the tract for the nation. He made his appeal as a scientist and an expert. But his zeal was that of an artist who had stumbled by accident upon an ancient and incredible masterpiece in a perfect state of preservation.

Doctor Hall's plea boiled down to this: Here, and only here is a perfect forest. To fail to preserve it would be a calamity. Doctor Hall pleaded his cause well. The commissions voted to provide the additional money needed to repurchase the tract from the lumber company—about half of a necessary $25,000 total—on condition that it would be preserved by the Forest Service as a forest museum. There was jubilation in Paoli, and no doubt Uncle Joseph's restless spirit found peace at last. Now he could sleep. His trees were safe.

But the public furor stirred by the threat to the trees created new problems. Thousands of visitors flocked to the tract. They parked their cars on the fringe of the woods and went floundering through the green jungle of its underbrush.

This had two results. One was a physical threat to the forest from people who insisted on cutting their initials on trees and uprooting sample plants. An additional problem was curious. The majority went away disappointed. They had been led to believe that they would find a grove of enormous trees, of spectacular girth and height, dwarfing California's redwoods. They found big trees, but most seemed to their unschooled eyes like those that would be found in any woods. They found the forest carpeted by a tangled mat of vines and plants, which made walking difficult. They were like the thousands who flock to stare at the Venus de Milo and go away wondering why anyone would get excited over a statue without arms.

The Forest Service is planning to make it clear to all who visit it just why this particular forest is in a class by itself. To that end, experts have completed a detailed and comparative classification of its trees and plants.

The Forest Service inventory points out that nowhere else in the country are there so many black walnuts so large and so perfect. In one particular grove they tower well over 100 feet, sheer and unblemished. Someone named it Cathedral Cove. It was Uncle Joseph's favorite spot.

Some of the oaks are notable for size and for age, though there are larger and perhaps older oaks elsewhere. One particular giant is estimated to be more than 600 years old, with a bole six feet in diameter and a vast spread of mammoth limbs that reach the sunlight at more than 110 feet above the ground. Other trees that have grown to unusual size are the yellow poplar, the white ash, and the beech.

Already more than 25 species have been catalogued, and there are probably more. These include the chestnut, the black oak and the red oak, several species of maple, the black and the honey locust, the sycamore with its silver bark—the buttonwood tree of the pioneers—the black gum, the blue ash, the red elm; the butternut, and the pignut and the shagbark hickories; the wild cherry, the ruddy wood of which was a favorite with Joseph Cox in his pioneer workshop; such oddities as the Kentucky coffee tree, and the aromatic sassafras.

There is the wild grape, one enormous vine with a main stem larger than the trunks of most trees. There is the spicebush, the wahoo, the bittersweet with its orange berries, Salomon's seal and stoneroot, the devil's walkingstick; the tough ironwood, which made fine tool handles; the flowering creamy dogwood, and its satellite, the redbud, which the pioneers called the Judas tree; there is the pawpaw with its mouth-puckering fruit.

The floor of the forest is a carpet of delicate shade-loving plants. Botanists know of no other spot where so many grow in such balanced perfection. Underfoot are the filmy white flowers of the bedstraw; the yellow buttercup, known as the hooked ranunculus; the Indian turnip called jack-in-the-pulpit; the May apple, sought as a medicinal herb; the common purple violet and the yellow dogtooth violet; the hardy pink, or sweet William; the roselike avens; the chocolate-colored flowers of the wild ginger; the bluebell, meadow rue; the rate forest orchid, which is known locally as moccasin flower, or lady's slipper; the shy jewelweed called touch-me-not, and a wild profusion of forest ferns.

Acquisition of the Cox Forest at this particular time seems peculiarly providental for the Forest Service. It provides the dramatic accent needed to bring into sharp focus the whole vast program of land restoration throughout the Ohio Valley—a project involving several million acres, designed to bring into practical commercial service as forest areas eroded and cutover land of little or no present value.

The Forest Service will provide no picnic ground or camp-site. No road will be cut through it. There will be forest trails. There will be benches here and there. There will be rangers on hand to guard against fire and vandalism, and explain the forest's mysteries and its special wonders. The Forest Service likes to think that the plans worked out for the trees would suit Uncle Joseph.

(The 1942 Post cost five cents. The current Post sells for $2.55 plus 15 cents tax in Pennsylvania or a total of 53 times more than it cost in 1942. The $25,000 paid for Uncle Joseph's 88 acres of timber would equal $6,625,000 using a Post index.)

Appendix II

Black Walnut Recipes

Homemakers and professional bakers agree that black walnuts add a delicious flavor and texture to cakes, cookies, rolls, and other baked goods. Because the Eastern black walnut retains its flavor during baking, it is a traditional favorite with people who enjoy good baked foods. There is little to compare with the full rich flavor of Eastern black walnuts in candy. They can be used as a flavor ingredient for any candy from fudge to brittle, or as a fancy topping. Whether the candy is chocolate, caramel, vanilla, or any other flavor, black walnuts will enhance its taste. Black walnuts also lend a unique flavor to salads and casseroles.

Black walnut kernels are rich in nutritional value, being extremely high in fats (polyunsaturated), protein, and carbohydrates. One ounce of black walnut nutmeats contains 180 calories, 8 grams of protein, 3 grams of carbohydrates, 15 grams of fat, of which 9 grams are polyunsaturated, and no cholesterol. They compare favorably with meat in vitamins A, B and C and are the highest of nearly all foods in linoleic acid. Black walnuts are often referred to as the "Heart Food" as they contain virtually no cholesterol. They provide so much body energy in such a compact form that they are particularly suited for use by hikers, bicyclers and runners. Eastern black walnuts, as opposed to English or California walnuts, have a full, rich robust flavor that millions of people have come to know and love.

Black walnuts can be substituted for other nuts in any recipe calling for nuts. They can be added to standard commercial cake, muffin, or bread mixes for an added flavor treat. They can be added to any homemade ice cream.

There are two cookbooks currently in print and offered for sale that specialize in recipes using nutmeats of the Eastern black walnut. These are:

Cooking with Black Walnuts
$7.95 plus $3.00 postage and handling
from Missouri Dandy Pantry
P.O. Box A
Stockton, MO 65785
1-800-872-6879

Black Walnut Festival Cookbook
Award-Winning Recipes
$8.00 plus $2.00 postage and handling
from The West Virginia Black Walnut Festival Inc.
Black Walnut Festival Cookbook
Post Office Box 1
Spencer, West Virginia 25276

For those who would like to try a black walnut recipe before they purchase one of the above cookbooks, here are some samples.

Missouri's Best Black Walnut Oatmeal Cookie

3/4 c. brown sugar	1 tsp. soda
1/2 c. sugar	3 c. oatmeal
1 1/4 c. butter	1 1/4 tsp. cinnamon
1 egg	1/3 tsp. nutmeg
1 tsp. vanilla	2 c. Eastern black walnuts
3/4 tsp. salt	1/2 c. raisins (optional)
1 1/2 c. flour	

Mix sugar, egg, butter, vanilla together. Stir in dry ingredients and Eastern black walnuts. Spoon onto a cookie sheet. Bake at 350 degrees for 10 minutes. Makes 3 dozen. Let cool, then enjoy.

"Best Ever" Black Walnut Pie

3 eggs	1 c. dark corn syrup
2/3 c. sugar	dash salt
1/3 c. butter, melted	1 c. Eastern black walnuts

Beat eggs thoroughly with sugar, salt, syrup and melted butter. Add black walnuts. Pour into unbaked pastry shell. Bake in 350 degree oven for 50 minutes or until knife inserted halfway between center and edge of pie comes out clean. Cool.

Guter Nuszkucvhen
(Good Walnut Cake)

1 1/2 c. sugar	3/4 c. butter
1 1/2 c. milk	3 eggs
3 c. flour	3 tbs. baking soda
1 1/2 tbs. vanilla	2 1/4 c. black walnuts

Beat butter til fluffy, then add sugar, eggs and vanilla. Mix baking powder with flour. Mix milk and flour mixture with other ingredients. Blend well, add nuts, pour into 9 x 13 inch pan, bake for 30 minutes at 350 degrees. Use a powdered sugar frosting and sprinkle with chopped Eastern black walnuts.

Zucchini Black Walnut Bread

3 eggs
2 c. sugar
1 c. cooking oil
1 tbs. vanilla
1 tbs. cinnamon
1 tsp. salt

2 tsp. baking soda
1/4 tsp. baking powder
2 c. grated, peeled zucchini
2 1/4 c. sifted flour
1 c. chopped black walnuts

Sift together all dry ingredients except sugar. Beat eggs til foamy, add oil, sugar, and vanilla. Mix well. Add dry ingredients alternately with grated zucchini, mixing well after each addition. Add black walnuts. Turn batter into one greased 9 x 5 or two 8 1/2 x 4 1/2 loaf pans and bake at 350 degrees for 1 hr. 10 min. Cool in pans on rack 15 min. then turn out and cool completely before cutting. May be frozen for months and eaten cool or warm. Delicious for breakfast or afternoon tea.

Black Walnut Ice Cream

2 1/2 c. sugar
4 tbs. flour
1/2 tsp. salt
5 c. milk, scalded
6 eggs, beaten

4 c. cream
4 1/2 tsp. vanilla
2 cups black walnuts
3 tbs. butter

Saute black walnuts in the 3 tablespoons butter, and cool. Combine sugar, flour and salt, slowly stir in hot milk. Cook 10 minutes over low heat, stirring constantly. Stir small amounts of cooked mixture gradually into beaten eggs and cook 1 minute. Chill in refrigerator, then pour in freezer and add cream and vanilla. Churn in freezer for about 15 minutes, then add black walnuts and finish freezing.

Black Walnut Pancakes

3/4 c. milk
1 egg
2 tsp. baking powder
1/2 tsp. salt
1 medium, ripe banana
  peeled and sliced 1/2 in. thick
oil

2 tbs. butter, melted
1 c. flour
3 tbs. sugar
1/2 cup toasted chopped
  black walnuts, see note.
maple syrup

Beat together milk, melted butter and egg in medium bowl. Stir together flour, baking powder, sugar and salt in separate bowl, Stir into milk mixture just to mix. Stir in nuts and banana slices. Lightly oil pancake griddle. Heat over medium heat 1 to 2 minutes. Pour out batter for 4 pancakes. Cook until top side has air bubbles and underside is golden, 3 to 5 minutes. Flip pancakes over and cook second side, 1 to 2 minutes longer. Serve with maple syrup. Makes 1 generous or 2 regular servings.

Note: To toast walnut, place on baking sheet and bake at 350 degrees until lightly browned and aromatic, about five minutes. Immediately remove from oven and from cookie sheet.

Favorite Farm Black Walnut Cookies

1 c. margarine	1 tsp. salt
1 c. sugar	1 tsp. baking soda
1 c. brown sugar	1 tsp. cinnamon
2 eggs	1/4 tsp. nutmeg
1 tsp. vanilla	3 c. oats
1 1/2 c. flour	1 c. raisins
1 1/2 c. black walnuts	

Cream margarine and sugars. Mix in eggs and vanilla. Stir together flour, salt, soda and spices. Mix into creamed mixture. Stir in raisins, oats and black walnuts. Drop by teaspoonsful onto a greased cookie sheet. Bake at 350 degrees for 10-12 minutes or until golden brown. Makes about 4 dozen cookies.

Missouri Black Walnut and Bourbon Pie

3 eggs	1/2 c. butter, melted
1 1/4 c. sugar, divided	1 1/4 c. black walnuts
4 tbs. cornstarch	1 6-oz. package of semi-
5 tbs. bourbon	sweet chocolate morsels
1 9" unbaked pie shell	

Beat eggs with 3/4 c. sugar. Mix remaining 1/2 c. sugar with cornstarch and add to egg mixture. Fold in bourbon, butter, black walnuts and chocolate morsels. Pour filling into unbaked 9" pie shell. Bake in a preheated 375 degree oven for 15 minutes. Reduce oven temperature to 325 degrees and bake 15 minutes or until filling is set and crust is golden.

Appendix III
Directory

Organizations

American Forest Foundation, Suite 780, 1111 19th Street, NW, Washington, D.C. 20036, 202-463-2462.

American Forestry Technology, Inc. 1001 North 500 West, West Lafayette, IN 47906, 317-583-331. Walnut seedlings.

American Forests, P.O. Box 2000, Washington, D.C. 20013-2000, 202-667-3300.

American Walnut Manufacturers Association, 260 South First St. Suite 2, Zionsville, IN 46077-1602, 317-873-8780.

Association of Consulting Foresters, Inc. 5410 Grosvenor Lane, STE. Bethesda, MD 20814, 301-530-6795.

Indiana Forestry and Woodland Owners Association, Inc., P.O. Box 2102, Indianapolis, IN 46206.

Museum of Appalachia, P.O. Box 0318, Norris, TN 37828, 615-494-0514.

National Arbor Day Foundation, 100 Arbor Avenue, Nebraska City, NE 68410, 402-474-5655.

National Woodland Owners Association, 374 Maple Ave. E. STE 210, Vienna, VA 22180, 703/255-2700.

Nebraska Nut Growers Association, 122 Mussehl Hall-East Campus, University of Nebraska, Lincoln, NE 68583, 402-472-3674.

North Central Forest Experiment Station, Forestry Sciences Laboratory, SIU Carbondale, IL 62901-4630, 618-453-2318.

Northeastern Forest Experiment Station, 5 Radnor Corporate Center, 100 Matsonford Road, Suite 200, Radnor, PA 19087, 610-975-4045.

Northern Nut Growers Association, Kenneth Bauman, Treasurer, 9870 S. Palmer Road, New Carlisle, OH 45344.

Purdue Research Foundation, Office of Technology Transfer, Purdue University, 1650 Engineering Admin. Bldg. Room 328, West Lafayette, IN 47907-1650, 317-494-2610.

Shepherd Hills Walnut, P.O. Box 909, Lebanon, MO 65536, 417-532-9450. Walnut wood products.

Walnut Council, 260 South First Street, Suite 2, Zionsville, IN, 46077, 317-873-3780.

West Virginia Black Walnut Festival, P.O. Box 1, Spencer, WV, 25276, 304-927-3580.

Products

"Extractor," Gaston G. Fornes, 2400 Bennington Road, Charlottesville, VA 22901. 804-293-9598.

"Get Crackin' Nutcracker," The Missouri Dandy Pantry, 212 Hammons Drive East, Stockton, MO 65785, 800-872-6879.

Hunt's Black Walnut Nut Cracker, P.O. Box 3, Hartford, IA, 50118, 515-989-0117.

Walnut Meats and Candies, The Missouri Dandy Pantry, 212 Hammons Drive East, Stockton, MO 65785, 800-872-6879.

Walnut Wood Products, Independent Stave Company, P.O.Box 104, Lebanon, MO 65536, 417-532-6186.

Walnut Wood Products, Shepherd Hills Walnut, P.O. Box 909, Lebanon, MO 65536, 417-532-9450.

Publications

American Forests, American Forests, P.O. Box 2000, Washington, D.C. 20013-2000. 202-667-3300.

Arbor Day, The National Arbor Day Foundation, 100 Arbor Avenue, Nebraska City, NE 68410.

Black Walnut Festival Cookbook, Award-Winning Recipes, $8.00, The West Virginia Black Walnut Festival, Inc. P.O. Box 1, Spencer, WV 25276.

Cooking with Black Walnuts, $7.95, Missouri Dandy Pantry, P.O. Box A, Stockton, MO 65785, 800-872-6879.

Journal of Forestry, 5400 Grosvenor Lane, Bethesda, MD 20814-2198, 301-897-8720.

National Woodlands, National Woodland Owners Association, 374 Maple Ave. E., STE 210, Vienna, VA 22180, 703-255-2700.

Nutshell, The, Quarterly Publication of the Northern Nut Growers Association, Tucker Hill, 654 Beinhower Road, Etters, PA 17319-9774, 717-938-6090.

Planting Black Walnut for Timber, Leaflet No. 487, Forest Service, U.S. Dept. of Agriculture, Superintendent of Documents, U.S. Government Printing Office, Washington, D.C. 20402. $.35.

Thinning Black Walnut, North Central Forest Experiment Station, Forest Service, UDSA, 1992 Folwell Avenue, St. Paul, MN 55108.

Tree Farmer Magazine, American Forest Foundation, Suite 780, 1111 19th St. N.W. Washington, D.C. 20036, 202-463-2462.

Walnut Council Bulletin, George Rink, Ph.D. Editor, USDA Forest Service, Mailcode 4630, Forestry Sciences Laboratory, SIU, Carbondale, IL 62901-4630, 618-453-2927.

Walnut Notes, Forest Service, U.S. Dept. of Agriculture, 1992 Folwell Avenue, St. Paul, MN 55108.

Walnut Notes, Superintendent of Documents. U.S. Government Printing Office, Washington, D.C. 20402.

Woodland Stewardship: A Practical Guide for Midwestern Landowners, MES Distributors, University of Minnesota, 1420 Eckles Ave., St. Paul, MN 55108-6069. $14.95

Visual Aids

"Black Walnut From Nut Seed to Timber Tree"
Leo C. Bird, Dibble Creek Tree Farm, P.O. Box 181, Stockton, KS 67669, 913-425-6043. VCR Tape. $37.50.

"Pruning Black Walnut Trees For Profit"
Black Walnut Videotape, 101 Agricultural Communications Bldg. University of Nebraska-Lincoln, Lincoln, NE 68583-0918. $45.00

"Woodlot Management: How it Grows"
"Woodlot Management: Helping It Grow"
"Harvesting and Renewing It"
"Selling Timber"

These four VCR tapes are currently available at $15 each from the West Virginia University Extension Service, Timothy L. Pahl, P.O. Box 6125, Morgantown, WV, 26506-6125, 305-293-7550 Ext. 450.

Companies

Amana Furniture Shop, David Rettig, P.O. Box 189, Amana, IA 52203, 319-622-3291.

Atlantic Veneer Company, P.O. Box 660, Beaufort, NC 28516, 919-728-3169. Timber buyers and veneer processors.

Berea College Crafts, CPO 2347, Berea, KY 40404, 606-986-9341. Ext. 5220. Furniture and novelties in black walnut.

Black Walnut Festival, P.O. Box 1, Spencer, WV 25276, 304-927-1780. Festival 2nd Weekend in October.

Capital Machines International Corp. 2801 Roosevelt Ave., Indianapolis, IN 46218, 317-638-6661. Veneer equipment.

Cascade Forestry Nursery, Route 2, Cascade, IA, 52033, 319-852-3042. Full range of forest services.

Charley's Nut Tree Nursery, Charles A. Richcrick, R.D. 10, Box 316-N, York, PA 17404. Grafted walnut cultivars.

Fenn Wood, Dan Fenn, P.O. Box 344, Amana, IA 52203, 319-622-3710.

Forest Management Services, Inc. 4120 Haythorne Avenue, Terre Haute, IN 47805, 812-466-4445. Full range of woodland owner services.

Goby Walnut Products, 5016 Palestine Road, NW, Albany, OR 97321, 503-926-7516.

Good Hope Hardwoods, Inc., 1627 New London Road, Landenberg, PA 19350, 215-274-8842. Hardwoods for craftsmen.

Hammons Products Company, 217 Hammons Drive East, Stockton, MO 65785, 417-276-5181. Buys walnut nuts and sells shells and meats.

Henkel-Harris Company, Inc. P.O. Box 2170, Winchester, VA 22601-1370, 703-667-4900. Manufacturers of fine walnut furniture.

Henredon, P.O. Box 70, Morganton, NC 28655, 704-437-5261.

Independent Stave Company, P.O. Box 104, Lebanon, Missouri, 65536, 417-532-6186. Offers black walnut wood products and novelties.

Irion Company Furniture Makers, 1 S. Bridge St. Christiana, PA 17501, 610-644-7516. Fine black walnut furniture.

Krauss Furniture and Clock Factory, Steve Krauss, 2783 HWY 6 Trail, South Amana, IA 52334, 319-622-3223.

Lohr, Jeff, 242 North Limerick Road, Schwenksville, PA 19473, 610-287-7802.

Museum of Appalachia, P.O. Box 0318, Norris, TN 37828, 615-494-7680. Museum, craft shop and Tennessee Fall Homecoming (2nd Weekend in October).

Nolin River Nut Tree Nursery, John and Lisa Brittain, 797 Port Wooden Road, Upton, KY 42784, 502-369-8551. Large selection of black walnut cultivars.

Oikos Tree Crops, P.O. Box 19425, Kalamazoo, MI 49019, 616-342-2759. Black walnut nuts, seedlings and grafted cultivars.

Pike Lumber Company, Box 255, Carbon, IN 47837, 812-448-3961. Buyers of standing lumber.

Reinhart Fajen Inc. 1000 Red Bud Drive, P.O. Box 338, Warsaw, MO 65355, 816-438-5111. Fine black walnut gunstocks.

Schanz Furniture and Refinishing Shop, Norman Schanz, 2773 HWY 6 Trail, South Amana, IA 52334, 319-622-3529.

Swartzendruber Hardwood Creations, 1100 Chicago Ave. P.O. Box 180, Goshen, IN 46526, 219-534-2502. Fine walnut furniture.

Tree Pro, 3180 W. 250 N. West Lafayette, IN 47906, 800-875-8071. Offers tree shelters and walnut planting kits.

Tubex Treeshelters, P.O. Box 7097, 75 Bidwell Street, St. Paul, MN 55107, 800-248-9239. Treeshelters.

Waterford Furniture Makers, P.O. Box 11888 Lynchburg, VA 24506, 804-847-4468. Quality solid black walnut furniture.

Webb, David, R. Co. Inc. 206 S. Holland St. P. O. Box 8, Edinburgh, IN, 46124-0008, 812-526-2501. Buys walnut and cuts veneer.

Below are applications for membership in the Walnut Council and the Northern Nut Growers Association.
Prices listed are effective through 1995.

APPLICATION FOR MEMBERSHIP

Please add my name to your membership list and advise me of future activities of the Walnut Council.

I have contacted the following individuals and believe they are interested in becoming members of the Walnut Council. I understand that the Walnut Council will follow up with a form invitation from our Executive Director Larry Frye.

Name

Title or Business

Address

City	State	Zipcode

☐ NEW MEMBER   ☐ MEMBERSHIP RENEWAL
Please make your check out for the appropriate dues category as determined by your country or state of origin, listed below

REGULAR MEMBERS		OTHER MEMBERSHIP CATEGORIES
U.S.A.*	**International**	
Illinois	$30	Canada	$20	
Indiana	$30		Student Member	$5
Iowa	$30	All Other	Supporting Member	$50
Kentucky	$30	Countries	$30	Life Member	$300
Maryland	$25		
Michigan	$20		
Missouri	$25		
Nebraska	$30		
Oregon	$30		
Wisconsin	$20		
All Other States	$20	*INCLUDES STATE CHAPTER DUES	

CHANGE OF ADDRESS _____

COMMENTS _____

Name

Title or Business

Address

City	State	Zipcode

Name

Title or Business

Address

City	State	Zipcode

Send information to: Walnut Council
260 South First Street, Suite 2
Zionsville, IN 46077
317/873-8780

The *Walnut Council Bulletin* (ISSN 1041-5769) is published quarterly by the Walnut Council, an organization dedicated to advancing knowledge of walnut culture, encouraging the planting of walnut and the management of established walnut, and perpetuating the utilization of all walnut products. A subscription is included in the annual dues paid by members of the Council. (Please include old address when sending change-of-address notice). Contributions of gifts to the Walnut Council are not deductible as charitable contributions for federal income tax purposes. However, dues payments are deductible by members and non-members alike as an ordinary and necessary business expense. Address all correspondence and information to George Rink, Editor, *Walnut Council Bulletin*, Forestry Science Laboratory, Mailcode 4630, Southern Illinois University at Carbondale, Carbondale, Illinois 62901-4630. Telephone 618-453-2927.

This application form is included with each issue of *The Nutshell* for you to share with a friend. All current members will be supplied an application form and envelope each fall. You should use that form for your annual renewal. The two digits after your name on the mailing label indicate the year for which your dues are paid.

Membership Application
☐ New Member   ☐ Renewal

Send to: Kenneth Bauman, Treasurer
Northern Nut Growers Association
9870 S. Palmer Rd.
New Carlisle, OH 45344
USA

Name _____ Date _____

Address _____

City _____ State/Province _____

ZIP/Postal Code _____ Amount Enclosed _____

Phone Number (_____) _____ - _____

Dues must be payable in U.S. funds. Make check payable to NNGA.

Dues in U.S. Funds	
Individual	$15.00
Family	20.00
Canadian	17.00
Overseas & Mexico	20.00
Contributing	25.00
Sustaining	35.00
Life	200.00

All memberships carry the same privileges: a copy of the current *Annual Report* and four issues of *The Nutshell*.

Members joining between 1 October and 31 December will receive all *Nutshells* of that period and will be credited with membership for the following year.

Bibliography

American Forestry Technology, Inc. Undated. *Questions & Answers Frequently Asked about Genetically Superior Black Walnut Trees.* Sales brochure. West Lafayette, IN: American Forestry Technology, Inc.

Angela, Piero, and Alberto Angela. 1993. *The Extraordinary Story of Human Origins.* Buffalo, New York, NY: Prometheus Books.

Arnow, Harriet Simpson. 1960. *Seedtime on the Cumberland.* New York, NY: MacMillan Company.

Author unspecified. June 1977. "Is This the Oldest Working Machine in the Furniture Industry?" *Wood and Wood Products.*

Auvergne, Caroline. October 1986. "The American Black Walnut," *Early American Life.*

Ballantine, Betty, and Ian Ballantine, Eds. 1993. *The Native Americans.* Atlanta, GA: Turner Publishing, Inc.

Bartram, William. 1908. *The Travels of William Bartram.* Naturalists Edition. Frances Harper, Ed. New Haven, CT: Yale University Press.

Beineke, Walter F. February 1989. "Black Walnut Plantation Management," *Woodland Managment.* Forestry and Natural Resources Bulletin 119. West Lafayette, IN: Purdue University Cooperative Extension Service.

Beineke, Walter F. 1984. *Characteristics of Purdue University's Patented Black Walnut Trees.* Forestry and Natural Resources Bulletin 115. West Lafayette, IN: Purdue University Cooperative Extension Service.

Beineke, Walter F. Undated. *Corrective Pruning of Black Walnut for Timber Form.* Forestry and Natural Resources Bulletin 76. West Lafayette, IN: Purdue University Extension Service.

Berry, Edward W. 1912. "Notes on the Geological History of the Walnuts and Hickories," *The Plant World.* Vol. 15, No. 10. Baltimore, MD: The Johns Hopkins University.

Bey, Calvin F. October 1980. "Growth Gains from Moving Black Walnut Provenances Northward." *Journal of Forestry.*

Bird, Leo C. Summer, 1991. "Why Grow Trees." *Walnut Council Bulletin.*

Bly, Robert. 1990. *Iron John, A Book About Men.* Massachusetts: Addison-Wesley Publishing Company.

Bormann, F. Herbert, Diana Balmori, and Gordon T. Geballe. 1993. *Redesigning the American Lawn: A Search for Environmental Harmony.* New Haven, CT: Yale University Press.

Bromfield, Louis. 1948. *Out of the Earth.* New York, NY: Harper & Brothers.

Brooks, Maurice. 1965. *The Appalachians.* Boston, MA: Houghton-Mifflin Company.

Brooks, Maurice. 1951. *Effect of Black Walnut Trees and Their Products on Other Vegetation,* Morgantown, WV: West Virginia University Experiment Station.

Brower, Kenneth. 1990. *One Earth.* San Francisco, CA: Collins Publishers.

Burbank, Luther, and Wilbur Hall. 1931. *The Harvest of the Years.* New York, NY: Houghton-Mifflin Company.

Burde, E. Lucy, Ed. 1988. *Walnut Notes.* Forest Service, North Central Forest Experiment Station. St. Paul, MN: U.S. Department of Agriculture.

Burke, Bob. Winter, 1990. "Walnut Estate Sale Yields Over Half Million Dollars," *Walnut Council Bulletin*.

Callahan, John C. 1990. *The Fine Hardwood Veneer Industry in the United States 1838 - 1990*. Lake Ann, MI: National Woodlands Publishing Company.

Callahan, John C., and Robert P. Smith. August 1974. *An Economic Analysis of Black Walnut Plantation Enterprises*. Research Bulletin No. 912. West Lafayette, IN: Purdue University Agricultural Experiment Station.

Calvin, William H. 1986. *The River That Flows Uphill, A Journey From the Big Bang to the Big Brain*. San Francisco, CA: Sierra Club Books.

Caraway, Cleo. 1976. *A Forestry Sciences Laboratory and How It Grew*. North Central Forest Experiment Station, Forest Service. Carbondale, IL: U.S. Department of Agriculture.

Caufield, Catherine. May 14, 1990. "A Reporter at Large, The Pacific Forest." *The New Yorker*.

Collier, James Lincoln. 1991. *The Rise of Selfishness in America*. Oxford: Oxford University Press.

Cronin, William. 1983. *Changes in the Land, Indians, Colonists and the Ecology of New England*. New York, NY: Hill and Wang.

Desmond, Adrian, and James Moore. 1991. *Darwin, The Life of a Tormented Evolutionist*. New York, NY: Warner Books.

Dietrich, William. 1992. *The Final Forest, The Battle for the Last Great Trees of the Pacific Northwest*. New York, NY: Simon & Schuster.

Eldredge, Niles. 1991. *The Miner's Canary, Unraveling the Mysteries of Extinction*. New York, NY: Prentice Hall Press.

Epps, Lor. 1984. "Tree sale sets record in state," Danville, IL, *Danville Commercial News*.

Faragher, John Mack. 1992. *Daniel Boone, The Life and Legend of an American Pioneer*. New York, NY: Henry Holt and Company.

Fletcher, Stevenson Whitcomb. 1950. *Pennsylvania Agriculture and Country Life 1640-1840*. Harrisburg, PA: Pennsylvania Historical and Museum Commission.

Fornes, Gaston G. 1988. *Instruction Manual and Other Useful Information for Use With The New Patented Fornes Nut Kernel Extractor for the Hard Shell Edible Nuts*. Charlottesville, VA.

Frankl, Viktor E. 1992. *Man's Search for Meaning, An Introduction to Logotherapy, Fourth Edition*, Boston, MA: Beacon Press.

Frueh, Leo H. 1992/1993. *Cascade Forestry Nursery, Trees: The Environmental Crop*. Price list.

Giono, Jean. 1985. *The Man Who Planted Trees*. Chelsea, VT: Chelsea Green Publishing Company.

Goreau, Angeline. April, 1993. "Natchez," *Gourmet* magazine.

Grey, Zane. 1910. *The Young Forester*. New York, NY: Grosset & Dunlap Publishers.

Hahn, Jerold T. July 31, 1987. *Illinois Forest Statistics, 1985*. Resource Bulletin NC-103. North Central Forest Experiment Station, Forest Service. St. Paul, MN: United States Department of Agriculture.

Hahn, Jerold T., and John S. Spencer, Jr. 1991. *Timber Resource of Missouri '89*. Resource Bulletin NC-119. North Central Forest Experiment Station, Forest Service. St. Paul, MN: U.S. Department of Agriculture.

Half A Century in Wood: 1920-1970, The Woodenworks of Wharton Esherick. 1988. The Warton Exherick Museum, P.O. Box 595, Paoli, PA, 19301.

Hall, William L. 1900. "Forest Extension on the Middle West," *Yearbook of Agriculture.* Washington, D.C.: U.S. Government Printing Office.

Halls, Lowell K. 1984. *White-Tailed Deer, Ecology and Management, A Wildlife Management Institute Book.* New York, NY: Stackpole Books.

Hammons Products Company. Undated. *Premium Soft Abrasive Grit.* Sales brochure. Stockton, MO: Hammons Products Company.

Hammons Products Company. Undated. *The Company.* Stockton, MO: Hammons Products Company.

Havighurst, Walter, 1956. *The Heartland, Ohio, Indiana and Illinois, 1673-1860.* New York, NY: Harper and Row.

Havighurst, Walter. 1970. *River to the West, Three Centuries of the Ohio.* New York, NY: G. P. Putnam's Sons.

Heiman, A.W., Editor. *The Hoosier Kernel.* Anderson, IN: Indiana Nutgrowers Association.

Henredon Furniture Company. 1989. *Henredon Versailles.* Morganton, NC: Henredon Furniture Company.

Hepburn, Andrew H. January 31, 1942. "Joe Cox's Trees Live On." *The Saturday Evening Post.* Philadelphia, PA: The Curtis Publishing Company.

Hine, Thomas. 1991. *Facing Tomorrow, What the Future has Been, What the Future Can Be.* New York, NY: Knopf.

Hoadly, R. Bruce. 1980. *Understanding Wood, A Craftsman's Guide to Wood Technology.* Newton, CT: Taunton Press.

Howard, Robert P. 1972. *Illinois, A History of the Prairie State.* Grand Rapids, MI: William B. Eerdmans Publishing Company.

Indiana Forestry and Woodland Owners Association, Inc. 1991-1992. *Directory of Professional Foresters.* Indianapolis, IN: Indiana Forestry and Woodland Owners Association, Inc.

Johnson, Robert. April 25, 1989. "Walnut Trees Now Are Often Grown for Different Nuts." *The Wall Street Journal.*

Jonas, Gerald. 1993. *The Living Earth Book of North American Trees,* Pleasantville, NY: The Reader's Digest Association, Inc.

Josephy, Alvin M. Jr. Ed. 1992. *America in 1492, The World of the Indian Peoples Before the Arrival of Columbus.* New York, NY: Alfred A. Knopf.

Kalisz, Paul J., Jeffrey W. Stringer, and Deborah B. Hill. March 1989. "Growth of Young Black Walnut Plantations in Kentucky," *Northern Journal of Applied Forestry,* Vol. 6, No. 1.

Karges Furniture Company. 1991. *Karges by Hand, A Concert of Wood and Design.* Evansville, IN: The Karges Furniture Company, Inc.

Kennedy, Roger G. 1994. *Hidden Cities, The Discovery and Loss of Ancient North American Civilization.* New York, NY: The Free Press.

Kinkead, Eugene. 1980. *Squirrel Book.* New York, NY: E. P. Dutton.

Lillard, Richard G. 1947. *The Great Forest.* New York, NY: Knopf.

Lindsey, Alton A., Ed. 1966. *Natural Features of Indiana.* Indiana State Library. Indianapolis, IN: Indiana Academy of Science.

Logan, Clay S. Spring 1992. *Stark Bro's Fruit Trees & Landscaping Catalog, 175th Anniversary.* Louisiana, MO: Stark Bro's Nurseries and Orchards Co.

Mackay, Charles, LL.D. 1972. *Extraordinary Popular Delusions and the Madness of Crowds*. Reprinting of 1841 issue, Nineteenth Printing, 1972. Wells, Vermont, Fraser Publishing Company.

McGuire, John R. 1958. "Our Vital Private Forest Lands," *Land, The Yearbook of Agriculture 1958*. Washington, D.C.: U.S. Department of Agriculture.

McPhee, John. 1967. *Oranges*, New York, NY: Farrar Straus & Giroux, 1967.

McPhee, John. 1986. *Rising From the Plains*. New York, NY: Farrar Straus & Giroux.

Michaux, Francois André 1865. *The North American Sylva*. Philadelphia, PA: W.M. Rutter & Company.

Mills, W.L., and B. C. Fischer. 1985. "The Economics of Timber Stand Improvement." *Woodland Managment*. Forestry and Natural Resources Bulletin 86, Cooperative Extension Service. West Lafayette, IN: Purdue University.

Missouri Dandy Pantry. Undated. *Black Walnut Recipes*. Stockton, MO: Missouri Dandy Pantry.

Missouri Dandy Pantry. Undated. *Missouri Dandy Pantry, "For gifts with perfect taste."* Quarterly sales brochure. Stockton, MO: Missouri Dandy Pantry.

Moize, Elizabeth A. December 1985. "Daniel Boone, First Hero of the Frontier." *National Geographic*. Washington, D.C.: National Geographic Society.

Morgan, Ted. 1993. *Wilderness at Dawn, The Settling of the North American Continent*. New York, NY: Simon & Schuster.

Nakashima, George. 1988. *The Soul of a Tree, A Woodworker's Reflections*, New York: Kodanska.

National Geographic Society. October 1991. "1491, America Before Columbus." *National Geographic*. Washington, D.C.: The National Geographic Society.

Northern Nut Growers Association. 1990. *The 81st Annual Report of the Northern Nut Growers Association, Inc.* Lincoln NE: University of Nebraska.

Northern Nut Growers Association. 1991. *The 82nd Annual Report of the Northern Nut Growers Association, Inc.* Corvalis, OR: Oregon State University.

Northern Nut Growers Association. *The Nutshell, The quarterly newsletter of the Northern Nut Growers Association*. Etters, PA.

Noweg, Tonga A., and William B. Kurtz. September 1987. "Eastern Black Walnut Plantations: An Economically Viable Option for Conservation Reserve Lands Within the Corn Belt." *Northern Journal of Applied Forestry*, Vol.4, No.3.

Paine, Thomas. 1918. *The Crisis*. New York: Peter Eckler Publishing Company.

Peattie, Donald Culross. 1966. *A Natural History of Trees of Eastern and Central North America*. Boston, MA: Houghton-Mifflin Company.

Peattie, Donald Culross. 1936. *Green Laurels, The Lives and Achievements of the Great Naturalists*. New York, NY: Simon and Schuster Inc.

Peattie, Donald Culross. 1943. "Men, Mountains, and Trees." *The Great Smokies and the Blue Ridge*.

Pennington, Steve. Undated. "Learn How You Can Benefit From State Nurseries: Reforestation Takes Root in Indiana." *Outdoor Indiana*.

Pennsylvania Nut Growers Association. *The Nut Kernel, Official Publication of the Pennsylvania Nut Growers Association*. Allentown, PA.

Platt, Rutherford. 1965. *The Great American Forest*. New Jersey, Prentice-Hall, Inc., 1965.

Pope, P.E., B.C. Fischer, and D. L. Cassens. Undated. *Timber Harvesting and Logging Practices for Private Woodlands*. Forestry and Natural Resources 101, Cooperative Extension Service. West Lafayette, IN: Purdue University.

Reaman, G. Elmore. 1957. *The Trail of the Black Walnut*, Pennsylvania German Society, McClelland & Stewart Limited.

Reich, Robert B. 1992. *The Work of Nations, Preparing Ourselves for the 21st Century Capitalism*. New York, NY: Alfred A. Knopf.

Reid, William. 1988. "Eastern Black Walnut: Potential for Commercial Nut Producing Cultivars." *Advances in New Crops*. Proceedings of the First National Symposium NEW CROPS: Research, Development, Economics, Indianapolis, Indiana, Oct 23-26, 1988. Portland, OR: Timber Press.

Reinhart Fajen Inc. Undated. *Reinhart Fajen Inc., The Finest Quality Gunstocks Since 1951*. Catalog 9. Warsaw, MO: Reinhart Fajen Inc.

Richter, Conrad. 1966. *The Awakening Land, The Trees, The Fields, The Town*. New York, NY: Alfred A. Knopf.

Rink, George. May 1985. *Black Walnut, An American Wood*. Forest Service, Washington, D.C.: U. S. Dept. of Agriculture.

Rink, George. 1987. "Heartwood Color and Quantity Variation in a Young Black Walnut Progeny Test." *Wood and Fiber Science*. USDA Forest Service. Carbondale, IL: North Central Forest Experiment Station, Forestry Sciences Laboratory.

Rink, George, and John E. Phelps. 1989. "Variation in Heartwood and Sapwood Properties Among 10-year-old Black Walnut Trees." *Wood and Fiber Science*. USDA Forest Service. Carbondale, IL: North Central Forest Experiment Station, Forestry Sciences Laboratory.

Rue, Leonard Lee III. 1989. *The Deer of North America*. Danbury, CT: Grolier Book Clubs Inc.

Sagan, Carl. 1994. *Pale Blue Dot: A Vision of the Human Future in Space*. New York, NY: Random House.

Sander, Ivan L. 1966. "Natural Reproduction." *Black Walnut Culture*. Report of the 1966 Walnut Workshop, North Central Forest Experiment Station.

Savage, Henry, Jr. 1970. *Lost Heritage, Wilderness America Through the Eyes of Seven Pre-Audubon Naturalists*. New York, NY: William Morrow & Co.

Savage, Henry, Jr., and Elizabeth J. Savage. 1986. *Andre' and Francois Andre' Michaux*. Charlottesville, VA: University Press of Virginia.

Schiffer, Nancy, and Herbert Schiffer. 1977. *Woods We Live With*. Exton, PA: Schiffer Limited.

Schultz, R.C., and J.R. Thompson, J.R. 1990. "Nursery Practices That Improve Hardwood Seedling Root Morphology." Paper presented at the Northeastern Area Nurseryman's Conference, Peoria, Illinois, July 24-27.

Sesser, Stan. 1993. *The Lands of Charm and Cruelty, Travels in Southeast Asia*, New York, NY: Alfred A. Knopf.

Severeid, Larry. Winter, 1992. "Direct Seeding Using Tree Shelters: Establishing Walnut and Oak Plantations." *Woodland Management*. Wisconsin Woodland Owners Association.

Silverberg, Robert. 1968. *Mound Builders of Ancient America: The Archaeology of a Myth*. Greenwich, CT: The New York Graphic Society, LTD.

Sloan, J. M. Undated. *Johnny Walnutseed & Growing Black Walnut.* New York, NY: Vantage Press.

Sloane, Eric. 1965. *A Reverence for Wood.* New York, NY: Ballantine Books.

Sloane, Eric. 1979. *Legacy: The Providence of God in My Inheritance.* New York, NY: Thomas Y. Crowell.

Smith, W. Brad, and Ronald L.Hackett. 1991.*Veneer Industry and Timber Use, North Central Region, 1988.* Resource Bulletin NC-125,North Central Forest Experiment Station, Forest Service. St. Paul, MN: United States Department of Agriculture.

Spencer, John S. Jr., Neal P. Kingsley, and Robert V. Mayer. 1990. *Indiana's Timber Resource, 1986: An Analysis.* Resource Bulletin NC-113. North Central Forest Experiment Station, Forest Service. St. Paul, MN: United States Department of Agriculture.

Stringer, J.W., and R.F. Wittwer. 1985. "Release and Fertilization of Black Walnut in Natural Stands." Paper presented at the Fifth Central Hardwood Forest Conference held at Urbana, Illinois on April 15-17.

Stringer, J.W., Ed. 1984. *Proceedings 15th Annual Meeting of the Walnut Council.* Lexington, KY, July 29-Aug 2, 1984. Lexington, KY: University of Kentucky Dept. of Forestry.

Stuart, Reginald. December 30, 1976. "'Perfect' Walnut Tree is Among 18 Sold for $80,000," *The New York Times.*

Tetreault, Fred. Summer 1991. *Tree Farmer.* Washington, D.C.: American Forestry Council.

Ulrich, Alice H. December 1990. *U.S. Timber Production, Trade, Consumption, and Price Statistics 1960-88.* Miscellaneous Publication No. 1486, Forest Service. Washington, D.C.: United States Department of Agriculture.

University of Nebraska. Undated. *Pruning Black Walnut Trees for Profit.* Videotape. Cooperative Extension Institute of Agriculture and Natural Resources. Lincoln, NE: University of Nebraska.

U.S. Dept. of Agriculture. 1973. *Black Walnut as a Crop.* Black Walnut Symposium, August 14-15. North Central Forest Experiment Station, Forest Service. Carbondale: U.S. Dept. of Agriculture.

U.S. Dept. of Agriculture. 1976. *Planting Black Walnut for Timber.* Leaflet No. 487. Forest Service. Washington, D.C.: U.S. Dept. of Agriculture.

U.S. Dept. of Agriculture. 1982. *Black Walnut for the Future.* General Technical Report NC-74. North Central Forest Experiment Station. St. Paul, MN: U.S. Dept. of Agriculture.

U.S. Dept. of Agriculture. 1924. *Black Walnut for Timber and Nuts.* Farmer's Bulletin 1392. Washington D.C.: U.S. Dept. of Agriculture.

U.S. Dept. of Agriculture.*Quick Reference For Thinning Black Walnut.* St. Paul, MN: North Central Forest Experiment Station, Forest Service.

Van Sambeek, J.W., and George Rink. "Physiology and Silviculture of Black Walnut for Combined Timber and Nut Production." *72nd Annual Report of the Northern Nut Growers Association.*

Walker, Aidan. 1989. *The Encylopedia of Wood: A Tree-by-Tree Guide to the World's Most Versatile Resource.* New York, NY: Facts on File.

Walnut Council. 1989. *Walnut Symposium, The Continuing Quest For Quality, Proceedings of the Fourth Black Walnut Symposium.* Carbondale, IL: Southern Illinois University.

Walnut Council. Spring 1983 to Spring 1993. *Walnut Council Bulletin*. George Rink, Ed. USDA Forestry Sciences Laboratory. Carbondale, IL: Southern Illinois University.

Warton Esherick Museum. 1988. *Half a Century in Wood: 1920-1970. The Woodenworks of Warton Esherick*. Paoli, PA: Warton Esherick Museum.

Wertz, Halfred W., and M. Joy Callender. 1981. *Penn's Woods 1682-1982*. Wayne, Pennsylvania and Birchrunville, Pennsylvania: Green Valleys Association.

West Virginia Black Walnut Festival Inc. 1980. *Black Walnut Cookbook: Walnut Winners*. Spencer, WV: West Virginia Black Walnut Festival Inc.

West Virginia University. Undated. *Managing Your Woodlot: How it Grows*. Publication and videotape. College of Agriculture and Forestry. Morgantown, WV: West Virginia University.

West Virginia University. Undated. *Managing Your Woodlot: Helping it Grow*. Publication and videotape. College of Agriculture and Forestry. Morgantown, WV: West Virginia University.

Zinkhan, F. Christian, William R. Sizemore, George H. Mason, and Thomas J. Ebener. 1992. *Timberland Investments, A Portfolio Perspective*. Portland, OR: Timber Press Inc.

Index